W9-DFH-859

Japan's Postwar Economic Recovery and Anglo-Japanese Relations, 1948–62

The origins of Japan's 'miraculous' economic growth in the 1960s has been a topic that continues to interest academic inquiry. The initial focus upon internal factors has been supplemented by greater emphasis on the role played by the United States and the Western allies in promoting Japan's economic welfare. This book provides the British perspective on Japan's postwar economic recovery. It refutes the accepted view that Britain's policy towards Japan was driven by fears that the latter's economic recovery through greater trade relations with Southeast Asia would encroach upon Britain's sphere of influence. Through a close examination of Britain's sterling and trade policies towards Japan, the book illustrates the complex, often contradictory, yet daring British vision of Asia as a whole in the immediate postwar world.

Noriko Yokoi received her Ph.D. from the London School of Economics and Political Science. She has taught Asian history at Pace University in New York. Her research interests include international history and Japanese history.

RoutledgeCurzon Studies in the Modern History of Asia

1 The Police in Occupation Japan
Control, corruption and resistance to reform
Christopher Aldous

2 Chinese Workers
A new history
Jackie Sheehan

3 The Aftermath of Partition in South Asia
Tai Yong Tan and Gyanesh Kudaisya

4 The Australia-Japan Political Alignment
1952 to the present
Alan Rix

5 Japan and Singapore in the World Economy
Japan's economic advance into Singapore, 1870–1965
Shimizu Hiroshi and Hirakawa Hitoshi

6 The Triads as Business
Yiu Kong Chu

7 Contemporary Taiwanese Cultural Nationalism
A-chin Hsiau

8 Religion and Nationalism in India
The case of the Punjab
Harnik Deol

9 Japanese Industrialisation
Historical and cultural perspectives
Ian Inkster

Japan's Postwar Economic Recovery and Anglo-Japanese Relations, 1948–62

Noriko Yokoi

RoutledgeCurzon
Taylor & Francis Group

LONDON AND NEW YORK

First published 2003
by RoutledgeCurzon
11 New Fetter Lane, London EC4P 4EE

Simultaneously published in the USA and Canada
by RoutledgeCurzon
29 West 35th Street, New York, NY 10001

RoutledgeCurzon is an imprint of the Taylor & Francis Group

© 2003 Noriko Yokoi

Typeset in Times by Taylor & Francis Books Ltd
Printed and bound in Great Britain by Antony Rowe Ltd,
Chippenham, Wiltshire

British Library Cataloguing in Publication Data
A catalogue record for this book is available from the British Library

Library of Congress Cataloging in Publication Data
A catalog record for this book has been requested

ISBN 0–415–29721–4 (hbk)

To my parents

Contents

Illustrations

Figures

Tables

Acknowledgements

This book is a result of my Ph.D. thesis in international history at the London School of Economics, which was funded in part by the British Council and the Japan Foundation. I should like to thank my supervisor, Dr Antony Best, for his guidance and advice throughout the writing of the thesis. I would like to thank him for directing me to William Borden's *The Pacific Alliance* at the beginning of my doctoral programme and challenging me to write a British perspective on Japan's economic recovery. I am also very grateful to the late Professor Ralph Smith for introducing me to the Bank of England archives and encouraging me to incorporate a financial angle to the thesis. I wish to also extend my appreciation to Professor Sugihara Kaoru for guiding me to invaluable Japanese sources. My appreciation also goes to my examiners, Professor Anthony Stockwell and Dr Stephen Large, for their constructive comments and suggestions, many of which have been incorporated into this book.

I would like to express my appreciation to archivists at the Bank of England, the Birmingham University Library, the Bodleian and Rhodes House Libraries in Oxford, Durham University Library, Manchester Central Library, the Modern Records Centre at Warwick University, the Public Record Office, and Trinity and Churchill Colleges in Cambridge. Records from the Public Record Office appear by permission of the Controller of Her Majesty's Stationery Office.

I wish to also extend my appreciation to the staff at the Ministry of Foreign Affairs Archives in Japan, and in particular to Mr Nomoto, who expedited my research requests. In the United States, I wish to thank the archivists at the Dwight D. Eisenhower and Harry S. Truman Libraries, the National Archives in College Park, Maryland, and the Seeley G. Mudd Library at Princeton. A grant from the Royal Historical Society and the Truman Library made it possible for me to conduct research in the United States in the summer of 1996.

This manuscript has been a long time in coming; thus there are many people to whom my appreciation is overdue both regarding the writing of the thesis and in the preparation of the manuscript. In the United Kingdom, I wish to thank Dr Janet Hunter, Dr John Kent and Professor Ian Nish for their comments on earlier drafts of the thesis. Robert W. O'Hara and Imelda Lauris deserve a special mention for their assistance in locating and dispatching documents from the Public Record Office. Chiara Levrini was, as always, the perfect host during my stay in London. In Japan, Dr Aaron Forsberg, Dr Takahiko Tanaka, Professor Kibata Yôichi and Professor Nakanishi Hiroshi all gave valuable advice. In the United States, I am grateful to the co-heads of the Strategic Planning Department at Rapp Collins Worldwide, Andrew N. Jones and Russell L. Lapso, for granting me the one-month sabbatical to complete the manuscript. I would also like to thank Professor Barbara Blumberg, Professor Joan Rowland and Dr Ronald Frank of Pace University for their support and encouragement. Peter Sowden remained understanding throughout as I was beset by delays relating to the challenges of working in corporate America and my many close calls with downsizing. My husband, Dele Akinla II, encouraged me through the most challenging of times with his optimism and faith as I juggled full-time work and adjunct professorship with the writing of this manuscript. Without his humour and patience, the project would not have come to fruition. Of course, none of the individuals mentioned above bear responsibility for any errors that remain.

Last but not least, my parents have supported me in all my endeavours, including this one. Without them, this would never have been written. I thus dedicate this book to them.

Usage and Abbreviations

The usual conventions concerning Japanese names are observed throughout this book with the family name followed by the given name. The exceptions are for Japanese scholars who publish in English. The terms Far East and East Asia have been used intermittently in the book due to the popular usage of the term Far East in the 1950s. An attempt has however been made to use East Asia wherever possible.

AA	Automatic Approval
cif	cost, insurance, freight
COCOM	Coordinating Committee
CHINCOM	China Committee
CLC	Commonwealth Liaison Committee
CPCE	Committee on Preparations for Commonwealth Economic Conference
ECA	Economic Cooperation Administration
ECAFE	Economic Commission for Asia and the Far East
ECOSOC	Economic and Social Council
EPB	Economic Planning Board
EPC	Economic Policy Committee
EPU	European Payments Union
ERP	European Recovery Program
ESB	Economic Stabilisation Board
ESC	Economic Steering Committee
ESS	Economic and Scientific Section
FEC	Far Eastern Commission
FECB	Foreign Exchange Control Board
FE(O)C	Far Eastern (Official) Committee
FOA	Foreign Operations Administration
GARIOA	Government and Relief in Occupied Areas
GATT	General Agreements on Tariffs and Trade
IBRD	International Bank for Reconstruction and Development
IC/DV	Import Certificate, Delivery Verification
ILO	International Labour Organisation

ISA	Independent Sterling Area
IMF	International Monetary Fund
ITO	International Trade Organisation
IWA	International Wheat Agreement
IWC	International Wheat Council
l/c	letter of credit
MFN	Most Favoured Nation
MITI	Ministry of International Trade and Industry
MOF	Ministry of Finance
MOFA	Ministry of Foreign Affairs
NAC	National Advisory Council
NATO	North Atlantic Treaty Organisation
NSC	National Security Council
OGL	Open General License
ONC	Overseas Negotiations Committee
OPA	Open Payments Agreement
PRC	People's Republic of China
RFB	Reconstruction Finance Bank
ROC	Republic of China
RSA	Rest of the Sterling Area
RTA	Reciprocal Trade Agreements
SCAP	Supreme Commander of the Allied Powers
SEATO	Southeast Asia Treaty Organisation
UKLM	United Kingdom Liaison Mission
UN	United Nations
VER	Voluntary Export Restrictions

1 Introduction

Since Japan's high-speed growth in the 1960s, there has been a growing amount of scholarly work on Japan's postwar success, and this peaked in the 1980s when Japan became the world's second strongest economy and the world's largest creditor nation. The focus of the inquiry was the Western desire to understand how a country deficient in raw materials, devastated in the Second World War and stripped of its empire could have recovered so quickly from defeat and risen to become one of the strongest economies in the world in a matter of few decades.[1] Much of the focus on Japan's so-called economic miracle examined the peculiarities of Japan's political and economic framework, such as the emphasis on consensus and cooperation between the ruling party, the bureaucracy and big business.[2] There have also been studies of institutional characteristics such as the seniority wage system and the practice of life-time employment.[3] Other factors that have been highlighted are Japan's education system, the 'paternalistic orientation behind the notion of labour and management ... enthusiastic acceptance of benevolent guidance, the work ethic and an inclination to save'.[4] Although there have been numerous works emphasising one aspect of Japan's society or the other to explain the reasons for Japan's economic miracle, these explanations have become clichéd over the years. At times, they have fuelled the notion that Japan is unique which has not been very constructive nor particularly insightful.

Diplomatic historians, with their reliance on publicly released government documents, have had an opportunity to contribute to this body of literature since the thirty-year rule availed them of postwar documents. Hence historians have been publishing books on Japan's economic recovery since the mid-1980s. Initial research results have identified the Cold War in Asia as the major factor behind the US decision to 'reverse' its postwar policy towards Japan in order to maintain a balance of power in the region. A subsequent wave of historical inquiry has shifted the emphasis to economics and trade as the reason for the US decision to sponsor Japan's economic recovery. Scholars representing this view have argued that the United States saw urgency in sponsoring the economic recovery of key countries in Europe and Asia as a means of pursuing its vision of a multilateral trading system, even in a compromised form in the immediate postwar period. The impetus behind this decision was both to enable the United States to sustain the Western economic trading system, and also to maintain the health of the US economy during the period of trade disequilibria known as the dollar gap.

This book follows the historical inquiry pursued by the latter group of historians, but the focus of the research will be on the British perspective, which has been mentioned tangentially but not addressed fully in the existing works. Specifically, the book will focus upon the argument cited frequently by US historians that Britain opposed the US-sponsored Japanese economic recovery due to a conflict of interest with its own policies. The book will explore the two themes that have been presented by scholars as examples of British opposition to Japan's economic recovery. The first is the impact of Japan's economic recovery on Britain's sterling policy in Asia; the second is British fears of a revival of the cut-throat competition of the pre-war period and its effects upon British industries if Japan were allowed to pursue its economic recovery with little restraint from the postwar international trading community at large.

Britain has often been viewed as being opposed to US attempts to resuscitate the Japanese economy through an intricate triangular trading system whereby the United States supplied raw cotton to Japan, which was used to manufacture cotton goods for export to Southeast Asia in exchange for raw materials that were sold on to the United States for dollars. This was because the US plan allegedly impinged upon the postwar British triangular trading system, which was centered on its Southeast Asian colonies as the dollar-earning pivot. It has been argued that Britain subsequently regulated Japan's economic activity with the countries that fell within the Sterling Area's jurisdiction in order to stifle Japanese competition, thereby limiting Japan's chances of resurrecting its economy through trade with the Sterling Area members, who were far-flung across Southeast Asia, South Asia, Australasia, the Middle East, Europe and Africa,[5] and accounted for a quarter of the world's trade between 1951 and 1957.[6]

Moreover, scholars argue that Britain's attempts to postpone Japan's GATT (General Agreement on Tariffs and Trade) entry in the postwar period represents further evidence of Britain's opposition to Japan's economic recovery. British industrial representatives, particularly those representing Lancashire's textile concerns, lobbied for protection against perceived as well as actual Japanese competition. They were particularly fearful of the repetition of the pre-war, unfair trade competition, which consisted of price dumping, government subsidies and copyright infringement, which contributed to the overall erosion of Britain's export market share. Their views were represented by the Board of Trade, which was responsible for Britain's commercial policy; in this way the industry lobby withstood internal cabinet opposition to postpone Japan's GATT membership until 1955. In addition, Britain refused to base its trade relations with Japan on the spirit of the postwar multilateral trading system of free and fair trade until 1962 – a full six years after the most-favoured-nation treatment clause in the 1951 peace treaty had expired.

This book will explore the two inter-related issues between 1948 and 1962, in order to assess whether Britain's overall policy towards Japan was based upon a comprehensive effort to block the latter's economic recovery. The year 1948 has been chosen as the starting point of the research because it was the year that official trade relations began between the two countries in the postwar period. The year 1962 is seen as the natural end of this research because it was the year that the two countries signed the treaty of commerce, establishment and navigation that formalised bilateral commercial relations. The intervening years are treated chronologically to analyse the validity of the hypothesis, and to examine the impact of Britain's decisions upon its relations with Japan and its postwar sponsor, the United States.

The book's structure follows the evolution of Anglo-Japanese sterling and trade relations, which can be divided into three phases: the Open Payments Agreement (1948–51), the Sterling Payments Agreement (1951–7), and bilateral trade agreements (1958–62), with an expanded focus upon the middle phase. The book follows the development of each of the three agreements – albeit loosely – to illustrate the strategies formulated by British policymakers and to assess how closely they adhered to, or how far they deviated from, the original blueprint. The middle phase, from 1951 to 1957, has been covered in most detail because that period encompassed Britain's greatest activity and investment in the success of the postwar Sterling Area and by extension, its interest in Japan as an important sterling partner in East Asia.

The first phase, covered in Chapter 2, was characterised by bilateral agreements between the respective Sterling Area countries and Japan. The trading countries controlled trade balances with little supervision from the United Kingdom. The bilateral nature of the agreement, however, restricted countries from expanding their trade relations with Japan. To circumvent the limitations, Britain invited sterling countries that had a rough balance of payments with Japan into a participant pool, where members grouped their trade volume for economies of scale. Sterling Area relations with Japan never exceeded the minimum during this first phase because the dollar clause in the agreement permitted the SCAP (Supreme Commander of the Allied Powers) to convert any excess sterling into dollars twice a year. Although the SCAP never activated the dollar point, the potential for a dollar drain through Japan deemed the latter a hard currency country, thus the Sterling Area countries were discouraged from expanding their trade relations beyond the necessary level.

The second phase, covered in Chapters 3 to 8, was characterised by Japan's signing of the Sterling Payments Agreement. Britain initiated the change in order to introduce Japan to an established Sterling Area trading system of the postwar period. As part of this transition process, the dollar clause was abrogated to open the way for Japan to become a soft currency country. Britain's aim behind the shift from the Open Payments Agreement to the Sterling Payments Agreement was governed entirely by self-interest. The postwar Sterling Area and its vitality was Britain's paramount concern. Britain realised Japan's potential role for stimulating intra-Asian trade as the regional 'workshop', and in the process, revitalising sterling as the trading currency of choice in the region. Thus she encouraged Japan's use of sterling as an international currency for multilateral trade. The additional benefit of inviting Japan to expand trade relations with the Asian Sterling Area countries was the affordability of Japan's manufactured goods, which were appropriate in price and quality for many of the 'under-developed' colonies. The results of Britain's strategy are clearly illustrated in Figures 1.1 and 1.2, where 67 per cent of Japan's imports from the Sterling Area are shown to have come from the Asia-Pacific region, which included Australia, New

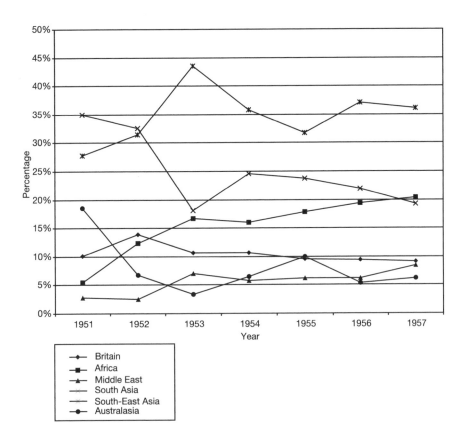

Figure 1.1 Japan's exports to the Sterling Area, 1951–7

Source: Bank of Tokyo 1969.

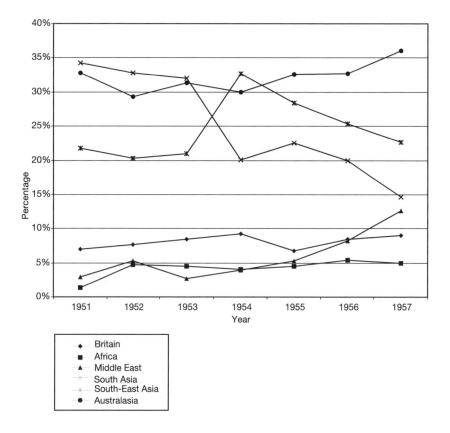

Figure 1.2 Japan's imports from the Sterling Area, 1951–7

Source: Bank of Tokyo 1969.

Zealand, Pakistan, India, Ceylon, Burma, Malaya, Hong Kong and Singapore.[7] Exports to these countries accounted for 81 per cent of Japan's exports to the Sterling Area. Thus the British policymakers' blueprint reveals that Britain saw Japan as an important economic partner in Asia, who could contribute to the resuscitation of sterling in the region, which underlies the fact that Britain did not pursue a comprehensive plan to thwart Japan's economic recovery.

Britain's sterling policy towards Japan in the second phase was clouded, however, by its inability to reconcile Japan's membership in a postwar multi-lateral trading system that was governed by liberal economic principles. The three underlying components of economic liberalism were the open door policy, the most-favoured-nation treatment and the principles of compara-tive advantage.[8] During the 1950s Britain was unable to extend a single component of these postwar ideals to Japan due to strong domestic resistance. The open door policy, for example, was never truly functional, because most soft currency countries took advantage of the temporary privilege extended to them to use quantitative restrictions to limit imports of goods from certain hard currency countries, during their balance of payments crises or the dollar gap. In some instances, quantitative restrictions were used as an excuse to limit imports of manufactured goods that competed with their domestic production, as in the case of Britain and its restrictive licensing of Japanese goods. Moreover, Britain reserved its rights to extend *de jure* MFN (Most Favoured Nation) rights to Japan throughout the 1950s through its decision not to apply the GATT rules to Japan. The decision stemmed from two factors. The first was Britain's hopes of protecting its market share in the Commonwealth bloc against Japanese competition via the continuation of a preferential tariff system that discriminated in favour of Commonwealth goods. Britain's plans to engineer lower Commonwealth tariffs were not granted due to the GATT's no-new-preference rule, which precluded any member from increasing preferential treatment without extending it to all members. Thus Britain felt that it could not invite Japan into an association that did not allow for protection in its traditional market. Second, Britain felt that the GATT rules on adverse competition by a member country relied too heavily on consensus building and discouraged swift action by a country wronged by unfair competition. Unable to reconcile herself to the proposed rule, Britain felt uncomfortable inviting Japan into the GATT until a more decisive regulation was enforced within the GATT framework or until Japan exhibited more 'responsible' behaviour within the trading community. Last, the US vision of a multilateral trading system based upon competitive advantage failed to function in regard to Britain in the 1950s because the latter could not come to terms with the fact that more competitive labour and raw material sources existed elsewhere for the production of inexpensive manufactured goods for the world market. This was especially true in the case of textiles manufacturing, where Britain asked countries such as India, Pakistan, Hong Kong and Japan to adhere to voluntary export restrictions in order to protect its own domestic industry from losing market share to foreign competition. Thus the second phase saw a conflict of interest between British policymakers who saw opportunities to be gained from Japan's economic recovery, and those who sought to protect themselves from its revival. Thus Britain sent mixed messages to Japan and the United States about its policy. This second phase lasted for seven years, but came to an end with Britain's decision to abrogate the outdated Sterling Payments Agreement and the accompanying exchange of letters.

The final phase, treated in Chapter 9, was characterised by the unravelling of the postwar Sterling Area as a result of the diminishing importance of a centralised dollar reserve. This was due to the return of dollar convertibility, and to the increasing independence of individual Sterling Area members' economic policies. Britain, which viewed itself as providing strategic guidance to the postwar Sterling Area, viewed Japan with less importance as a result of Britain's diminished role in the Asian Sterling Area. Thus, by the third phase, Japan's relevance to British policy became proportionate to the actual level of Anglo-Japanese trade, which was miniscule in comparison to their respective total trade (see Figures 1.3 and 1.4). This explains why Britain did not prioritise the signing of a formal commercial policy to legitimise trade relations after the lapse of the Sterling Payments Agreement. The period of lull continued from 1956 until 1959, when Britain's export potential in the booming Japanese market became an opportunity that the former could not resist. Thus this period saw a shift in emphasis, as British exporters gained greater national influence while the political impact of domestic manufactures such as textiles waned in comparison.

Survey of the literature

As mentioned in the introductory paragraph, most of the research on Japan's economic recovery has focused on internal factors. In spite of this trend, the last fifteen years have seen a steady output of scholarly study of the external factors behind Japan's economic recovery, with the release of American and British government documents. Works of note are Michael Schaller's *The American Occupation of Japan*; Andrew J. Rotter's *The Path to Vietnam*; and William Borden's *The Pacific Alliance*. Schaller's work focuses on Washington's decision to reverse the course of the occupation due to the intensifying of the Cold War, and places the role of the Supreme Commander of the Allied Powers during the occupation, Douglas MacArthur, firmly back in its proper perspective. Moreover, Schaller highlights the decision by American policymakers to promote Japan's 'greater co-prosperity sphere' by linking its economy with that of Southeast Asia, in order to promote its economic recovery and to ensure that Southeast Asia did not enter the communist orbit. Rotter has gone one step further by linking American policymakers' decision to sponsor Japan's economic recovery with the eventual American involvement in the Vietnam War. Although Borden also argues that the United States actively supported Japan's economic recovery, he highlights the importance of Japan's economic recovery to America's plans for a multilateral trading system in the non-communist world. For such a system to succeed, the United States needed to provide sufficient economic aid to Europe and Asia, to enable the 'free' world to continue purchasing American products.

All of the three works cited above refer in passing to Britain's postwar Asian interests. Schaller has dealt the least with Britain's perspective, while Borden has conducted some research based on American documents. Rotter, who has conducted archival research at the Public Record Office in Kew, deals in greater detail with Britain's interests in Southeast Asia. All three indicate the importance that Britain placed on its economic ties with Southeast Asia, and argue that British industrialists felt threatened by Japan's economic

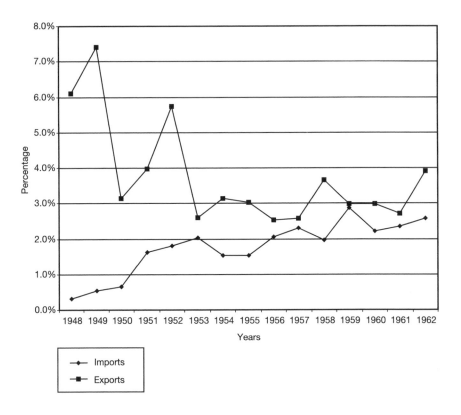

Figure 1.3 Britain's share of total Japanese imports and exports, 1948–62

Source: United Nations 1952–67.

links with the region, but they produce little research on Britain's response to Japan's trade recovery. The problem with the approach of the three scholars mentioned above has been their acceptance of the argument that Britain felt threatened by Japanese competition in Southeast Asia. This is largely due to the fact that these scholars accepted the contemporary American view of British policy. In fact, this argument, cited as early as 1979 in John Dower's *Empire and Aftermath*, has become proverbial in that it has been widely accepted by American scholars dealing with this area of research. This is evident in the work of scholars such as Sayuri Shimizu and Aaron Forsberg, who have published studies on the Eisenhower administration's policy towards Japan in the 1950s.[9]

Conversely, there has been comparatively less interest in Britain with regard to Japan's economic recovery and Britain's role *vis-à-vis* Japan in the

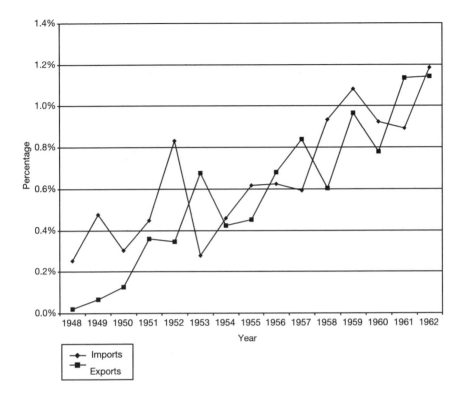

Figure 1.4 Japan's share of total British imports and exports, 1948–62
Source: United Nations 1952–67.

postwar period. The most comprehensive study undertaken in the 1980s was Roger Buckley's *Occupation Diplomacy*. Buckley undertook research on Britain's occupation policy towards Japan from 1945 to 1952 in order to highlight an alternative perspective on the Allied occupation experience. He elucidated the differences between the American and British policymakers' views towards the occupation, and British policy towards Japan in the immediate postwar period. Although Buckley argues that Anglo-Japanese relations in the postwar period were primarily based on commercial relations, his work is lacking in Treasury, Board of Trade and Bank of England document citations. Buckley has managed to argue his case using Foreign Office documents (primarily FO 371 papers) but one is left wondering about the views of the other ministries in Whitehall.[10] Another scholar who has been working extensively on Britain's policy towards East Asia in the 1950s is Peter Lowe. Lowe has undertaken extensive research on British policy towards Korea, China and Japan, but his focus has been primarily diplomatic.[11] There has been a small but growing collection of works on Britain's business relations with Japan in the 1950s, starting with Davenport-Hines and Jones' *British Business in Asia since 1860*, as well as case studies of Anglo-Japanese commercial relations in the recently published volume of *The History of Anglo-Japanese Relations, 1600–2000, Volume 4*, edited by Janet E. Hunter and S. Sugiyama. These provide a greater understanding of British commercial interests in Japan and the strategies undertaken by selected companies with various degrees of success in penetrating a highly protected and regulated market; but a comprehensive work on Britain's commercial policy towards Japan in the 1950s has yet to be published.[12]

The reason why Anglo-Japanese relations have not enjoyed greater academic interest in Britain is the fact that historians have expressed a stronger interest in topics relating to its former empire and the decolonisation process. One of the topics which has fuelled an extensive amount of research among scholars has been the Sterling Area system. The Sterling Area, as an informal economic and financial 'club', has been seen as one of the factors that kept the British empire together, and thus a number of scholars, such as Cain and Hopkins,[13] have conducted research on the ties between the City of London and Britain's formal and informal empire, while others have concentrated on the Sterling Area system. The most comprehensive work on banking and the Sterling Area in the 1950s has been carried out by Catherine Schenk. John Singleton and Paul L. Robertson have recently published a more concentrated study on the relations between Australia, Britain and New Zealand. All these works have provided the author with a more solid conceptual understanding of the workings of the Sterling Area.[14] Moreover, they have provided a framework for evaluating whether Japan's dealings with the Sterling Area was unique or whether it was part of the overall sterling strategy towards non-Sterling Area countries. This study will show that the overall sterling policy was decided by Britain with the consensus of the core Commonwealth countries. Thus the decisions that drove Anglo-Japanese trade relations were taken by the Sterling Area policy makers or by the members of the Overseas Negotiations Committee, which was in charge of the high-level strategies, thus substantiating Cain and Hopkins' thesis that decisions were made at the centre, not the periphery. Where Cain and Hopkins' argument concerning gentlemanly capitalism does not apply to Britain's relations with Japan, is in the importance that the latter placed upon 'salesmanship' from foreign exporters and their drive to enter the Japanese market. Such characteristics matched the 'entrepreneurial drive' found in the manufacturing sector, and were not those of gentlemanly capitalists from the financial sector. Thus the later years hinged upon the success of a different group of British capitalists.

In Japan, although there has been an increasing number of historians conducting research on Japan's postwar external relations, most have concentrated on her relations with the United States for obvious reasons.

Some academics have, however, focused on British and Commonwealth policy towards Japan – scholars such as Hosoya Chihiro and Kibata Yôichi. The former has written an outstanding account of the lead-up to the San Francisco Peace Treaty, but does not deal with post-occupation relations. The latter has conducted extensive archival research in Britain, Malaya and Australia, but his emphasis has been on Malaya.[15] On Japan's entry to the GATT, Akaneya Tasuo's work is the most comprehensive to date in any language.[16] Akaneya has, however, gathered most of his documentary evidence in Australia, and thus his perspective on British policymaking is limited. Although there has been growing interest in Japan's trade relations with the Sterling Area, publications to date suggest that scholars are examining Japan's bilateral relations with former Sterling Area countries without reference to Britain's sterling policy.[17] An exception to this is Junko Tomaru's work on Japan and Malaya's postwar rapprochement, which is by far the most comprehensive work to date on Britain's gradual acceptance of Japan's return to Southeast Asia.[18] Tomaru's meticulous research is apparent from the range of sources used to build her argument. She argues convincingly that Britain allowed Japan back into Malaya by 1954 because of Britain's overall focus on Malayan stabilisation ahead of its independence. Her study thus refutes the view that Britain was opposed to Japan's return to Southeast Asia. This book will support Tomaru's central argument, but where our works differ is in her reliance on the Colonial Office and Foreign Office documents and the views of British officials in the region, whereas this book will focus on the views of British officials who made the strategic decisions concerning Sterling Area-Japanese trade in the Economic Policy and the Overseas Negotiations Committees. Thus this book will provide an overlay to Tomaru's research by providing the views of officials at the centre.

Last, although this study deals primarily with foreign economic diplomacy, one cannot ignore the voluminous amount of research that has been generated on Japan's postwar economic development. The research has provided the author with a better understanding of the key elements in Japan's economic success, which were a combination of bullish Japanese companies, technology imports from abroad, and government planning authorities' efforts to remove barriers to economic growth.[19] Nor can any research on Japan's economic recovery be conducted without the author being fully aware of the decades of research that have led to an accumulation of knowledge concerning the developmental versus the liberal forms of capitalism, with particular emphasis upon the Japanese institution that has underpinned the developmental form of capitalism, namely the Ministry of International Trade and Industry, or MITI.[20] In more recent years, much of the admiration for Japan's economic model has been replaced by criticism, as the country's economic woes have highlighted weaknesses in the developmental economic model. These criticisms aside, one cannot ignore the important role that industrial policy played in Japan's miraculous economic growth in the immediate postwar period.

2 The Open Payments Agreement with Japan

Introduction

The postwar economic system was designed to prevent the world from returning to the economic nationalism, discriminatory trading blocs and 'beggar-my-neighbour-policies' of the inter-war period.[1] In order to achieve international stability it therefore aimed at full employment and economic growth on the domestic front, and beyond this the establishment of a stable world economic order where countries had fixed exchange rates and fair and competitive tariff rates.[2] The plan for the postwar economic order was discussed as early as 1942, and negotiations for the blueprint of such a world order began between Britain and the United States in 1943. The two economic experts who prepared documents for the negotiations were John Maynard Keynes and Harry Dexter White.[3] Disagreements occurred between the two sides during the course of discussions, but US economic dominance guaranteed that the American plans would be implemented at the Bretton Woods Conference of 1944.[4] The two institutions established at Bretton Woods were the IMF (International Monetary Fund) and the IBRD (International Bank for Reconstruction and Development). The IMF's role was to monitor exchange stability and balance of payments, while the IBRD's function was 'to encourage long-term international investment'.[5] As a by-product of the conference, the GATT was established in 1946.[6] It was initially a temporary meeting between the original member countries until the ITO (International Trade Organisation) Charter was ratified. However, with the failure of the United States to ratify the charter, the ITO was never realised as an organisation.[7] Instead, the GATT became the alternative body that replaced the ITO as the third pillar of the postwar economic system. The two aims behind the GATT were first 'a multilateral and non-discriminatory approach to international trade' and second, 'condemnation of quantitative trade restrictions'.[8]

Although much planning and discussion had taken place to establish the Bretton Woods system, in reality, the world that emerged after the war was in no condition to implement it. The reason behind this was the physical devastation in Europe and Asia, which meant that governments were far more concerned with domestic reconstruction than with liberal international trade. One of the countries most affected by the war was Britain. During the war, it had run down its gold and dollar reserves as well as its overseas assets. Furthermore, Britain had accumulated huge sterling liabilities with the Sterling Area countries in order to finance the war. The loss of its overseas assets, continuing military commitments abroad and the sterling liabilities meant that Britain faced a very serious balance of payments problem. In addition, Britain, like so many other countries, was facing a dollar shortage or a 'dollar gap', where it sought American goods but did not have enough foreign exchange to buy them. Furthermore, the abrupt decision by the United States to end the Lend-Lease (Mutual Aid) programme on 17 August 1945, in order to prevent the recipient countries from using American aid for reconstruction, only exacerbated British difficulties.[9]

Recognising Britain's financial problems, the United States agreed to extend a loan, which was signed on 6 December 1945.[10] There were several conditions to the loan. First, the loan of $3.75 billion was not interest-free. Britain was to pay 2 per cent interest on the loan from 31 December 1951 in fifty annual installments. Second, Britain had to pledge to make sterling convertible to countries outside of the sterling and dollar areas on all current transactions after 31 December 1946. Third, an attempt was made to solve the sterling balances, and it was agreed that 'some balances would be written off, some funded, and some immediately released'.[11]

After the signing of the loan agreement, Britain made preparations for the convertibility of sterling by concluding bilateral agreements with holders of sterling, starting with the Anglo-Argentine Agreement of September 1946.[12] Britain expected the convertibility of sterling to be carried out in an orderly fashion, and furthermore, expected many countries to continue holding sterling as a medium of foreign exchange. However, when convertibility was put into place on 15 July 1947, dollars began to drain rapidly from Britain. In order to stop the tide of the dollar drain, convertibility was suspended from 20 August and full convertibility did not take effect until 1958. The failure of attempts to make sterling convertible signified that convertibility of currencies was premature. Given that there was an overall sterling surplus and dollar shortage, it should have been clear to officials that sterling convertibility would not work. Furthermore, an attempt to convert sterling in a world where most currencies were inconvertible was a recipe for disaster.

For the first half of its period of inconvertibility, therefore, the Sterling Area was established into a trading bloc with four different account areas: the sterling, the American, the transferable and the bilateral. Sterling transfers within each bloc were permissible, with the exception of the bilateral account. Bilateral account countries were able to transfer sterling automatically to sterling account countries, but were unable to transfer sterling to another member of the bilateral account without the approval of the Bank of England. Transferable account countries were able to transfer sterling within the account group and to sterling account countries, but they were not permitted to transfer sterling to the American account group, whose sterling holdings were the most flexible because they were able to exchange their sterling into dollars and vice-versa. They were also allowed to transfer their sterling to the sterling account or the transferable account groups. This complicated division of countries into different groups was designed to restrict convertibility of sterling into dollars (see Table 2.1).[13]

Currency convertibility was not the only deviation from the postwar international economic model. The United States' attempt to rid the postwar international economic order of unfair trade practices was also unsuccessful. As mentioned above, the ITO was never ratified because of differences in British and American aims. The United States wished to see an end to quota restrictions and imperial preferences. In the negotiations for the charter of the ITO, the United States agreed that quota restrictions should be applied only because it was uncertain of the conditions which might prevail after convertibility; therefore, Britain was determined to keep quota restrictions indefinitely. The United States wanted an end to imperial preferences. Commonwealth imperial preferences dated back to the Ottawa conference of August 1932, and it was these that the US wished to eliminate,

Table 2.1   Sterling Area account system, 1952

Sterling Area	American account	Transferable account	Bilateral account
Australia	USA	Austria	Argentina
New Zealand	Bolivia	Chile	Belgium
South Africa	Canada	Czechoslovakia	Brazil
India	Central America	Denmark	China
Pakistan	Venezuela	Egypt	Formosa
Ceylon	Ecuador	Ethiopia	France
Burma	Philippines	Finland	East Germany
Iceland	Colombia	West Germany	Hungary
Iraq	Dominica	Greece	Iran
Jordan		Italy	Israel
Libya		The Netherlands	Japan
Persian Gulf		Norway	Lebanon
territories		Poland	Paraguay
British colonies		Spain	Peru
		Sweden	Portugal
		Thailand	Romania
		USSR	Switzerland
			Syria
			Tangier
			Turkey
			Uruguay
			Yugoslavia

Source: Schenk 1994.

but it was unsuccessful in this. At the Geneva Conference of 1947, the US was able to terminate preferences for Commonwealth goods going to Britain, but it was unable to terminate preferences for British goods going to the Commonwealth. The former was easy to accomplish, as the Commonwealth countries were not very enthusiastic about imperial preferences. During tariff negotiations Britain terminated a mere 5 per cent of its pre-war preferences to the Commonwealth, while 70 per cent of them were retained intact.[14] Imperial preferences were important for Britain to ensure favourable export markets for its goods, and to maintain full employment. Although the United States was also concerned with full employment, it was to America's advantage to press for free trade in order to achieve full economic activity in the United States. With the breakdown of the ITO talks, Britain was allowed to maintain quantitative restrictions, and to continue the practice of imperial preferences for existing agreements.

Although Britain was able to keep the United States and its multilateral trading system at bay, it was faced with an additional challenge as the Cold War intensified. This was Japan's economic recovery under US sponsorship. When the United States realised that its former wartime ally, the Soviet Union, was not to be trusted in Eastern Europe, it became determined that East Asia should not fall into the Soviet sphere. The area, which particularly concerned the US was Northeast Asia and Japan. The wartime allies had originally agreed to allow the Soviets to establish a sphere of influence over Manchuria in return for Russian entry into the Pacific war three months after Germany's defeat. After the defeat of Germany however, the American position shifted. It sought to curtail Soviet influence in Manchuria, and even became ambivalent about Soviet entry into the Pacific war.[15]

On 6 August 1945 the US dropped an atom bomb on Hiroshima. This was followed by a bomb on Nagasaki a few days later. The bombs were used to avoid the unnecessary deaths of allied combatants, but also had the potential to end the war without the need for Soviet entry. The Soviet Union declared war on Japan, however, a few days before Japan's surrender. With the end of the war, there was a scramble by the Guomindang, with the assistance of the United States, and the Chinese Communists for the key cities in Northeast China. Initially, both the Soviet Union and the United States supported the Guomindang government, and only with the support of both countries was the national party guaranteed future control over the country. The growing rift between the two countries, however, cast a shadow over the Guomindang's ability to govern China. Moreover, domestic instability raised doubts about China's ability to fulfil its role as one of the four 'policemen' in the postwar period. By the end of 1945, Guomindang and Chinese Communist forces were clashing over territory in Northeast China. In an attempt to find a peaceful solution, US President Harry Truman asked George Marshall to mediate. In January 1947, however, Marshall announced the failure of his mission.[16] The uncertainty in China, together with the continued division along the Korean peninsula, had a direct effect on America's policy towards Japan.

From September 1945 to 1947, the SCAP (Supreme Commander of the Allied Powers), General Douglas MacArthur, followed the postwar reform programme produced by the State-War-Navy Coordinating Committee entitled the 'Initial Post-Surrender Policy for Japan' (SWNCC 150/4/A).[17] The reforms set out in SWNCC 150/4/A were far-reaching. They included destroying Japan's military power, building a representative government, changing the constitutional role of the monarch[18] and establishing free labour unions – to name but a few.[19] One of the occupation force's main aims was the dissolution of Japan's large business conglomerates or *zaibatsu*, as many believed that their business interests and influence had enabled the militarists to wage war. In addition, during the early period of the occupation, there was talk of transferring Japan's industrial capacity to the rest of Asia as reparations. This undertaking would ensure that Japan would have to rely on Asia for manufactured goods, and it would also guarantee that its economic strength would be no higher than that of its Asian neighbours.[20] During this period, Japan was only able to conduct trade under the strict control of the occupation authorities (also referred to as SCAP).[21] Trade was a means to enable Japan to feed its population and to maintain a minimum standard of living, but Japan faced huge economic problems as it was cut off from its traditional trading areas in Northeast Asia. It had a growing population restricted to the four main islands, and the postwar years saw domestic crop failures which resulted in famine. Furthermore, Japan was faced with a dollar shortage due to its inability to sell silk to the United States, which had been Japan's main export destination in the pre-war period. With the advent of the production of cheap synthetic fibre such as nylon, Japan's silk was no longer in demand; therefore Japan had to rely extensively on the US Army's GARIOA (Government and Relief in Occupied Areas) programme for humanitarian aid.[22]

With the failure of the Marshall mission and increasing tension between the United States and the Soviet Union, the Truman administration begun to view very seriously the idea of reconstructing Germany and Japan, the so-called 'workshops' of Europe and Asia. The idea was a development of George Kennan's containment strategy, which argued that US national security could only be maintained by protecting as many as possible of the five world centres of industrial power. The five were the United States, Great Britain, the Soviet Union, Germany and Japan. With the Soviet Union, Eastern Europe and later the PRC (People's Republic of China) firmly entrenched in the communist sphere, it became all the more important to safeguard Japan and Germany.[23] It was hoped that the two economies would act as economic pivots in Europe and Asia, and encourage economic integration between the 'free' countries in their respective regions, thereby preventing more countries from going communist. Building up Japan's economy was, however, not only motivated by strategic reasons. Another motive was to aid the US economy by overcoming the postwar dollar gap. The dollar gap was created by the fact that 'the United States made the products that the rest of the world wanted to buy ... both for present consumption and for reconstruction but the devastated areas did not have suitable goods and services to exchange'.[24] In order to safeguard American interests, it was imperative that European and Asian countries be given financial aid to purchase American goods. Thus the United States was motivated by two concerns: strengthening the economies of the 'free' countries in Europe and Asia against communism, and ensuring that those countries had enough dollars to continue purchasing American goods. The change in American attitude towards the two defeated nations meant the urgent formation of new policies. The new policy towards Japan was drawn up by Kennan, who was the head of the State Department's PPS (Policy Planning Staff). Kennan visited Japan in early 1948 to see the situation prevailing there for himself. His visit overlapped with that of the Under-Secretary of the Army, William H. Draper. The findings of the Kennan and Draper mission were incorporated into the NSC document 13/2, which was approved and signed by Truman on 9 October 1948. This document was the beginning of the 'reverse course' in Japan.

The new role created for Japan was that of a bulwark against the spread of communism in Asia. In order to fulfill this role, Japan's economic recovery became crucial, which meant reorganising Japan's domestic economy, and encouraging her trade with the outside world. The postwar period, however, saw rampant inflation in Japan, since the 'wartime governments had printed money to finance arms production and the collapse of the civilian goods sector drove consumer prices skyward'.[25] Inflation was also encouraged by Japanese businesses, which wished to reduce the real burden of their financial debts to the government via increased prices. Moreover, the RFB (Reconstruction Finance Bank), established in October 1946, provided generous loans to various industries, further exacerbating the inflationary situation in Japan.[26] This inflation was a prime obstacle to Japan's economic recovery, as the economic conditions increased the cost of production in Japan, making her products uncompetitive abroad. The person brought in to solve the Japanese economic problem was Joseph M. Dodge, a Detroit banker. The policy implemented by Dodge was a nine-point stabilisation programme, which was aimed at balancing the budget and reducing inflation. The three main points of the Dodge plan were, first, a balanced budget through government expenditure and an increase in taxes; second, the phasing out of the RFB and its replacement by the Counterpart Fund, which would be under Dodge's control as it was thought that a more stringent loan system would prevent unnecessary government expenditure; and third, the establishment of a single exchange rate, set at 360 yen to the dollar, to enable Japan to enter the Western economic system.[27]

One idea behind this programme was that Japan should achieve economic recovery without US aid. Therefore, emphasis was placed on Japan's trade expansion with its neighbouring countries.[28] America's plan was to see an expansion of Japan's trade with Southeast Asia so that Japan could gain access to raw materials there, and sell the raw materials to the United States to alleviate Japan's dollar gap. A key difficulty for this policy was, however, that Southeast Asia was not only linked to Japan's economic recovery, it was also linked to that of Britain. Britain, as a Southeast Asian colonial power, relied on sales of raw materials, such as Malayan tin and rubber, from this region to the United States for dollars. As Britain was experiencing a shortage of dollars in the postwar period, there was an attempt to re-establish this pre-war trade link, which was known as the triangular trade.[29] Therefore, America's plans for the expansion of Japan's exports to Southeast Asia raised fears in some industrial sectors in Britain.

These fears were not unfounded, as Japan had been one of Britain's major competitors in the 1930s, particularly in the area of textiles. In the aftermath of the First World War, Britain had been unable to regain its pre-war share of the world's cotton goods export market. This was due to various reasons, ranging from the establishment of indigenous cotton industries in Britain's former traditional markets, Japan's successful penetration of the East Asian textiles markets, and the demand for cheaper textiles during the depression when quality became a secondary issue for most consumers.[30] By 1933, Japan had overtaken Lancashire as the world's largest exporter of cotton piece goods. As the Lancashire cotton industry became increasingly threatened, its representatives began to accuse Japan of dumping goods, exploiting its labour, and of supplying heavy state subsidies to the cotton industry. From 1932 onwards a number of MPs representing Cheshire and Lancashire began making 'bitter attacks' against Japanese competition in the House of Commons.[31] In order to assist Britain's beleaguered industries, protectionist measures were implemented, including the Ottawa Agreements of 1932, and colonial quotas against foreign textile imports, which began in 1934. Although these measures checked Japanese exports, British exports were never able to regain their pre-war market share.[32]

The British textiles industry continued to have a voice in Britain in the immediate postwar period, as cotton textiles exports played a vital role in balancing Britain's trade between 1945 and 1951. It should also be noted that the cotton textiles interests had representation inside and outside of government through bodies such as the Manchester Chamber of Commerce and the Cotton Board, which kept the textiles issue alive. There was also an element of racial prejudice linked with the belief that Japan had started the war unfairly in East Asia, and this concept seems to have translated into the idea of Japanese 'unfair competition'; thus the textiles issue became representative of anti-Japanese feeling as a whole rather than just concerning the plight of Lancashire's textile workers.[33]

Private trade between citizens of the allied countries and Japan was permitted from the summer of 1947.[34] In the autumn of that year, a limited trade agreement was signed between the Sterling Area and Japan.[35] Official trade began on 31 May 1948 in the form of the OPA (Open Payments Agreement) a government-operated trade agreement. The British and

Japanese objectives behind the opening of trade relations were different. For Japan, it was a means to purchase scarce raw materials from pre-war trading partners with a view to re-establishing commercial relations with them. For Britain, trade with Japan was not crucial, but it was an important non-dollar source of cotton textiles for two reasons. First, it alleviated domestic demand for textiles, which enabled the British textiles industry to concentrate its manufacturing efforts on dollar-earning overseas markets. Second, grey cloth imports from Japan were re-exported as finished cotton textiles, accounting for nearly 20 per cent of Britain's total exports of these types of cotton goods in the first year of the agreement alone.[36]

The initial trade agreement between the Sterling Area and Japan was established only after lengthy administrative and banking negotiations. The sticking point was the pressure on SCAP to earn dollars from all of Japan's exports, because she could only obtain dollars from her trade with the United States. SCAP relented and broke the 'dollar-import ergo dollar-export sequence'.[37] It decided to trade in sterling on the condition that SCAP be allowed to convert surplus sterling into dollars at six-monthly intervals (on 30 June and 31 December). The only exception to this arrangement was Sterling Area purchases of cotton textiles, which had to be paid in dollars until July 1948 because the raw materials originated from a dollar source.[38] Sterling Area countries agreed to this arrangement in the knowledge that any serious imbalance in their bilateral trade would lead to a dollar drain. In short, the Open Payments Agreement was severely regulated because trade was based on convertible sterling, which designated Japan a hard currency country. Thus trade was restricted to goods which were deemed essential, and less essential items were justified only on the ground that such trade was 'useful' to the Sterling Area.[39] The OPA between the Sterling Area and Japan was further complicated by the fact that the Sterling Area signatories were divided into participants and non-participants. This division had been established at the outset, when certain dominions agreed to join a trade pool, which was designed to enable Britain and the 'participants' to scale their purchases from Japan so that they could collectively afford to import beyond the austerity level.[40] Participant countries had representation in the initial negotiations and on the Tokyo working party, which was an administrative group that ensured the smooth running of the OPA. Participants included countries such as Australia, New Zealand, South Africa, India and the United Kingdom. The non-participants, such as Burma, Pakistan and Iraq, were sterling countries, who traded in sterling and whose trade affected the overall sterling balance with SCAP, but who did not participate in either the negotiations or in the working party. These countries were excluded because their trade imbalance deemed them destabilising members of the core Sterling Area group.[41] The one Sterling Area territory that operated outside of the sterling pool was Hong Kong. It was deliberately left out of the OPA arrangement because of concerns that its entrepôt trade with mainland China would lead to a serious dollar drain.[42]

Each year the participants submitted their forecast of trade with Japan to Britain, which negotiated the agreement on behalf of the collective group. The administrative nature of the agreement meant that the three government bodies in charge of running the agreement, namely the Treasury, the Bank of England and the Foreign Office, had to maintain constant communication with SCAP and the participant countries to ensure that agreed levels of trade were being transacted. To ensure communication on the ground, representatives of the Sterling Area and SCAP met in Tokyo to discuss pertinent issues, but the group in Tokyo had no influence on decision making. Many of the strategic decisions were discussed in the Cabinet's Overseas Negotiations Committee and sometimes in the Economic Policy Committee, and if an issue warranted ministerial action, discussion was raised to Cabinet ministerial level.

Once both sides had agreed on the trade level, import licences were issued. The Board of Trade issued licences in the United Kingdom and MITI issued comparable licences in Japan. Different types of licences were available for importers, and these ranged from the most flexible to the restrictive. In Japan and the United Kingdom, the most flexible form of import licences were called AA (Automatic Approval) and OGL (Open General Licence) respectively.[43] These were less frequently used in restrictive bilateral trade relations, where specific licences were more likely to be issued.[44] In the first year, the sterling bloc had a trade deficit with SCAP because the latter bought seasonally (purchases were divided into the October–March and April–September budgets respectively) and around 60 per cent of the trade was conducted between December and March. In contrast, the Sterling Area bought on a continual basis and gave out import licenses much more freely. SCAP's purchases, however, did not reach the estimates reached at the time of the agreement; thus SCAP accumulated excess sterling, which raised the convertibility issue from the first year of the agreement. The sterling bloc did not wish to see a dollar drain and hoped that SCAP would retain sterling as part of their capital. SCAP was divided between two schools of thought: those who believed that Japan must earn dollars from the Sterling Area and those, including General MacArthur himself, who believed that the main objective of the agreement was to increase Japan's trade with the Sterling Area to a maximum, and therefore supported surplus sterling holdings, even when the pound was devalued against the dollar.[45]

Assurances from MacArthur were not enough to calm British fears. In Whitehall, the OPA with Japan was discussed in July 1949 by an inter-departmental working party,[46] where the collective group proposed that SCAP be allowed to hold a minimum of £10 million sterling balance before they converted it into dollars.[47] The proposal was approved by the Overseas Negotiations Committee (ONC) and the Chancellor of the Exchequer, and eventually accepted by SCAP. Despite these guarantees, the Treasury was not going to take any chances in the next set of negotiations for the year 1949/50. Its aim was to prevent any form of dollar liability, even if this meant reducing trade with Japan to negligible amounts. This very stringent approach was a reflection of the overall British policy adopted at the Commonwealth Economic Conference of July 1949, where Britain asked individual sterling Commonwealth countries to set national import programmes and abide by their respective targets. The aim behind this approach was to keep down sterling-dollar expenditures and minimise the dollar drain.[48]

While the Sterling Area continued to manage its trade relations with occupied Japan, profound economic changes were taking place as a result of the US 'reverse course'. In February 1949 Joseph Dodge arrived in Japan to carry out the nine-point stabilisation programme, which included balancing the budget, cutting off loans from the Recovery Finance Bank, and reducing subsidies.[49] In April Dodge established the official exchange rate at 360 yen to the dollar, a rate which remained in place until 1971, and implemented a deflationary policy by cutting down on demand.[50] His basic premise was that Japan should not continue to rely on US aid for economic recovery, but focus instead upon her own productivity. The year 1949 also saw the arrival of three US trade missions in Japan.[51] Two of these recommended an import-first policy on the premise that increased imports would 'stimulate production and eventually increase exports'.[52] This policy was implemented in 1950 and early 1951. Placed in this difficult situation, Japan needed cheap raw materials from a soft currency area. The result was greater SCAP purchases from the Sterling Area.

In short, Britain was faced with unexpected changes in 1950. American sponsorship of Japan's economic recovery meant that Japan would be expanding its exports to the West. By gradually weaning Japan from American aid, the United States' aim was to encourage Japan to look towards Southeast Asia and the Sterling Area for its raw materials. Until 1950, the OPA between the Sterling Area and Japan was a useful agreement by which the Sterling Area countries could buy non-dollar cotton textiles. With the expansion of Japanese exports, however, the bilateral agreement became a much more complex issue. If Japan increased its purchases, the Sterling Area would have to reciprocate and purchase more goods in order to balance payments. The consequence of not doing so was the possibility of SCAP converting its sterling into dollars, or SCAP using participant sterling to purchase non-participant goods. Britain's problem was how to reach a trade balance with Japan without a loss of dollars and without a threat to British industries; she also had to ensure the Sterling Area that she had its interests at heart rather than the welfare of her domestic industries.

Britain was, therefore, under pressure to balance the various interests effectively during the trade negotiations, which began on 7 June 1950. Some of the issues on the agenda were discussed and settled early in the negotiations, such as the question of the establishment of official Japanese overseas agencies throughout the Sterling Area. This was rejected because the British colonies were still not ready to give MFN treatment with respect to the free entry of Japanese nationals. The peoples of Southeast Asia held bitter memories of their occupation and maltreatment at the hands of the Japanese during the war.[53] They were ready to accept Japanese products but not Japanese nationals.[54] Furthermore, SCAP's request for a Sterling Area-wide MFN treatment in shipping, together with guarantees of non-discriminatory trade and tariff treatment, as rejected because it was a matter to be considered by the individual Sterling Area countries.[55]

What was more complicated was agreeing to an estimated amount of trade between the two sides for the period 1 July 1950 to 30 June 1951. The eventual agreed amount was £92.6 million in each direction, approximately £38 million more than in the previous year.[56] The increase in trade was due to Japan's increased imports from the Sterling Area.

The significance of these new trade levels was in the political problems that arose from the Sterling Area's obligation to increase its purchases from Japan. For instance, colonial estimates for increased Japanese purchases became a point of contention between the Colonial Office and the Board of Trade, because the latter thought colonial intentions for increased textile purchases breached the intra-sterling agreement which stipulated imports of strict essentials only. Given that the six West African colonies had fourteen months' supply of textiles either in production or in transit, the Board of Trade deemed that further textile imports were unnecessary.[57] More importantly, the Board of Trade's opposition was driven by the alarm that would be triggered in Lancashire as a result of increased Commonwealth and colonial cotton purchases.[58]

The Colonial Office could not accept the Board of Trade's position. They understood the importance of restricting imports in order to save gold and dollars, but opposed restrictions, which were predominantly based on the British government's wish to 'secure sheltered position for UK manufacturers'.[59] Furthermore, the Colonial Office argued that the colonies themselves were far better equipped to judge the amount of textiles they should be importing, and that, in fact, increased Japanese textiles exports were necessary because both India and Germany had priced themselves out of the colonial market by raising their textile prices. Japan was the only source of textiles in the appropriate price range.

The ONC was unable to help the Board of Trade's position, as the colonial estimates were based on essentials and therefore there was no ground on which the ONC could ask them to revise the figures. Furthermore, Britain could only ask the colonies to reduce their imports on balance of payments grounds and not on the basis of protecting British manufacturers.[60] The issue was finally settled two months later at an Economic Policy Committee (EPC) meeting on 28 July 1950 chaired by the Prime Minister, Clement Attlee. It was agreed after much discussion that the 'estimates of colonial textile requirements by direct shipment from Japan should be increased to the figure proposed by the Secretary of State for the Colonies'.[61] The deciding factor was the political consequence of the colonies discovering that their import estimates had been scaled down for the benefit of UK manufacturers.

The other problem, which became apparent during the negotiations, was the rising suspicion and the dissatisfaction among the participants over trade allocations with Japan. Britain, as head of the Sterling Area, was the controller of the agreement and therefore responsible for balancing trade plans. Britain's role was becoming more difficult as the dominions, such as Australia, India and Ceylon, were anxious to see greater trade flexibility with Japan because they felt constrained by the limits placed on their purchasing power.[62] There were even grievances raised by the dominions' representatives when Britain decided, during the meeting of the Sterling Area delegation in Tokyo, that UK and colonial figures for the trade plan should be a single figure instead of separate figures. The representatives of the dominions believed that Britain's motive for the change was to reserve the right to raid colonial purchasing power for her own benefit.[63]

These incidents indicate the difficulties Britain faced in allocating purchasing powers that were satisfactory to all the member countries. They also highlighted the fact that many members did not entirely trust the system led by Britain. Australia and Ceylon wished to see a liberalisation of trade, but had it been carried out, there would have been major setbacks to the system, the main one being the potential for a major trade imbalance if bilateralism was replaced by more liberal trade which could have led to a drain in Britain's precious dollar reserves.

The most serious problem in the talks arose as a result of differences between SCAP and the Sterling Area concerning SCAP's sterling holdings. The position taken by SCAP was that it should be free to

> spend its holdings as it pleased with either participant or non-partici- pant sterling countries, subject only to the area's normal currency controls and the agreement that trade under the Sterling Area-Japan plan reach an approximate balance by the end of the year.[64]

Britain was of the view that rigid controls had to be put in place because Japan's 1949 purchase of Burmese rice using participant balances had reduced the availability of sterling for the participants, and they wished to avoid a repetition of this. The deadlock was lifted in October when it was decided that £3 million would be put aside in case difficulties arose in 'maintaining an exact trading balance at all times'.[65] Both sides also agreed that sterling balances could not be diverted from one account to the other; both SCAP and partici- pant representatives believed that they had secured their respective positions. SCAP officials believed they could still divert some sterling from the partici- pant account if it was discussed with the participants in advance, while the negotiators for the participant countries were convinced they had 'won their point on restricting Japan's free usage of participant sterling'.[66]

Tensions between SCAP and the Sterling Area were not eased by the fact that SCAP requested increased rice purchases again in 1950. Alvary Gascoigne, head of the UKLM (United Kingdom Liaison Mission), vigorously opposed this. His argument was that in the first instance, rice production in Southeast Asia was below normal because the region had been ravaged by Japan during the war and its economies were still disrupted. Second, he believed that the Southeast Asian countries, which relied on Burma's rice production in the past, had prior claim over that of Japan. Moreover, Southeast Asian countries had a higher priority because Japan had a considerable indigenous production and the Japanese had a greater tolerance for other grains. Finally, heavy demand by Japan threatened to raise rice prices, making it difficult for Southeast Asian countries to purchase foodstuffs; consequently, Southeast Asia would become more vulnerable to communist pressure and infiltration. In spite of Gascoigne's opposition, Japan was allocated large supplies of Burmese rice. This was because Burma was a non-participant and therefore free to reach trade agreements independently of Britain.

Britain thus faced numerous problems in regard to Japan in 1950. These included increased raw material purchases by Japan and the possible revival of Japanese competition. There was rising frustration on the part of the participant countries, who wished to see a greater flexibility of trade between themselves and Japan. The mounting issues eventually necessitated a long-term approach to the Sterling Area's trade relations with Japan. Thus in July, the ONC set up a working party to study the long-term relations between the Sterling Area and Japan.[67] In the meantime, Britain and Japan faced more difficulties concerning raw materials, namely Japan's attempt to enter the International Wheat Agreement.

Japan's application to the International Wheat Agreement

Rice was not the only food in short supply in the postwar period. A parallel set of negotiations was taking place in 1950 with regard to Japan and Germany's application to join the International Wheat Agreement (IWA). The International Wheat Council was an international organisation established in 1931 when the first meeting was held in Rome. Although several meetings were held throughout the years, it was not until the seventh meeting of the IWC in 1949 that the IWA was signed and ratified by all participants.[68] The IWA was made up of both wheat exporters and importers, and the organisation's aim was to stabilise wheat prices so that exporters were guaranteed a set price for their wheat while importers were guaranteed an agreed amount of wheat for the duration of the agreement. The signatories agreed to buy or sell wheat at a price which would not exceed $1.98 Canadian as a maximum and $1.65 Canadian as a minimum for the four-year duration of the agreement, from 1 July 1949 to 31 July 1953.[69] In November 1949, Germany and Japan applied to join the Agreement under US sponsorship. In order to become members, Germany and Japan needed the approval of two thirds of the wheat exporters and importers respectively. Their application was turned down in November due to the opposition of the wheat importers. Thus the joint German and Japanese application was postponed until January 1950.[70]

In the meantime, Britain was working on its policy with regard to Japan and Germany's application. On 5 January 1950, the issue was raised at the EPC and it was decided that Britain would be prepared to agree to the accession of Germany and Japan only if this did not adversely affect Britain's position.[71] Five days later, the British delegation met representatives of the major wheat exporters, the United States, Canada and Australia, and came to the conclusion that none of the wheat exporters understood Britain's concerns. Therefore she had no other choice but to oppose Japan and Germany's entry to the IWA.[72] The issue was discussed on 12 January at a meeting of the IWC. The condition of Japan's entry was that she would be guaranteed 900,000 metric tons of wheat and that Germany would be guaranteed 1,800,000 metric tons annually for the four-year duration of the IWA. An objection was raised at the meeting by the United Kingdom, because it feared that if Japan bought wheat from Australia, the amount available for Britain would decrease. This in turn meant that Britain would have to look to the dollar area for wheat. In order to address Britain's opposition, Australia proposed to sell wheat to Britain at the beginning of the year and sell whatever was left to Japan. Although SCAP was unhappy with this compromise, it was ready to accept any agreement that could be reached in order to enable Japan and Germany to become members of the IWA. Britain, however, argued that the mere possibility that Japan would buy Australian wheat would send sterling wheat prices up, and asked that Japan agree to buy only a specified amount from Australia. Britain wanted Japan and Germany to agree to restrict their purchases from Australia and France to the extra amount created by the two producers for their benefit. On 20 January, the German representative wrote a note to the Wheat Council agreeing to Britain's demand. The deadlock continued, however, due to Australia's opposition to Britain's formula.

The question of Japan and Germany's membership was raised again on 13 March. A vote was taken in which all of the exporting countries (the USA, Canada, Australia, Uruguay and France) and twelve of the nineteen importing countries agreed to their membership. Those who opposed the motion, thereby preventing the membership of Germany and Japan, were Ceylon, Greece, India, Israel, New Zealand, the Philippines and the UK. At a subsequent meeting two days later, German and Japanese membership were considered separately. As Germany had written a letter to the Council expressing its intention to self-regulate its wheat purchases from Australia, it became a member of the IWA. Conversely, Japan, which did not furnish a similar letter to the Council, was not admitted. The next meeting of the IWC was scheduled for 19 June.

Meanwhile, British officials were continuing their talks with the Australians in order to reach an agreement which would not only safeguard Britain's purchases but also satisfy Australia. They were also conducting talks with officials in Washington and with SCAP, hoping that they would agree to Japan's conditional entry to the IWA. At a meeting on 3 May the Americans proposed a Japanese undertaking, addressed privately to the British government, not to buy excess Australian wheat. All the Commonwealth importers, including Britain, approved the idea. The only affirmative answer needed to break the deadlock was SCAP's.

SCAP initially decided to leave the decision to the Japanese. On 25 May, representatives of Japan's ESB (Economic Stabilisation Board), the Ministry of Agriculture and Forestry and MOFA (the Ministry of Foreign Affairs) met to discuss the conditional entry. However, before the Japanese could come to a decision, they received the news that MacArthur had decided against the offer without prior consultation with the Japanese or other SCAP officials.[73] MacArthur's motives behind his unilateral approach were based on two points. First, under conditional membership, Australia's wheat would be contracted to the United Kingdom and other Sterling Area countries; thus the amount of non-dollar wheat available to Japan would be too small to be of any advantage. Second, British documents indicate that MacArthur had linked the wheat issue with the difficulties SCAP was facing in regard to rice purchases from Burma. The IWA was a bargaining chip against difficulties he was encountering in negotiating the new trade plan with the sterling participants.

When the IWC met again on 19 June, Japan's application for unconditional membership was turned down due to the opposition votes of importers such as the UK, India, Ceylon, Egypt, New Zealand, Saudi Arabia and Greece.[74] The case of Japan's attempts at IWA membership highlights the shortage of food supplies in the postwar period, and the high demand for non-dollar foodstuffs. It also underscored Britain's fears of a decrease in non-dollar wheat sources if Japan was accepted unconditionally to the IWA.

MFN treatment for Japan

To expand its international trade, Japan needed the assistance of its foreign trade partners. What this assistance entailed was equal tariff rights for Japan. Without better tariff rates, Japan's produce would continue to be in a disadvantageous position, and for this reason the United States wished to see Japan granted MFN rights and eventual accession to the GATT. Clearly, the United States' motive for Japan's entry was to see the latter's products receive equal tariff rates abroad so that it could undertake economic recovery without American assistance. Another reason behind American eagerness for Japan to enter the GATT as soon as possible, was the anxiety that stemmed from the fact that if an agreement was not concluded quickly US manufacturers would rise up in opposition to the increased level of Japanese goods on the US market. In order to prevent complications, the State and Army Departments wanted to rush the matter through and establish an international agreement to grant MFN treatment to Japan. There were even greater reasons why Japan wished to become a GATT signatory. First was the political prestige linked to membership, because this would signify the return of Japan into the international community. Second, Japan could gather information and exchange information with other countries concerning international trade.[75] But more important was the realisation in Japan that negotiating tariffs through the GATT was fairer and more practical than attempting to regulate trade with each individual trading nation through bilateral agreements.[76]

America's first step towards Japan's GATT application was very modest; it was to gain MFN treatment for the duration of the US occupation. Although West Germany was granted MFN treatment for goods in 1948, Japan was not extended the same right in that year. The major obstacle to Japan was Britain and its dominions, who opposed Japan's temporary membership for the following reasons. First, MFN treatment should only be given to sovereign states; second, Japan would have to conform to a uniform exchange rate; third, bitterness towards Japan was a major political obstacle to extending MFN treatment; and fourth, Japan's trade practices and labour costs in the postwar period were a cause for concern in Britain.[77]

Even after the uniform exchange rate was established between the dollar and the yen, and the pound and the yen, Britain remained opposed to granting MFN treatment to Japan.[78] The US State and Army Departments decided not to discuss the Japan issue at the GATT talks in Geneva in February 1950 because of opposition from various quarters. Instead, they decided to continue with the original approach of acquiring MFN treatment for Japanese merchandise through bilateral agreements. By 1950, eight countries had extended MFN treatment to Japan. These were Austria, the French zone of occupation in Germany, Greece, Ireland, Italy, Norway and Turkey. Those countries that had agreed in principle to extend MFN treatment were South Korea, Hong Kong and Burma.[79] Having gained this degree of support, the United States decided to place the Japan issue before the GATT session in Torquay in November. Conversely, Britain was still against granting MFN treatment to Japan. The issue was, thus, scheduled for discussion at the EPC in September in order to decide on Britain's position.[80] The Board of Trade prepared a memorandum for the committee, in which it recommended that Britain should stop stalling and tell the United States outright that it was unable to extend MFN treatment to Japan. The main reason behind the Board of Trade's opposition to Japan was the low cost of Japanese products as a result of 'low wages combined with modern and efficient plants and methods'.[81] Although the President of the Board of Trade, Harold Wilson, did not wish to support a policy which 'nursed inefficient UK industries', he did not wish to undertake a policy which might lead to 'widespread unemployment problems' in the United Kingdom. Thus his policy was to protect the UK against Japanese competition. He also hoped the Commonwealth countries would follow Britain and retain their freedom of action. If the Commonwealth countries extended MFN treatment to

Japan, there was the chance that they would have to take action to protect their own industries against Japanese competition. This meant they would be forced to take equal discriminatory action against British goods. Furthermore, Wilson indicated that it was inappropriate for the United States to propose the MFN issue independently of the issue of Japan's GATT application. Thus he thought the issue should be postponed until such a time when Japan's GATT membership could be discussed.

On receiving the Board of Trade's memorandum prior to the scheduled meeting of the EPC, the Foreign Office prepared its argument to counter the Board of Trade's proposal. The Foreign office prepared two sets of objections. One was based on international political implications. The Foreign Office's argument rested on the fact that if Japan continued to rely on American charity, it would consequently strain Western resources as a whole. In addition, if Japan did not become economically viable, there was a chance that the Japanese communists might take advantage of general disgruntlement to cause civil unrest and disrupt industrial production through their association with the trade unions.[82] There was, therefore, always the potential threat of a communist uprising from within, which could lead to the eventual loss of Japan from the 'Western camp'. Furthermore, the Foreign Office highlighted the significance of cheap Japanese exports for the colonies, whose people depended on them. Moreover, the Foreign Office emphasised the importance of pursuing a policy of eliminating restrictions on world trade as a whole, and this included giving MFN rights to Japan.

The second objection concerned the protection of British industries. The Foreign Office viewed the British refusal to give MFN rights to Japan as unproductive, as it would only encourage a few other countries such as Australia and New Zealand to follow its lead. It was also pointed out that the UK would only be able to protect its industries in the UK and the colonies; thus there was little point in refusing to give MFN treatment to Japan. Furthermore, the Foreign Office indicated that they did not see any signs of the textiles industry being threatened from Japanese competition, especially as the order books of most industries were still full.[83]

In short, the Foreign Office was aware of the American position on the issue and saw a need to align British policy with that of the United States. They were also aware from the UK Liaison Mission's reports that without greater trade relations with Western countries, Japan's economy could collapse, leading to internal chaos and creating the perfect opportunity for communism to rise from within. The Foreign Office's concern was well justified, as the Japanese Communist Party had been instructed by the Cominform to carry out a violent revolutionary struggle in Japan. Moreover, the SCAP clampdown on communist activities had driven many members underground.[84]

Despite preparing a full set of arguments, the Foreign Office was unable to dissuade the EPC from endorsing the Board of Trade's position on 15

September.[85] The decision in the EPC was not taken very well by Foreign Office officials, and one of them noted that 'an open refusal at present will, in addition to the offence it gives to the Americans, appear as most uncalled for in the Japanese eyes and may cause us embarrassment in future relations after the conclusion of a Peace Treaty'.[86]

The result was that the US attempt to have the Japan issue discussed at the GATT conference in Torquay was derailed once again in November 1950. This time, the British position was a firm 'no' to the prospect of an international obligation to extend MFN treatment to Japan. In short, what the issue highlighted was the importance of reassuring British industrial concerns about their future and protecting British exports to the Commonwealth, over and above Britain's relations with the United States. Although the United States was no nearer to getting MFN treatment for Japan, it nevertheless persisted with its endeavour. At the Torquay meeting, America began to campaign for Japan's observer status with each contracting member country, in the hope of raising the issue successfully at the GATT conference in 1951.[87]

Conclusions

1950 saw the continuing US sponsorship of Japan's economic recovery that had begun with the 'reverse course' in 1948. It was the first year since the beginning of the OPA that Britain and the Sterling Area countries experienced the full impact of Japan's economic recovery, because Japan sought increased food purchases from Southeast Asia and the Sterling Area countries. The consequence of this was a possible imbalance in the OPA as SCAP sought to buy extra raw materials from Burma using participant sterling. In order to prevent SCAP using its sterling reserves from the participant pool, it became all the more important for participant countries to increase their trade levels with SCAP. Although this was the most sensible solution, it led to other problems such as increased purchases of cotton textiles direct from Japan. This led to the Board of Trade raising alarm bells over the possible demise of the Lancashire cotton industry due to competition from Japan's cheap and efficient labour force. Furthermore, by the third year of the trade plan, there was an accumulation of dissatisfaction by all participants who felt constrained by the controls placed on their purchases. The anger was directed at Britain, as the various participants thought that Britain was reducing their trade allocations for its own benefit. Moreover, there was the constant sterling anxiety over SCAP's right to convert its sterling balances into dollars. All these issues led officials in Whitehall to take the initiative, and in July an inter-ministerial working party was set up by the ONC to study the Sterling Area's long-term relations with Japan.

A feature of 1950 was the political issues that arose from the scarcity of raw materials. The rice issue and Japan's attempt to enter the IWA highlighted Britain's inability to accept the former's presence in its trading sphere. Britain was afraid that Japan might buy up the limited, non-dollar raw materials and raise prices. In the end, however, it was not Japan, but the outbreak of the Korean War on 25 June that caused raw material prices to skyrocket.

Another reason why Britain was against the extension of the MFN treatment to Japan was the fear that cheap Japanese goods would flood the market, thereby, threatening Britain's industrial livelihood. Britain feared that this would force the Commonwealth to raise tariffs against all imports regardless of their origin, thus nullifying any imperial preferential rights enjoyed by British goods and eventually driving Britain out of its traditional trading area.

What the above three issues highlight is the nature of the challenge presented to Britain by the gradual return of Japan into the Western comity of nations through US assistance. On the surface, Britain seemed less than friendly to Japan's economic recovery. In reality, there was no unanimity between the ministries concerned. The Board of Trade had the interests of British industries at heart with regard to MFN treatment. The Treasury expressed its concern with the overall balance in Britain's financial affairs. Conversely, the Foreign Office was concerned with Britain's relations with foreign countries. If there was any major discrepancy, it was over the MFN issue between the Board of Trade and the Foreign office. It was inevitable that the Board of Trade would gain the upper hand because it had been responsible for commercial treaties since the 1920s, and the question of MFN rights was in the Board of Trade's sphere of responsibility.[87] Britain's relations with Japan and the United States thus depended very much on whether a compromise could be reached between Britain's domestic and external interests.

3 Embarking on the Sterling Payments Agreement

Introduction

If the division between the East and the West had taken shape at first in Europe, it was the outbreak of the Korean war in June 1950 that solidified the communist threat in East Asia. The events of 1950 had several consequences for the United States' attitude towards the region. First, America's perception of a communist threat shifted from a Soviet threat to that of a Chinese threat. Second, there was a growing conviction that if the United States did not intervene in the various wars in the region, Chinese communists would overrun all of Southeast and East Asia. Other consequences of the Korean War were the signing of a liberal peace treaty with Japan in September 1951 and the introduction of the Mutual Defense Assistance Control Act of October 1951. The Battle Act, as it was commonly known, stated that if any of America's allies were found to be exporting strategic materials to the Soviet bloc at any time, their economic and military aid from the United States would be terminated.[1] The act made it increasingly difficult for Japan to resume its trade with mainland China, and it therefore became even more important for Japan to explore other markets. Thus there were attempts made in 1951 to assess Japan's trade potential with Southeast Asia, through missions such as the joint SCAP-Japan mission of July, which incidentally was unsuccessful because British officials in the colonies refused entry to Japanese citizens.[2]

It is incidents such as the above that have endorsed the view that Britain's policy was to protect its trading interests in Southeast Asia against Japanese competition. This argument has been accepted so widely that no one has ventured to examine the different strands of Britain's policy towards Japan. This chapter, therefore, examines Britain's sterling policy towards Japan in order to elucidate Japan's importance to the Sterling Area in 1951. Conversely, the negotiations towards Sterling Area-Japan trade and their aftermath are examined to highlight Japan's perception of Britain as banker to the Sterling Area.

The year 1951 saw Japan's entry into the IWA and the ILO (International Labour Organisation). Japan was invited to be present as an observer to the

GATT in October, but not without a three-hour debate about the implications of this. Britain, which was fearful of any Japanese affiliation with the GATT until all trade issues were resolved, expressed opposition with support from Australia, Southern Rhodesia and Czechoslovakia. The opposing group eventually relented in order to prevent a serious division within the contracting parties. With the British compromise, Japan was invited as an observer from the sixth session. Although Japan was no nearer to joining the GATT, the invitation was still interpreted by the Japanese as a foot in the door.

Long-term relations between the Sterling Area and Japan

In July 1950, a working party was set up under the ONC to undertake a study of the long-term relations between the Sterling Area and Japan.[3] Such a study was long overdue, as traders and participants had become increasingly frustrated by the restrictive and short-term nature of the Open Payments Agreement. The study was thus an attempt by the United Kingdom to establish a long-term strategy for the Sterling Area's trade relations with Japan. The working party was instructed to write a joint report demonstrating probable Sterling Area-Japan trade relations in 1953, basing its predictions on Japan's balance of payments and earnings.

The working party spent seven months compiling the report. During the process, members expressed differences of opinion, as expected, over the future of Britain's trade relations with Japan. The final version of the report was, however, a comprehensive and highly strategic document, which focused on the long-term framework of Britain's policy. If anything, the lack of Board of Trade representation on the committee enabled the working party to compile an objective assessment of Anglo-Japanese trade relations, without undue consideration for the interests of domestic manufacturers.

The report was submitted to the Economic Steering Committee on 6 February 1951. It considered future patterns of trade and payments arrangements between Japan and the Sterling Area under the following points:

(i)   The Sterling Area balance of payments with Japan; the United Kingdom's overall balance of payments; and the general position of sterling as an international currency in the Far East
(ii) Competition between the United Kingdom and Japanese exports
(iii) The impact on Britain's political and economic interests of Japanese purchases of rice in Burma and Thailand, and of cotton and possibly raw materials in the Sterling Area
(iv) The interest of the underdeveloped countries in cheap imports of consumption and capital goods from Japan[4]

With regard to the first point, the report identified Britain's long-term financial policy as one whose goal should be to restore and encourage the widest possible use of sterling in East Asia. In order to achieve this aim, the report recommended Japan's eventual inclusion in the transferable account area, which meant that Japan would eventually be able to apply automatic sterling transferability from and to any third country, whereas she was unable to do so whilst a member of the bilateral account group.

The report identified several points which precluded Japan from joining the transferable account area immediately. First, there was the possibility that Japan might accumulate an uncontrollable amount of sterling as a result of the demand for Japanese goods from the Commonwealth countries. Second, there was uncertainty over whether automatic transferability would lead to a net inflow or outflow of sterling from Japan over a period of time. The report thus recommended that Japan's convertibility rights should be forfeited, and while Japan would be given freedom to use its sterling with third countries it would be restricted to administrative transferability, which meant that transfers had first to have the permission of the Bank of England.[5] Therefore, despite plans for the eventual inclusion of Japan in the transferable account area, Japan was to remain in the bilateral account area for the foreseeable future.

Concerning competition between the United Kingdom and Japanese exports, the report observed that British textiles manufacturers would not be able to compete with Japanese cotton and rayon manufacturers in the long run for two reasons; first, Japan's labour costs were a fraction of those of Britain, and second, Japan was being allocated American raw cotton on a more favourable basis than Britain. The report expressed uncertainty over the future position of British industries such as pottery and steel, and therefore concluded that more information on Japan's main industries was needed and that these should be monitored carefully. In the meantime, the report saw little reason for Britain to block Japan from the GATT or to refuse MFN rights to Japan in order to protect British trade, as it had been doing since 1948 and 1950 respectively, as neither measure would be of any use for the protection of British goods in third markets. Instead, the report recommended that British industries improve their technical and commercial lead over Japan in the sectors where they were ahead. In the short-term, however, the report expressed the hope that the Commonwealth countries would follow the British example and apply import restrictions on Japanese manufactured goods to enable Britain to preserve its market share in the Sterling Area.

The report was sympathetic to the difficulties faced by Asian Sterling Area countries in importing Southeast Asian rice when SCAP, on behalf of Japan, was outbidding everyone else. The working party viewed the problem as outside its jurisdiction, because Britain did not have the power to dissuade SCAP from heavy purchases of raw materials in the interest of Southeast Asian stability or to persuade Thailand and Burma to revive the rice allocation system. Thus it concluded that the colonies and Ceylon would simply have to outbid Japan in their rice purchases from Thailand and Burma.[6]

The final point in the report focused on the issue of 'underdeveloped' countries. It outlined the difficulty of dissuading 'underdeveloped' countries within the Sterling Area from purchasing cheap Japanese goods when the United Kingdom had already publicised their policy of assisting the development of those areas through the Colombo Plan. Thus the report recommended that these colonies be allowed to purchase cheap Japanese goods.

The working party's recommendations were channelled through to various Cabinet committees and boards, starting with the Economic Planning Board and the Economic Steering Committee on 15 February, followed by the ONC on 23 February and finally to the Chancellor of the Exchequer. In each instance the recommendations were approved with minor changes. Thus, by the end of the bureaucratic approval process, it was decided that Britain's long-term aim would be to transfer the Sterling Area-Japan payments relations to a non-dollar agreement where Japan's convertibility rights would be abolished. Britain would negotiate trade levels on behalf of the entire Sterling Area; thus Britain would be the sole negotiator in the newly envisioned relationship. In order to prevent any sudden Japanese accumulation of sterling, a bilateral balance of payments exercise would be conducted periodically. Finally, given Japan's probable future independence from the United States, the new agreement would be signed by Japan, instead of SCAP.[7]

The report prepared by the working party between July 1950 and February 1951 underscores the British decision to sign the Sterling Payments Agreement in place of the OPA, and to end Japan's rights to convertibility. The overarching impetus for Britain's decision was her desire to expand the use of sterling in East Asia. This was an extension of Britain's sterling policy of the early 1950s, when British policymakers thought that sterling could still provide a viable alternative to the dollar bloc. If one looks at Britain's overall sterling policy, it is understandable that with mainland China lost to Western trade after 1950, it was obvious that Britain should look for another anchor in East Asia to help the expansion of sterling in the postwar world. A country like Japan was also important because expanded trade relations between Japan and the sterling countries in the region would facilitate a reduction in the sterling balances of countries such as India, Pakistan and Ceylon. Therefore the main reason for the signing of the Sterling Payments Agreement was to facilitate Sterling Area-Japan trade.

After the Cabinet had approved the working party's recommendation, British representatives in the United States and Japan were instructed to approach the State, Treasury and Defense Departments in Washington, the Economic and Scientific Section of SCAP in Japan, and also members of the Japanese Cabinet, in order to inform them of Britain's payment plans. Christopher Steel, the Minister in Washington, and the Treasury representative, Allan Christelow, met with the American representatives in March. The meetings provided the British with valuable insights into the US perspective on the payments agreement. On the whole, all of the US officials expressed anxiety over their country's inability to influence Japan's trade policy if the latter decided to sign the new payments agreement. They expressed the hope that Japan would shift its entire trade into dollars, given the feasibility of such an option as a result of the Korean War boom.[8]

A report from Hugh Thomas, the Financial Advisor to UKLM in Tokyo communicated a similar negative reaction from SCAP's McDermott as well as the Japanese Finance Minister, Ikeda Hayato. Thomas detected a distinct anti-Sterling Area complex amongst SCAP officials, and by default this feeling was strongly held among Japanese politicians. The core of their discontent stemmed from the exclusion of convertibility in the proposed payments agreement between Japan and the Sterling Area, which they viewed as Britain's attempt to severely restrict Japan's trade options.[9]

This view was detailed in an Economic Counselor's report to the State Department dated 6 April. Carl H. Boehringer, the report's author, expressed uncertainty over the exact British arrangement but he was aware that Britain wished to obtain a new agreement which could continue without alteration in the post-treaty period. He wrote that 'instead of close integration with the Sterling Area, Japan might find it feasible and possibly more advantageous to assume American Account Status'.[10]

The arguments for shifting Japanese trade to a dollar basis were:

- Maximum transferability both within and without the Sterling Area and convertibility to dollars.
- Optimum competitive advantage in selecting and obtaining imports of critical raw materials from Sterling Area countries, several of which had direct or indirect preferential arrangements to maximise the export of desirable goods to hard currency areas.
- If Japan's trade shifted to a dollar basis, the United Kingdom would find it most difficult to influence Japan's trade with other areas, and would have only a limited ability to influence her trade with the Sterling Area.
- Close mutual defence arrangements with the necessary concomitant economic arrangements would be strengthened by having Japan a member of the Dollar Area. Japan's overall trade situation could be more effectively planned and directed in such manner as to best complement the US military aid programme.
- With Japan in the Dollar Area, America's ability to free Japanese trade from the numerous restrictions currently imposed by the UK would be directly enhanced. Furthermore, the US would be able to encourage the progressive freeing-up of world trade and an approximation of multilateral trade.[11]

The Economic Counselor's arguments were based on SCAP's firm belief that Japan would reap greater benefits from remaining in the dollar bloc because of its easier access to much needed raw materials. Japan's transition to the dollar bloc would also unshackle her from the many restrictions of the Sterling Area, and endorse US efforts to achieve a multilateral trading system.

Meanwhile, Britain's decision to abolish dollar convertibility in the forth-coming Sterling Payments Agreement spurred the Japanese government to undertake several studies of Japan's negotiating position. The view in Japan was that the abolition of the dollar clause would lead to an increase in trade with the Sterling Area, thus placing Japan in a dilemma over which currency bloc to base its exchange rate on, the Sterling Area or the Dollar Area. For example, the report compiled by Ichimada Hisato, Governor of the Bank of Japan, entitled 'Should Japan in future belong to the Dollar Area or the Sterling Area?', examined the pros and cons of the two blocs by raising questions concerning the two currencies' stability; the convertibility of the two currencies; the possible induction of foreign capital; the possibilities for Japanese trade with the two areas; and the prospects of acquiring foreign funds through invisible trade.[12] Responding to these questions, Ichimada acknowledged the improvement in the pound's position since the start of the Korean War. He realised, however, that this was due to a world-wide increase in the value of raw materials, which had subsequently helped increase the Sterling Area's dollar reserves. Furthermore, Ichimada noted that Japan would achieve greater stability by placing Japan's exchange base on the dollar rather than the pound, due to the dollar's stability. Moreover, Japan was assured of raw materials from the United States, whereas there was uncertainty over whether the Sterling Area would relax its trade restrictions with Japan. In the case of sterling trade restrictions, Ichimada foresaw difficulties in running down Japan's sterling reserves because sterling was not convertible. Another consideration was foreign capital for Japan's economic reconstruction and development. Ichimada knew that Japan could not rely on Britain and the Sterling Area to inject foreign capital into Japan, thus he thought that it would be wiser for Japan to place her foreign exchange base on the dollar. In conclusion, Ichimada considered that it was necessary for Japan to acquire dollars first by increasing exports to the United States; second, by increasing its exports to the open account countries in the area, as settlements were made in dollars; third, by expanding exports to countries within the Dollar Area; and last, by securing American credit from banks.[13]

The report elucidates Japan's dilemma about which bloc it should join. Japan's advantages in joining the Dollar Area were that the dollar was more stable and that it could provide the capital and foodstuffs necessary for Japan's economic development. Ichimada, however, expressed concern over the future of South and Southeast Asia. He was particularly anxious that if the Colombo Plan were to succeed, the whole of Asia might base its exchange on sterling, in which case Japan would face severe restrictions as the only dollar-based country surrounded by sterling-based countries. Thus he hoped that Truman's Point IV programme would succeed in encouraging Southeast Asia towards the dollar bloc.[14]

Another report prepared jointly by the FECB (Foreign Exchange Control Board), the ESB, MITI, the MOF (Ministry of Finance) and MOFA for submission to the Prime Minister, Yoshida Shigeru, indicated the extent to which the Japanese side was preparing for the negotiations. The report went into some detail about the merits and demerits of each of the Sterling Area account groups, and research was conducted into the amount of trade Japan could be expected to carry out with the Dollar and Sterling Areas in each respective account group. The purpose of the study was to establish Japan's negotiating position under every possible circumstance. The report clearly favoured Japan entering the American account (as encouraged by SCAP) or the transferable account group, because this would either encourage a closer economic relationship between Japan and the United States or enable Japan to trade with other sterling countries. The least favourable option was to remain in the bilateral group without convertibility, because of the uncertainty over whether Japan would be guaranteed the Sterling Area's raw materials, and the fear that Japan might be forced to take the Sterling Area's non-essential surplus instead of essentials. Moreover, the report indicated that if Japan were to remain in the bilateral group, she should press for a rise in the ceiling of the non-conversion limit instead of an end to convertibility.[15]

By early April, the ONC had compiled a set of instructions for the British negotiators Hugh Thomas and J. B. Loynes, a representative from the Bank of England.[16] They were instructed to sign a Sterling Payments Agreement without a convertibility provision. Although the new agreement would enable Japan to increase its trade with the Sterling Area, she was to remain in the bilateral accounts group, and third country transfers were to be processed through administrative transferability. The working party on Hong Kong had by this time decided to include Hong Kong in the agreement.[17] Initially, the negotiations were to start on 1 May and end by 30 June, so that a new agreement between Japan and the Sterling Area could be in place by the time that the existing OPA, which ran from June 1950 to June 1951, came to its natural end.

British negotiators were, however, faced with various difficulties: first, in starting the talks, and second, in reaching an agreement with their Japanese counterparts. The talks were delayed partly because SCAP, which was to chair the conference, was faced with a change in personnel when MacArthur was replaced by General Matthew Ridgeway, and also because of the imminence of the peace treaty, which necessitated detailed consultations with Washington over various issues. The talks finally began on 24 May and lasted until 31 August. There were several reasons why the negotiations dragged on for so long. First and foremost was the convertibility issue. Many dollar proponents in the Japanese Cabinet believed that the convertibility clause should be retained in order to prevent an uncontrollable amount of sterling reserves accruing in Japan. They were especially anxious that without a convertibility clause they would be unable to get rid of their excess sterling, especially after the termination of the agreement.[18] The other obstacle was opposition to the inclusion of Hong Kong in the Sterling Payments Agreement. The argument raised by Japan was that the inclusion of Hong Kong might increase Japan's sterling holdings and damage Japan's future trade with China via Hong Kong.[19] In short, Japan opposed the 'reining in' of Hong Kong within the payments agreement because this could potentially affect Hong Kong's role as an entrepôt trading centre.

An added complication arose due to Ikeda's public announcement on 21 April that the government would not abolish the 'dollar clause' in the Japan-Sterling Payments Agreement.[20] This announcement was not taken seriously by Thomas or the FEC (Far Eastern Commission), since the Kyodo News Agency's press release was not substantiated by the Japanese government. It was nevertheless a personal view expressed by Ikeda, and the convertibility issue became more complicated as it took on political importance in order to save his face.

Third, at the same time, the British and the Americans were drafting the Japanese peace treaty. By May 1951 considerable progress had been made in the formation of a draft treaty, and all the outstanding differences were ironed out during John Foster Dulles' visit to London in June.[21] Although Britain was unable to persuade the United States to adopt as strict a treaty as it desired, Britain was able to remain firm on some issues, such as compensation for allied POWs, the renunciation by Japan of her rights under the Congo Basin Treaty of 1919, and her removal from the Board of Directors of the Bank of International Settlement. Soon after the Anglo-American differences over the peace treaty were settled, there were statements were made in Britain about the treaty being a form of protection against Japanese competition. These statements were counterproductive to the British mission in Japan, because they hindered efforts to convince Japan that Britain harboured no ill intentions towards her in the postwar world.[22] Japan's main anxiety stemmed from the fact that Britain, as the chief nego-tiator for the Sterling Area, might restrict Japan's trade with the sterling bloc. Thus the statements emanating from Britain fuelled Japanese fears.

In the end, in place of dollar convertibility, the two sides agreed to an exchange of notes in which both would take responsibility for maintaining 'Japan's sterling balances within reasonable limits' and take measures to correct 'any chronic imbalance of payments in either direction'.[23] Both sides understood that Britain could not accept guarantees for Japan's use of ster-ling after the termination of the agreement. Furthermore, the British remained firm that they would not be obligated to offer credit facilities, and refused to guarantee any reconsideration of the dollar clause.[24] Either side could ask for a meeting at short notice to discuss any aspect of the agree-ment, and a payments review was scheduled to take place in six months time. Finally, Japan was given permission to transfer sterling to any country on the transferable account list subject to Bank of England approval.[25]

It was understood that the Japanese and British negotiators had been able to reach an agreement because Yoshida had given Takeuchi, the MOF repre-sentative to the conference, the authority to agree with Britain on all basic points. It was also revealed that Yoshida was ready to overrule Ikeda if he 'showed fight',[26] and that he had endorsed the British position because he thought that Britain could obstruct Japanese trade with the Sterling Area if Japan did not accede to British proposals.[27]

The other issue that delayed the signing of the agreement was Hong Kong. Although British negotiators made it quite clear that Hong Kong would be included in the new payments agreement from the start, the issue was not discussed during the main negotiations. It was agreed at the last meeting of the sterling financial conference that the drafting committee would discuss Hong Kong.[28] There was a delay in bringing the issue to the negotiating table on the British side because officials in Hong Kong were themselves reluctant to include the colony in the Sterling Payments Agreement with Japan. Under the OPA, Hong Kong had been an entrepôt trading port, whereby goods originating in China, Taiwan and Thailand would pass through Hong Kong on their way to Japan. The argument put forward by the governor of Hong Kong, Alexander Grantham, was that if Hong Kong were included in the Sterling Payments Agreement, third countries would either barter directly with Japan or use another open account country to conduct trade, thereby reducing the amount of goods which passed through Hong Kong.[29] It was only after the Colonial Secretary, James Griffiths, had assured Hong Kong that everything would be done to enable free trade transactions between Japan and Hong Kong, that officials agreed to the colony's inclusion in the Sterling Payments Agreement.

The Japanese opposed the inclusion of Hong Kong in the agreement because of fears that their country would accumulate an even larger supply of sterling through its trade with the colony. Furthermore, the Japanese feared that Japan's trade within the region would be siphoned off if Hong Kong were included in the trade agreement.[30] They also felt that they had a strong negotiating position because of the uncertainty voiced by Hong Kong officials, and also because they had the backing of US officials in Tokyo and Washington.[31] US officials were especially concerned about Hong Kong's inclusion in the payments agreement, because they felt this would undoubtedly change the trade patterns to the detriment of Japan's overall trade.[32]

After a two-week stalemate, the Japanese side finally agreed to include Hong Kong in the Sterling Payments Agreement. Their original position was overturned at a Cabinet meeting because ministers wished to settle the negotiations before the opening of the San Francisco Peace Conference. Furthermore, provisions in the payments agreement such as a ninety-day notice of abrogation, meant that Japan could opt out of the agreement if she became dissatisfied with the conditions.[33] Once again, it was clear to the British side that Yoshida's intervention during the stalemate had helped resolve the issue.[34]

The Sterling Payments Agreement was signed on 31 August 1951. On the same day, Britain and SCAP abrogated the OPA. The payments agreement was initially to last for a year, with the option of extension or renewal by

mutual consent. There was a provision of a three months' notice of termination by either side. The two sides also agreed to a payments review in six
months time. Although Japan was included in the bilateral account, she was
permitted to transfer sterling to the transferable account group with the
approval of the Bank of England. The agreement's special feature was the
exchange of notes, an outcome of the prolonged wrangling between
Japanese and British delegates.

Not long after the signing of the Sterling Payments Agreement, Britain
and Japan were to discover that they had respectively misunderstood a
fundamental element of the agreement, thereby causing misunderstanding
and distrust only a few months after the ink had dried on the paper. The
misunderstanding occurred during Kiuchi Nobutane's visit to the UK in
October. Kiuchi, who was the head of the FECB, embarked on an extended
visit to Europe to familiarise himself with the workings of European central
banks.[35] He met with David Serpell, of the Treasury, who was one of the key
officials in charge of formulating Britain's financial policy towards Japan,
and was very familiar with the recent sterling payments negotiations. The
meeting began innocently, but soon there emerged an apparent misunderstanding over the Sterling Payments Agreement. The Japanese side believed
that third country transfers had been introduced to Sterling Area-Japan
trade as a measure to control Japan's sterling balances. They had not imag-
ined that Japan would have to accept sterling from a third country.

Once the misunderstanding was relayed to Tokyo, the Japanese government convened an inter-ministerial meeting on 30 October in order to clarify
Japan's currency status. The Japanese remained convinced that Britain had
gone back on its word once it had got the 'financial agreement safely in the
bag'.[36] Soon the inter-ministerial meeting developed into a predictable
confrontation between MITI and MOF, where MITI supported sterling and
MOF took an anti-sterling stance. The differences between the two
ministries did not help resolve the issue, which was further compounded by
Japan's rising sterling balance, which had crept up from £38 million at the
end of August to £50 million by the beginning of November.[37] The high
sterling balances only confirmed Japan's fears that without a dollar convertibility clause, Japan would accumulate an unnecessary amount of sterling.
Furthermore, Britain's problems at Suez and Abadan, the drain on Britain's
dollar and sterling reserves and the growth of Britain's debtor position
within the EPU (European Payments Union)[38] all led to Japan's concern
that Britain's multiple problems would result in another devaluation of the
pound.[39] Fearful of holding on to too much sterling, Yoshida instructed the
implementation of the following six points on 1 December in order to
increase Japan's trade with the Sterling Area.

1   Priority foreign exchange allocations to importers wanting to buy goods
    from the Sterling Area
2   Dollar imports to be limited to goods that cannot be obtained elsewhere

3   Bank preference on loans to importers wanting to buy from the Sterling Area

4   Imports of raw cotton, wheat, phosphorous and iron ore from the Sterling Area to be encouraged; substantial raw cotton imports from the Dollar Area to be discouraged

5   No attempt to be made to limit sterling balances by withholding exports to the Sterling Area but all round trade to be expanded

6   Complicated domestic banking procedures to be revised to simplify buying from the Sterling Area[40]

Although the British representatives did not imagine that all six points would be fully implemented, it was a step towards a solution to the domestic Japanese wrangling over the Sterling Area. In the aftermath of the controversy, Treasury officials repeatedly justified their actions and underscored the fact that they had not been attempting to mislead their Japanese counterparts deliberately. But there was no doubt a bitter aftertaste among Japanese representatives after the completion of the first Sterling Payments Agreement between the UK and Japan.

The peace treaty and the China issue

The Sterling Payments Agreement of August 1951 and the adverse impact that overall distrust had on Anglo-American-Japanese relations were far-reaching. One such example was the China issue that followed the San Francisco Peace Treaty. It was one of the issues that had been unresolved by the United States and Britain before the signing of the treaty; thus it was agreed that 'Japan's future attitude towards China must necessarily be for determination by Japan itself in the exercise of the sovereign and independent status contemplated by the treaty. The treaty has been framed so as not to prejudice that important principle'.[41] The months following the signing of the San Francisco Peace Treaty, however, saw mounting pressure on Japan to recognise the Republic of China in line with the United States' decision of 1950. Japan's recognition finally came in the form of a secret letter written by Yoshida in December and made public in January, known as the 'Yoshida Letter'.

The history of the Yoshida Letter has been covered in length and breadth since US and UK government documents were made public in the early 1980s. Most studies have been written from the US angle, but some have examined the series of events from the British, and to some extent the Japanese, perspective. In spite of these different perspectives, all scholars have concluded that Japan's recognition of the ROC, regardless of how it came about, was inevitable, given Japan's alignment with the United States on all fronts – economic and political.[42]

This section does not intend to refute current historical interpretations as far as the outcome of Japan's recognition of the ROC is concerned. It does, however, raise the question of whether Britain was intent on obstructing the United States in the lead-up to the Yoshida Letter, as alleged by US officials at the time. Moreover, it raises the question of whether this was because Britain feared Japan's encroachment on its traditional trading area if it were to be permanently disassociated from mainland China. The chronology of events should at least provide some clues as to the validity of the allegations. Given that the only department involved in the three-month debacle was the Foreign Office, it is unlikely that this ministry would have been pressing for a protectionist policy to safeguard Southeast Asia from Japan. In fact, no documents recommending any form of protectionism can be found in the FO files leading up to the Yoshida Letter. What can be found instead are Britain's attempts to delay the American enforcement of a Japanese decision until the latter had regained sovereignty. Britain was disturbed by the potential long-term impact of a decision forced upon Japan based entirely upon America's short-term domestic goals, and how this would affect future Western relations with Japan. Thus the issue was not over trade and protectionism, as interpreted by US officials. As far as the British were concerned, it was about the interpretation of the Anglo-American joint statement on Japan's future attitude towards China and how to bridge the gap in this interpretation when one side, namely the United States, wished to rescind the agreement in order to achieve its political objectives.

The lead-up to the Yoshida Letter

In the lead-up to the San Francisco Peace Treaty, the United States and Britain worked together very closely to reach an agreement over the text.The issue which had the most far-reaching consequences for Japan was the China issue. The problem arose as a result of the Anglo-American dilemma over which China to invite to the peace conference. The question was difficult for one very good reason: Britain and the United States had recognised different Chinas. Britain had decided soon after the establishment of the People's Republic of China that she would recognise the mainland country, because she did not want to jeopardise her financial foothold there, while the United States had decided to continue to recognise the nationalist government of the ROC, now located on Taiwan, as the legitimate 'China', as a result of various factors such as the Angus Ward case, the PRC's decision to confiscate foreign property, and the outbreak of the Korean War.[43] Inviting one China to the conference and not the other had serious implications. If the PRC were invited, the issue of Taiwan and its return to mainland China would have been raised; while an invitation to Taiwan would have brought protests from the Soviet

Union and raised concerns about such an act strengthening the Sino-Soviet alliance.

Therefore, on 19 June 1951, Herbert Morrison, the British Foreign Secretary, and John Foster Dulles, the Consultant to the Secretary of State in charge of the Japanese Peace Treaty, agreed to invite neither China to the peace conference, in a joint statement now known as the Dulles-Morrison agreement.

Despite the drafting of a Dulles-Morrison agreement and a verbal assurance from Yoshida that Japan would not sign a peace treaty with the PRC, Dulles felt the need for a more concrete commitment from Yoshida. This was due to two contradictory statements made by Yoshida in Diet interpellations in October, after the signing of the treaty and prior to its ratification. In one statement he rejected a treaty with China, while in another he expressed his desire to sign a treaty with both the Soviet Union and the PRC.[44] Dulles was particularly concerned about the difficulties he might have in seeing the peace treaty ratified in the Senate if Japan were to appear equivocal about her relations with the two Chinas. The underlying reason was his fear that he would suffer the same fate that befell Woodrow Wilson at the 1919 Paris Peace Conference. Given his political ambitions to become a cabinet minister in any Republican administration, Dulles had to ensure success at any cost.

Before getting a written assurance from Yoshida, however, Dulles decided to consult the British government about his plans. Dulles hoped that the Conservative government, which took office on 26 October, would release the United States from its obligation under the Dulles-Morrison agreement, and enable Japan to make at least a limited peace treaty with the nationalist government.[45] Livingston Merchant, the US Assistant Under-Secretary of Far Eastern Affairs, who was then on holiday but familiar with the China issue, was instructed to go to London and discuss the problem with the Foreign Office. During the discussions on 13 and 14 November, Robert H. Scott, the Under-Secretary of the Far Eastern Department, gave three reasons why Britain could not endorse the American request. First, it would 'expose His Majesty's Government to the charge of conniving to a breach of a fundamental agreement in regard to China'[46] on which the peace treaty had been based. Second, he thought that in the long term it was unwise to influence Japan's future policy towards China, and wanted to avoid a situation where it 'would enable Japan to claim at a future date that her attitude to China had been determined for her by irresistible foreign pressure, while she remained an occupied country'.[47] Scott thought that it was crucial that the allies should not be placed in a situation where they could be blamed for Japan's failed China policy. Finally, he believed the United States should not be influencing Japan's policy for a short-term objective such as the ratification of the treaty in the Senate, because it might be 'laying up considerable trouble for the future'.[48]

On 14 November, two meetings were held in order to write a draft agreement of the joint Anglo-American approach to Sino-Japanese relations. The agreement was then passed on to Anthony Eden, the new Foreign Secretary, and Sir Esler Dening, the new head of UKLM in Tokyo. The reaction of Dening was adverse, but for Eden the memorandum came as a 'bombshell',[49] as he had been unaware that Scott and Merchant had gone so far and so fast. What Eden objected to was point 4 of the agreement, whereby both Britain and the United States permitted the Japanese government to engage in preliminary discussions with the Chinese nationalist government before the peace treaty came into force, 'providing that any treaty or agreement arising from such preliminary discussions were not concluded until after the Multilateral Peace treaty had come into force'.[50]

Eden thus supported Morrison's position, and refused to release America from its commitment. Due to the failure of the talks in London, Eden raised the issue with US Secretary of State Dean Acheson in Paris, where both were attending the sixth regular session of the UN General Assembly.[51] Neither Acheson nor Eden was able to settle the issue in Paris, and so the final decision on the Japan-Taiwan issue was delegated to Dulles and Dening during the former's forthcoming visit to Tokyo[52] with Senators John Sparkman (Democrat-Alabama) and H. Alexander Smith (Republican-New Jersey) of the Far Eastern Subcommittee of the Senate Foreign Relations Committee.[53]

By the end of November 1951, it was clear that the United States needed more than a verbal reassurance from Japan that she would open relations with the nationalists in Taiwan. In fact, what the Americans wanted was the start of peace negotiations between Japan and the nationalists so that Sparkman and Smith, the two Senators who had been appointed to defend the treaty, would be able to pass it through the Senate. The British, were, however, opposed to any form of recognition before the ratification of the peace treaty. Nothing conclusive was decided in London and Paris; therefore it was up to Dulles and Dening to come to a decision in Tokyo. By this time, however, there was a growing belief amongst American officials that Dening was working behind the scenes to prevent Japan from recognising the nationalists. In a memorandum to Dulles on the Anglo-American discussions held in London and Paris, Merchant concluded that:

> I believe Dening is the real fly in the ointment and that he has been actively attempting to influence the Japanese, not to a postponement of a choice on their part of which China, but actually to an ultimate choice of the Peiping [Beijing] government.[54]

America's Assistant Secretary of State for Far Eastern Affairs, Dean Rusk, who together with Sebald met Yoshida on 27 November, agreed with this view.[55] They perceived that the Foreign Office was against Japan's recognition of nationalist China lest it led to a renewal of Japanese competition in Southeast Asia and other areas of British interest.[56]

The increased suspicion towards Dening hindered the possibility of a successful meeting between Dulles and Dening. It can be deduced from the memoranda and telegrams being exchanged between the key US officials on this matter that that they thought Dening was not being entirely straightforward with them.

On their first meeting in Tokyo on 13 December, Dulles handed Dening a memorandum which reiterated the American position.[57] Dening objected to the memorandum and explained the British view, which Eden had expressed on previous occasions. After the meeting Dening observed in a telegram that:

> It looks as if the Americans are going to go ahead with this whether we like it or not. The Japanese certainly will not like it but they may well give in under pressure.[58]

In the same telegram he considered possible courses of action for Britain. The first was 'to refuse even to discuss Dulles' proposal', which would inevitably lead to a strain on Anglo-American relations. The second course was to examine the US proposal and 'to devise a formula which would enable Japan to make peace with Chiang Kai-shek [Jiang Jieshi, the nationalist leader] without irrevocably prejudicing her future relations with China'.[59] The third course of action was to persuade America to drop the whole idea. At the end of the telegram, Dening asked the Foreign Office for instructions concerning the issue.

The Foreign Office, perceiving that the matter would be more successfully handled in Washington, sent a telegram to Sir Oliver Franks asking him to try to 'persuade Mr. Acheson not to press the Japanese to take any action ... before the Peace Treaty comes into force'.[60] In the meanwhile, the Foreign Office instructed Dening not to continue the talks until Franks had had an opportunity to meet Acheson to convey British concerns over Dulles' action in Japan.[61] Acheson and Franks met on 18 December, and on concluding the meeting, Acheson sent Dulles a telegram informing him of the details of the meeting. As Franks had stressed that Britain was opposed to business arrangements between Taiwan and Japan being transformed into a peace treaty under pressure from the United States, Acheson asked Dulles to begin negotiations on an agreement, but one which 'did not in preamble appear as "Treaty of Peace"'.[62]

Unfortunately, by the time the telegram was written and sent to Tokyo, Dulles had departed for Honolulu, secure in the knowledge that Yoshida would write a letter confirming his desire to sign a peace treaty with nationalist China. What had led Dulles to ask Yoshida to write the letter was as follows.

Dulles, who flew to Korea on 13 December, returned hoping to continue discussing the Japan-Taiwan problem with Dening in order to reach a compromise solution between the two countries before his departure on 20

December. However, at an Anglo-American party on the evening of 17 December, Dening told Dulles that he was under instruction not to discuss the problem with the latter, and that the issue was being raised instead in Washington.[63] Dulles concluded that Dening and the British in London were being unreasonable, as the instructions given to Dening 'made it impossible to take advantage of my (Dulles) presence in Tokyo to arrive at a joint position with the Japanese government'.[64]

The conversation with Dening, together with Smith and Sparkman's view that a letter from Yoshida was necessary to get the treaty ratified, led Dulles to decide that a letter needed to be drafted by him, and signed by Yoshida.[65] At a meeting between Dulles, Sebald, Yoshida and Iguchi Sadao on 18 December, Yoshida agreed to write a letter, and it was decided that the letter would be given to Sebald at a later date. It was also agreed that the letter would not be published until after it was made known to Churchill and Eden during their visit to Washington in early January.

Dulles left Dening with the impression that nothing had been decided during his stay in Tokyo.[66] Unbeknown to Dening, however, Yoshida handed a copy of the letter to Sebald on 26 December, which was later dispatched by diplomatic pouch, to arrive in Dulles' hands on 7 January.[67]

The issue of Japan and Taiwan was discussed between the British and American heads of state and the foreign secretaries on 5 January during a meeting aboard the *S.S. Williamsburg*. It was agreed at the meeting that the differences should be ironed out between Acheson and Eden.[68] The letter was shown to Franks on 9 January at the preparatory meeting between Franks, Dulles and John Allison, prior to the meeting between Acheson and Eden on 10 January.[69] A copy of the letter, however, was not given to Franks to show to Eden, and the letter was only referred to indirectly on 10 January, when Dulles informed the British side that 'he had now received a direct communication from Mr. Yoshida, stating the intentions of the Japanese government, and that it would probably be necessary to make this known during the course of Senate's consideration of the peace treaty with Japan'.[70]

It was apparent from the meeting that although Eden understood and sympathised with the American situation, he could not compromise his position by reversing his stance. In the course of the meeting, Eden reiterated the view that nothing should be done to give Japan the opportunity in the future to say that it had been forced to recognise nationalist China against its own free will; and after further discussion, it was agreed that the British side would instruct Dening, if approached by Yoshida, to say that:

> The exchange between Mr. Acheson and Mr. Eden was full and cordial and there was complete mutual understanding. Though in this respect the result was an agreement to disagree this in no way affected the existing broad area of agreement between the two governments on all other matters relating to Japan.[71]

It now appears that Britain's response to the letter was interpreted as a green light for the United States, because Acheson sent a telegram to Sebald on the following day, instructing him to tell Yoshida to release the letter.[72] Yoshida agreed to publish the letter after he had received a telegram from Dulles stating that the letter had been shown to Eden in Washington and that 'there had been a general Anglo-American understanding on the China problem'.[73]

When the Yoshida Letter was released simultaneously by the Americans and the Japanese on 16 January 1952, it came as a great surprise to the British. It was especially embarrassing for Eden, as the letter was published on the day he returned to England. The publication led to speculations of a strain in Anglo-American relations over the China issue, but as emphasised by Eden and Acheson in their memoirs, the incident did not affect relations between the two ministers.[74]

When Dulles heard of Britain's adverse reaction to the Yoshida Letter, he asked Acheson to say at the next press conference that 'whatever was done in this matter was done not by me [Dulles] personally but by the United States government and that, in your [Acheson's] opinion, there is no basis whatever for any imputation of bad faith or breach of agreement by the United States government or any of its officials'. [75]

Later, Dulles justified his action in a memorandum. He wrote that

> the Dulles-Morrison Agreement of June 1951 never undertook that Japan would have a vacuum within which to decide its China policy. That would have been an unfulfillable undertaking. It did promise that Japan would have the right to reach its own decision as to what was in its best national interest, taking into account all the surrounding circumstances.[76]

The Yoshida Letter, in a nutshell, is a case study in foreign diplomacy in which two sides had to agree to disagree. The consequences for Britain and the United States were not of major proportions. Both sides recovered from the diplomatic bungle, but the impact on Japan was greater in that its relations with China had been decided for the next twenty years because of America's diplomatic requirement from Japan. Given Japan's postwar affiliations with the United States a conclusion such as this was inevitable. In other circumstances, however, the Japanese may have had more time to consider the long-term consequences of their decision and, perhaps, struck an agreement that was more palatable to Japan itself.

What is interesting from a British perspective is the level of misperception that American officials at the time had of Britain's motives in the case of the Yoshida Letter. Moreover, the existing literature elucidates the extent to which the American perception of events has dominated historians' interpretation of them. It is not surprising that officials and historians alike should reach this conclusion, given that Britain's main concern with Japan in this period typically focused on trade and the possible resumption of unfair competition. Furthermore, it should not be ignored that the United States had only recently taken part in Japan's first Sterling Payments Agreement, whereby Japan's trade and currency rights within the agreement had been severely limited, heightening the American perception that Britain was intent on restricting Japan's trade opportunities within the Sterling Area. It is ironic that in the one diplomatic arena where the Foreign Office dominated a policy whose focus was not on trade, it was so sorely misunderstood by the United States.

Conclusions

1951 saw Japan become a GATT observer and a signatory of the IWA and ILO. Although, on the surface, Japan's IWA entry seemed to indicate Britain's acceptance of Japan, it was made possible by the American commitment to provide Japan's wheat quota. Moreover, Japan's GATT observer status was procedural. The two cases indicate an overall British reluctance to admit Japan's re-entry to the Western comity of nations on an equal footing. The underlying fear was economic. This was evident in Britain's attempts to include a provision in the peace treaty which would prevent Japan from repeating its pre-war trade practices. Britain was unsuccessful in its attempt, thus it had to rely on Japan's adherence to the ILO and other international agreements.

Although Britain's policy towards Japan appeared defensive, this is not entirely accurate. A clear example is the Sterling Payments Agreement with Japan. Britain's policy objectives behind the agreement indicated that she thought Japan could play an important role for Britain. Although most literature on Japan's economic recovery has argued that Japan's trade expansion into Southeast Asia was at Britain's expense, the study compiled by the inter-ministerial group elucidates the government's attempt to use Japan's industrial potential to expand sterling usage in East Asia. Furthermore, there was growing British acceptance of Japan's presence in Asia, as indicated by Dening and MacDonald's conviction that Japan could play a useful role in Southeast Asia.

Unfortunately for the sterling policymakers, Japan misunderstood Britain's intentions and feared possible British discrimination against Japan in the sterling bloc. Japan's view derived from the assumption that as banker to the Sterling Area, Britain had unlimited control over sterling trade. The debacle in the aftermath of the negotiations probably heightened this view. Britain's link with the Sterling Area was, therefore, an indicator of its importance in the postwar period. For these reasons Yoshida was wary of upsetting Britain over other issues in case this should lead to further problems in Sterling Area-Japan trade.

4 Learning the rules of engagement

Introduction

When Japan finally became a sovereign nation in 1952, the political and economic landscape of the world that it re-entered was very different from the one that it had left in the 1930s. The most significant difference was the transformation of mainland China into a communist state. As a US ally in the Western economic sphere, Japan quickly learned the limits to its economic access to China, its former trading area. The most notable development was the US and Japanese release of the Yoshida Letter on 16 January 1952, and the subsequent bilateral pact with the ROC three months later, which precluded Japan from recognising the PRC (the People's Republic of China). Although Japan signed a purely symbolic private trade agreement with the PRC in June, this remained nominal because of Japan's membership of the newly established CHINCOM (the China Committee) two months later, which restricted any strategic exports from Japan to the mainland.[1]

In order to survive within the new Cold War reality, Japan had to become closely integrated into the Western comity of nations. This meant membership in Western international organisations as well as closer economic ties with Western countries. Japan was able to make headway in the former when it became a member of the IBRD (International Bank for Reconstruction and Development) and the IMF on 14 August 1952. Thus it became a signatory of two of the three pillars of the Bretton Woods system in the first year of sovereignty. It was to have greater difficulties entering the GATT.

Japan's attempts to forge greater economic ties with the Western world were mixed. In spite of the United States' support of Japan's economic expansion with the free nations as set out in NSC 125/2, convincing the free nations to trade with Japan was another matter. Especially challenging for Japan was its attempts to forge ties with Britain's Sterling Area, which encompassed many countries across the world, including Japan's neighbours in South Asia, Southeast Asia and Australasia. The primary obstacle was Britain and the Commonwealth's inability to view Japan as a trusted ally due to previous trade rivalries that had led to a deeply ingrained suspicion of Japan. This underlying suspicion led to an uneasy relationship, even as

Japan and the Sterling Area embarked on a Sterling Payments Agreement to expand trade relations. The year 1952 saw a continuation of the unease as Japan's misinterpretation of the 'rules of engagement' and Britain's inability to reach a comprehensive policy towards Japan failed to create a warmer relationship between the two. The distrust was also clearly evident in Britain's reluctance to support Japan's entry into the GATT. The two policies together thus gave the impression that Britain did not wish to pull its weight in supporting Japan's return to the Western comity of nations. This chapter examines the two issues in detail to underscore the fact that Britain's reluctance was based on its inability to reach a persuasive policy towards Japan. On both occasions, Britain's policy was dictated by a need for additional time to either correct larger economic and financial policies or to maintain the status quo in order to find a solution to its problems.

Japan's Rising Sterling Balance

At the end of August 1951, Japan's sterling holdings amounted to £38 million, but by end of January they had increased to £82 million and were accumulating at a rate of £9 million a month (see Table 4.1).[2] There were three reasons for the increase in Japan's sterling holdings. First, Japan was not making its annual seasonal purchases from the Sterling Area because it had enough dollar reserves from the Korean War to purchase its essentials from the Dollar Area, and thus Japan's sterling reserves, which usually fell between October and March, remained high.

Table 4.1 Japan's Sterling reserves, January 1950 –December 1953, £ thousands

	1950	1951	1952	1953
January	15,417	16,332	82,152	78,228
February	14,653	15,542	91,738	66,856
March	15,024	15,650	99,668	50,500
April	17,687	30,366	109,784	40,821
May	17,181	41,797	120,644	35,856
June	16,991	43,643	126,889	33,025
July	17,612	38,173	126,124	32,690
August	20,969	38,054	120,987	28,030
September	20,930	40,573	120,302	32,829
October	21,796	49,148	113,979	31,375
November	20,714	61,892	103,970	30,554
December	19,442	75,455	88,992	42,523

Source: Ministry of Finance 1978, 127

Table 4.2 Annual trade with Japan (selected Sterling Area countries) 1950–8, $millions

		1950	1951	1952	1953	1954	1955	1956	1957	1958
Australia	M	23.3	90	27.7	9	28.2	55.1	30.9	42.1	62.6
	X	76.4	126	132.6	172.3	117.1	177.7	248.4	362.8	225.6
Burma	M	16.2	18.2	21.2	33	45.6	38.3	36.3	75.9	46.4
	X	17.7	28.6	29.8	50.2	63.1	45.8	42.4	24.8	12.3
Ceylon	M	7.1	17.3	17.3	13.8	17.3	20.4	24.3	24.7	34.6
	X	0.2	1.3	2.3	2.2	2.6	2.8	3.3	6.3	7.3
Hong Kong	M		61.5	80.7	62.2	77.3	88.1	134.5	130.6	100.1
	X		5.7	6.8	7.9	4	6.2	18.7	26.7	11.6
India	M	20.3	51.7	36.7	27.4	43.9	84.7	105.3	113.3	84.8
	X	17.8	52.8	73	75.1	51.6	77.3	103.4	105	74.4
Malaya & Singapore	M	18.1	68.2	63	39.4	47.6	72.8	77.9	82.3	90.4(a)
	X	39.4	61.3	60.9	63.4	63.8	109.2	138.7	193.3	127.1(b)
New Zealand	M	1.2	8.6	8.1	1.3	2.6	7.9	5.9	7.6	7.4
	X	2.2	11.7	9.3	9.7	4.5	6.7	9.4	27.3	18.9
Pakistan	M	55.6	117	117.7	14.9	56	44	17.7	16.6	22
	X	38.9	95.5	82.4	108	36.2	47.1	50.6	47.2	34.2
South Africa	M	29.6	29.5	18	28.1	30.7	28.9	34.7	50.1	39.1
	X	3.3	5.9	13.1	19.5	10.6	17.5	26.5	34.1	16
UK	M	26	54	73.1	33.1	51.1	60.8	63.2	73.7	105.2
	X	6.4	31.8	36.7	49	37.1	37.9	66.6	98.5	59.4
Sterling Area	M	297	612.5	539.1	316.1	491.3	640.9	684.6	806.9	799.6
	X	221.5	446.6	500.4	602.5	433.7	588.6	817.7	1121.5	791.4

Source: Director of International Trade, United Nations.

Notes:
M imports; X exports.
Hong Kong's statistics for 1950 are excluded as it was an Open Account country.
Malaya and Singapore became the Malaya Federation and Singapore respectively from 1958.
(a) Malaya Federation: 13.1; Singapore: 77.3.
(b) Malaya Federation: 114.4; Singapore: 12.7.

Second, despite Japan's poor purchasing performance, the Sterling Area had been increasing its overall purchases from Japan. One of the worst culprits was Hong Kong, which had continued to purchase from Japan, despite its inability to sell goods in return (see Table 4.2). Hong Kong's trade imbalance, which amounted to £2.1 million between July and August of 1951, rose to £10.7 million between September and December of that year.[3]

Third, part of the reason why Japan was unable to decrease its sterling reserves lay in her opposition to the implementation of administrative transferability, because she was reluctant to set up a two-way sterling transfer system into and out of Japan. Japanese officials would have been much happier implementing a one-way system which would facilitate a fall in Japan's sterling reserves.

Japan's rising sterling balance was so serious that it was discussed at the Commonwealth Finance Ministers' meeting, which began on 15 January in London. Japan was part of a wider, global problem facing the Sterling Area in 1952. The problem was that the Sterling Area was facing an overall deficit with the rest of the world at an annual rate of £1,600 million. As a result, the Sterling Area's gold and dollar reserves were quickly receding to the 1949 level, when sterling had been devalued against the dollar. Thus, in order to solve this serious situation, Britain's goals were to convince members that it was to their advantage to remain in the Sterling Area and that the member states should work together to 'restore the strength of sterling and ultimately to achieve convertibility'.[4] The short-term remedies needed to attain the end goal were to implement overall import restrictions from non-Sterling Area countries, and work towards combating domestic inflation.[5]

The British delegation distributed a memorandum at the meeting advancing the reasons why the Sterling Area should curtail purchases from Japan. Outlined in the memorandum were four possible developments that could arise if Japan's sterling balances continued to rise. The first possibility was that Japan might make vigorous efforts to find sterling supplies, which would assist the Sterling Area's objective of expanding sterling usage in East Asia. The second was that Japan might ask the Sterling Area to restrict its purchases from Japan voluntarily. The third was the prospect that Japan might impose export restrictions upon the Sterling Area. The fourth, and the worst possible, scenario was the termination of the Sterling Payments Agreement while Japan still held huge sterling reserves.[6] The UK delegation presented its argument based upon the worst-case scenario, and urged the Commonwealth governments to prevent Japan from moving from the non-dollar to the dollar world, and to prepare to implement import restrictions, if necessary, following the conclusion of a payments review between Britain and Japan in March. Member countries were also encouraged to discuss their Sterling Area availabilities with Japan, in order to increase their exports,[7] as part of the Commonwealth countries' effort to remedy the immediate balance of payments crisis.[8]

It was imperative that the Sterling Area as a whole curb imports in order to prevent another devaluation of the pound against the dollar. Japan was a difficult case, because it began accumulating sterling reserves almost immediately after the signing of the payments agreement. With the dangerous decline in dollar reserves, and rumours of an imminent devaluation of the pound against the dollar, it was not known what action Japan would take. Therefore, Britain hoped to see an immediate decrease in Japan's sterling reserves, either through sterling's expanded exports to Japan or through Sterling Area import restrictions. On 3 March, however, Japan announced its decision to take unilateral action to restrict its exports of steel and textile products to the Sterling Area.[9] These products made up 60–70 per cent of all Japanese exports to the Sterling Area, but the MOF-initiated plan was presented and approved unanimously by the Cabinet as a measure to decrease Japan's sterling reserves.[10] Thus Japan took the first step towards reducing its sterling reserves.

As the talks in London were unfolding, British delegates in Tokyo were preparing their position for the March payments review. They were given clear instructions to steer the review away from any negotiations. If the Japanese side should insist on revising the agreement, the delegates were advised to stress the consultative nature of the agreement, which obliged the two sides to discuss differences before any revisions were made to the agreement. They were also encouraged to underscore the fact that six months was not enough time to give the agreement a fair chance to prove itself.[11] To further ensure that no negotiations took place, Hugh Thomas, the main negotiator, was instructed to limit the review to the initial expectations and the actual results, and to discuss the broad factual reasons for divergences from the forecast.[12]

Officials representing MITI, the FECB, MOF and MOFA attended the three-day meeting from the Japanese side, and W. W. Diehl of the Economic and Scientific Section represented SCAP. As predicted by the British delegates, the meeting became a forum for Japan to express its dissatisfactions with the agreement. Japan highlighted four main factors behind its poor performance. They were, first, the lack of availability of required goods in the Sterling Area; second, the higher price of goods in comparison to the Dollar Area; third, the difficulties Japan's merchants faced in buying from the Sterling Area, given their inability to enjoy an equal footing in their business activities because the principal sterling commodities were bought up under the Commonwealth preferential system, thus acting as an impediment to Japan's increased imports from the Sterling Area; finally, the Japanese side believed that the problem was a combination of Japan's exclusion from the MFN rights clause and its slow economic return in the Sterling Area.

Responding, Thomas defended the Sterling Area practices and refused to compromise on any of the four points mentioned by the Japanese delegates. Thomas maintained that Japan's adverse trade imbalance was mainly a result of the 'failure by the Japanese authorities to plan their importing policy properly with a view to effecting the maximum switch from dollar to sterling purchase'.[13] He assured the delegates that it was not only Japan which was facing discrepancies in dollar and sterling price differences, but that this was a problem faced by the rest of the world due to the general scarcity of dollars. Thomas declined to discuss Commonwealth preferential treatments, but did explain that Japan was facing difficulties because it lacked diplomatic and consular establishments. He underscored the fact that these would take some time to establish because many of the countries concerned had been overrun by Japan during the war and thus the general sentiment towards official relations was still unfavourable. Thomas rejected any links between the existing Sterling Area-Japan trade and the MFN question, given that Japan was receiving *de facto* rights via MFN treatment for goods.[14]

All other Japanese concerns, such as their inability to reduce their sterling holdings through administrative transferability and their dissatisfaction stemming from Hong Kong's entry in the Sterling Payments Agreement, were addressed by Thomas. In each case, he hinted at Japan's lack of commitment to persevere with the agreement by way of introducing alternative solutions to Japan's complaints.[15]

At the conclusion of the talks, Japan agreed to increase her sterling purchases as a remedial measure. In return, she asked Britain to help make goods available to Japan.[16] Although Britain assured Japan that it would cooperate through the UK mission, it was made clear that Britain could not discriminate in her favour.[17] Last, both sides put on record their dissatisfaction at the decision by the other to implement controls on trade. The British delegates complained that Japan had imposed export controls before it had availed itself of the machinery of consultation, while the Japanese side believed that its export restrictions were preferable to import restrictions by the Sterling Area.[18]

Britain was satisfied with the course of the payments review because the talks had progressed according to their original plans. The discussion did not lead to amendments, negotiations or compromises on Britain's part. To a certain extent it was right for Britain to avoid getting embroiled in trade questions or matters of policy, because this would have opened up a Pandora's box of issues that would have led to another long-winded discussion on the payments agreement. It was clear, however, that the payments review was far from satisfactory for the Japanese side. Not only did Britain not articulate any concrete solutions for Japan, but it also expressed little inclination to help Japan improve its trade relations with the Sterling Area.

At the completion of the talks, Britain sent instructions to the Commonwealth to curb imports from, but stimulate exports to, Japan.[19] Despite an immediate control on trade flows between the Sterling Area and Japan, the latter's sterling holdings continued to rise steadily. By 3 June they had exceeded £121 million and they amounted to £126 million by the end of June.[20] To Britain's surprise, Japan showed little reaction to the increased holdings. This delayed response was due to Japan's focus on renewing its diplomatic contacts and agreements with the United States following US ratification of the peace treaty.[21]

When the relevant ministries did meet to discuss the matter, they reverted to the anti-sterling and pro-sterling factions. Kiuchi of the FECB continued to expound his anti-sterling views in public, and demanded the return of the dollar clause as well as Hong Kong's exclusion from the general agreement. He did not hide his conviction that the root cause of the trade imbalance lay in the fact that trade was conducted at the official instead of the actual rate of exchange, and he lobbied for a revision to the latter.[22] MITI, on the other hand, supported an extension of the 1951 payments agreement for another year on the basis of £200 million of trade each way. MITI's views differed from the FECB's in that it believed it was the low volume, not the over-valuation, of sterling that was the reason for the trade inequity.

MOF was less willing to represent its views openly, but it was common knowledge that it was anti-sterling, and that it supported the FECB proposal. On 25 July, the Ministerial Council, the highest authority in charge of foreign exchange funds for imports and other payments, met and discussed the various ministerial proposals, and endorsed the MOF-FECB plan to press for a revision of the pound-yen cross-rate from the official to the real rate.[23] The Council also approved an import certificate system as well as an export-import price adjustment fund. The import certificate system was designed so that exports to the Sterling Area were possible only after traders produced a certificate proving that they had imported a certain amount of goods from the Sterling Area. The export-import price adjustment fund either penalised or rewarded merchants. For example, a tax or a levy was placed on sterling exports, and grants were awarded for sterling imports. The government approved both plans to stimulate Japan's Sterling Area purchases.[24] They became the FECB's last items of sterling-related legislation to be submitted to the government before it was abolished on 1 August.

Although the first anniversary of the payments agreement was approaching, neither the British nor the Japanese side had made any move to renew the agreement for another year. British Embassy officials in Tokyo proposed an extension of the agreement for four more months. The Japanese met the proposal with a lukewarm response, but without an alternative option, they had no other course of action; thus they accepted the British idea.[25]

Japan's inactivity was not due to lack of preparation so much as the political conflict within the Liberal Party between Yoshida and the former party leader, Hatoyama Ichirô. The situation arose from the fact that Yoshida refused to relinquish his leadership of the Jiyutô as he had promised in 1946 prior to Hatoyama's purge.[26] The combination of this factional contest and the possibility of a September election reduced the likelihood of any minister taking up a controversial issue, such as the payments agreement, before the elections.[27]

On 5 August, a *note verbale* was handed to Roberts by a MOFA official, expressing Japan's readiness to extend the payments agreement until 31

December 1952. Esler Dening and Okazaki Katsuo, the Japanese foreign minister, signed the document ten days later.

When Britain received the *note verbale* from the Japanese side, it also received a note entitled 'Japanese observations on the Anglo-Japanese Sterling Payments Agreement'. The content of the note was a reiteration of the Japanese position during the payments review in March. It stated that the reasons for Japan's imbalance with the Sterling Area were higher commodity prices in the Sterling Area in comparison to the Dollar Area, the limited supply of raw materials and foodstuffs available, discrimination against Japanese traders in the sterling market, and the rising practice of indirect purchases of goods by Thailand and Indonesia via Hong Kong. In order to alleviate these problems, the Japanese side made the following proposals: the return of a dollar point in the agreement so that Japan would be able to use its sterling balances freely, and an end to the Sterling Area's unilateral implementation of import restrictions to balance trade.[28]

Britain was faced with two tasks. First, to write a satisfactory reply to the Japanese observation, and then to devise a long-term Anglo-Japanese payments policy before the four-month renewal expired. Members of the Japan Working Party in Whitehall held several meetings in September and October but all were inconclusive. The only decision reached during the meetings was to exclude Japan from the agenda of the Commonwealth Economic Conference in November, due to Britain's reluctance to place undue significance on Japan while its policy towards the latter remained uncertain.[29]

On 30 October, nearly three months after Japan had presented its *note verbale* to Britain, Thomas handed the British reply to Oda Takeo, the Director of the Economic Affairs Bureau of MOFA.[30] The reply was basically a recapitulation of the British position at the March review, and nothing new was initiated. Oda remarked that it was as much as the Japanese had expected, and expressed his disappointment over Britain's inability to resolve the Hong Kong problem.

While Japanese officials were examining the British reply, British officials at the Bank of England and the Treasury were formulating alternative proposals to break the impasse with Japan. A Treasury proposal envisaged trade relations in which Britain and the Sterling Area would limit their import licenses to a certain fixed amount, and if the trade levels were either conspicuously higher or lower than the agreed amount, consultative machinery would be activated to correct the imbalance. Conversely, a Bank of England proposal supported the reintroduction of the convertibility clause, which would enable Japan to convert any sum in excess of £10 million held in a central Japanese account, provided that most of the existing balance could be tied down over a ten-year period so that Japan would be unable to convert all its reserves into dollars immediately.[31]

Both proposals were revised versions of earlier demands made by Japan – which underscored Britain's inability to find a viable solution for Japan's problems. Neither took into account Japan's growing anxiety over the import restrictions placed by the Sterling Area countries against Japanese products. The import restrictions had the desired effect of decreasing Japan's sterling reserves, but coincided with the end of the Korean War boom and Japan's dollar surplus. With both dollar and sterling reserves in decline, Japan was faced with an uncertain economic future.

A number of Treasury officials who had been following the declining rate of Japan's sterling reserves realised that the latter's position *vis-à-vis* the Sterling Area was weakening. They therefore suggested a renewal of the payments agreement without concessions. The Treasury's view was confirmed when on 27 November a MOFA *note verbale* was delivered to British officials in Tokyo. The note drew attention to the marked alteration in the trend of sterling payments, from a surplus of £29.359 million during the first five months of the year to a deficit of £35.428 million during the five months from June to October.[32] In light of this significant change, Japan declared that it would no longer adhere to the standard limit referred to in Kiuchi's letter of 4 October 1951, and hoped that the Sterling Area would also lift its restrictions against Japan. Furthermore, the note expressed a desire to hold an Anglo-Japanese conference in order to discuss various trade and payments issues.[33]

The Treasury's proposal was approved and Thomas was instructed to prolong the payments agreement for another year without any changes. If the Japanese side refused, Thomas was instructed to invite them to discuss the relevant issues after the payments agreement was signed.[34] On 2 December, Thomas met with Oda and conveyed the formal proposal to prolong the payments agreement for another year. Oda was shocked that he could be presented with an extension of the agreement without any preliminary discussion, and told Thomas that the Japanese negotiating line was to refuse a renewal if the Sterling Area refused to lift trade restrictions.[35] Japan's Cabinet discussed the issue, and agreed to support a one-year extension with the backing of MITI and MOFA, as they thought an extension of the agreement would lead to greater stability.[36]

On 12 December, Oda told Thomas that the Japanese government had decided to extend the payments agreement for another year, and two *notes verbales* followed seven days later. One confirmed Japan's extension of the agreement, while the other was a note proposing early discussions between Britain and Japan over various outstanding issues such as setting an equilibrium in trade levels, trade relations between Japan and Hong Kong, and other matters 'deemed necessary for the smooth operation' of the payments agreement. An exchange of notes took place on 27 December.

The four months between August and December 1952 saw a clear reversal of the Sterling Area and Japan's positions. Japan's sterling reserves had risen to over £100 million between July 1951 and June 1952, because of an expansion of Japan's exports to the Sterling Area. More importantly, Japan's accumulation of sterling had been due to the fact that Japan had established a pattern whereby it imported from the Dollar Area, and exported to the Sterling Area, which meant that Japan was not reliant on Sterling Area goods. It was possible for Japan to trade in this way as long as it was earning dollars through the Korean War boom.[37] Japan's sterling reserves began to fall because Japan's steel and textiles export restrictions and the Sterling Area's import restrictions were beginning to take effect from the middle of the year. The gradual decline of Japan's sterling reserves should have been a relief to the Japanese side, but the Sterling Area's decision to restrict purchases of Japanese goods came at a time when Japan was beginning to realise the short-sightedness of her policy to import from the Dollar Area and export to the Sterling Area. The impending end of the Korean War meant a decline in Japan's dollar surplus. Japan therefore had to rely more on imports from the Sterling Area, but in order to do so, she had to maintain a healthy balance of payments. It was for this reason that the *note verbale* of 26 November was handed to Thomas. The note indicated Japan's interest in extending the payments agreement, but more importantly, it indicated Japan's hopes for the lifting of the Sterling Area's import restrictions. Japan itself had lifted its own steel and textiles export restrictions from October,[38] and to ensure that the Sterling Area's import restrictions would be lifted at the Commonwealth Economic Conference, the *note verbale* was drawn up hastily by the Japanese government, with the inclusion of a paragraph stating that Japan would no longer subject trade to the standard limit established in October 1951.[39]

The Japanese *note verbale* of 26 November was delivered at a time when Britain was in a dilemma as to how to conduct future talks with the Japanese. There were fears that if negotiations took place before the end of the year, Japan would expect a major revision of the agreement. Britain was not enamoured by any of Japan's proposed revisions, and struggled to put together an alternative proposal. Once British officials realised that the balance had tipped in their favour, however, they seized the opportunity to continue with the existing payments agreement without concessions and without a preliminary discussion. Thus Britain was able to carry off a one-year renewal of the payments agreement with Japan. It was not a satisfactory agreement for Japan, as the renewal was not conditional on preliminary talks. As long as the existing agreement remained unrevised, Japan did not expect its situation *vis-à-vis* the Sterling Area to improve. But problems with the Sterling Area were not the only issues that Britain and Japan had to deal with. Another frustrating set of talks that dampened Anglo-American relations was Japan's attempt to enter the GATT.

The MFN issue

The MFN issue was never far from the minds of British officials in Tokyo. They knew that it was only a matter of time before Japan broached the subject in connection with Article 7 of the San Francisco Peace Treaty, which stipulated that signatories notify Japan about pre-war bilateral treaties or conventions they wished to continue or revive, within one year of treaty ratification.[40] On 26 April 1952, MOFA handed a *note verbale* to the UKLM in Tokyo, in which it inquired about Britain's intentions. MOFA wanted to know if Britain intended to renew its Commerce and Navigation Treaty of 1911 or if it were planning to negotiate new maritime and other commercial relations with Japan.[41] If neither of these was the case, MOFA wished to know to what extent Britain would accord MFN treatment to Japanese goods and nationals.[42]

In a letter to the Foreign Office dated 6 May 1952, Esler Dening, who had become the British Ambassador to Japan, wrote: 'this note puts us fairly and squarely on the spot'.[43] The note was discomforting because no specific policy had been formulated *vis-à-vis* Japan except that it had decided against giving MFN treatment to Japanese goods at the twenty-first meeting of the Cabinet's EPC in September 1950. Foreign officials were also aware that a revival of the 1911 commercial treaty would evoke great consternation among British manufacturers and at the Board of Trade.[44] Moreover, Britain was less than willing to sign a commercial treaty when it was uncertain about Japan's likelihood of reverting to the 'unfair' competition of the pre-war period. Britain was equally guarded in its judgement of the future of Sterling Area-Japan trade relations. Two months after receipt of the note, the British government was still unable to reach a decision. This was partially because the Foreign Office needed responses from interested ministries, such as the Board of Trade, the Treasury and the Ministry of Transport, but differences were bound to ensue at any inter-ministerial meeting. Therefore the government delayed its reply to the Japanese note. By 22 September 1952, however, the British had decided to dispatch a note to the Japanese government indicating their desire to 'continue to accord to the nationals, products and vessels of Japan most-favoured-nation treatment or national treatment as provided under article 12 of the Treaty of Peace'.[45]

Japan's *note verbale* placed Britain in a difficult position because it arrived when there was a strong likelihood of Japan applying for GATT membership. Britain had been able to stall US attempts to bring Japan into the GATT since 1948, but after Japan had signed the Peace Treaty in September, and was granted observer status in the GATT in October 1951, Britain knew that it was only a matter of time before Japan, with the encouragement of the United States, was accepted into the GATT.[46] Britain's problem stemmed from two related issues. First was the fear that if Japan became a GATT member, Britain would have to give MFN rights to Japan which included equal tariff treatment for Japanese goods, and would thus lead to strong opposition from the Lancashire textiles industry. Furthermore, Britain opposed Japan's entry because under the GATT rules, no contracting party was able to increase preferential tariffs. Therefore, if Japan became a GATT member, Britain and the Commonwealth would be unable to protect intra-Commonwealth trade by raising imperial preferential tariffs against non-Commonwealth countries. Britain saw this as a serious problem, as most of the preferences were in the form of specific duties rather than on an *ad valorem* basis.[47] By the 1950s inflation had eroded the value of many of the preferential tariffs that were still in place, and the average percentage margin of preference on all UK trade with the Commonwealth had been reduced to around 6 per cent.[48] Furthermore, the rules against preferential tariffs stipulated that if tariffs were raised against one country, they would have to be raised against all other contracting members. Thus Britain was in a 'catch-22' situation, where it would be unable to increase preferential tariffs and unable to discriminate against Japanese goods without having to increase tariffs across the board.[49] The GATT's restrictive nature even led to the question of whether Britain should remain in the GATT or whether she should set up an alternative organisation to regulate trade.

If Britain were to remain in the GATT, the immediate issue at hand was to find some way to protect British interests in case of Japanese membership. The proposals put forward at this time were to invoke one of the GATT treaty articles against Japan, such as Article 6, 12 or 35.[50] Article 6 stipulated that contracting parties had the right to apply 'counter-vailing duties against dumping'.[51] The problem with this article was the difficulty of substantiating dumping charges.[52] Article 12, which stipulated the balance of payments escape clause, was not considered entirely effective because the clause was limited to use against the world in general or in favour of a country or an area, while discrimination directed against specific countries was seen as 'highly suspect', and it was generally believed that this would lead to opposition from other GATT signatories.[53] Article 35 enabled a GATT signatory to withhold from another contracting party 'either all the provisions of the agreement or MFN rates in respect of goods appearing in negotiated tariff schedules'.[54] The drawback to this article was that it was tantamount to signifying the contracting party's unwillingness to see the other contracting party become a member.[55]

In the meantime, the Japanese side was preparing for GATT membership through the intersessional tariff negotiations procedure, which had been established at the sixth session of the GATT. The procedure was designed to enable minor countries to accede to the general agreement without having to wait for a large-scale tariff conference. Once a country asked to negotiate tariffs through the intersessional procedure, the contracting parties were to make their views known within thirty days, and at the latest sixty days, by postal vote. If three or more contracting parties objected to the procedure, the agenda was postponed until the following general session. This was a far shorter time period than if Japan opted for the regular Article 33 entry into the GATT. According to this procedure, Japan would have had to communicate its wish to enter into negotiations with a view to acceding to the agreement. Once the letter reached the GATT, a working party would be established to examine the application. The working party would then submit to the GATT Council its recommendation, including a draft protocol of the applicant's accession. This was to be followed by tariff negotiations, and when these were completed, the report of the working party, together with the draft tariff decision and the protocol of the accession would be submitted to the Council for approval. The final procedure was a decision on accession by a two-thirds majority of the contracting parties. Once an affirmative decision was reached, the protocol would take effect thirty days after being signed by the applicant government.[56]

The prospect of Japan's application via the intersessional tariff negotiations procedure ironically did not have the full support of the United States, because the latter wished to avoid any controversy over Japan's admittance to the GATT during an election year. Furthermore, the United States wished to avoid any entanglements over the GATT when the Reciprocal Trade Agreement was coming up for renewal in June 1953.[57] The United States' inability to support Japan's accession actively was communicated to the Japanese side on 4 July. Japan was also cautioned that Canada, France and Britain would most probably oppose Japan's application via the above procedure. Japan accepted that there would be three or more votes against her, but stuck to her decision to apply, due to the strong public and parliamentary support for GATT membership. On 13 July, Peyton Kerr, the First Secretary of the US Embassy, sent a note to MOFA in which he conveyed that 'the inclusion of the United States (as one of the countries which Japan wished to conduct tariff negotiations) would not be objectionable provided Japan does not state or imply that it has obtained the agreement of the United States'.[58] Japan was also reassured that US delegates at the October GATT session would be instructed not to 'oppose the outright rejection of Japan's application'.[59] Therefore, on 18 July, the Japanese government notified the Executive Secretary of the GATT, Eric Wyndham White, of its wish to enter into negotiations with twenty-eight countries, including the United States, Australia, New Zealand and the UK.[60]

The GATT contracting parties were immediately notified of Japan's application and asked to make their views known to the GATT Executive Secretary by 19 August. In order to decide on the British position, the issue was discussed at the twenty-third meeting of the Cabinet's EPC on 30 July. A Board of Trade memorandum strongly pressed for British opposition to Japan's application on the grounds that Japan was too significant a country to discuss at an intersessional gathering of the contracting parties. Therefore it was agreed at the EPC that Britain would oppose Japan's application, and the committee also decided that Britain should canvass enough votes to ensure a rejection of the application.[61] Britain subsequently approached various Commonwealth and European countries in order to canvass votes against Japan, and as a result Australia, New Zealand, France, the Benelux countries and Norway voted against the intersessional procedure.[62]

Britain's next hurdle was to persuade the other contracting parties to postpone tariff negotiations with Japan during the seventh session in

Geneva. This proved to be more difficult because, despite the opposition to Japan's accession through the intersessional procedure, many countries were not opposed to Japan's accession in principle. On 22 August, Truman approved a report by the Chairman of the Interdepartmental Committee on Trade Agreements that the United States should enter into tariff negotiations with Japan. Furthermore, Truman agreed to a 'full discussion of the question at the seventh session of the contracting parties'.[63]

On 2 September, the British government was informed by its Washington embassy that the United States did not object to the Japanese question being raised at the seventh session.[64] The US reversal of its position from reluctance to support meant that Britain had to arrive at a persuasive argument to delay Japan's application. A week later, the British stance towards the seventh session was discussed at the Cabinet's Far East (Official) Committee on 9 September, and at the Cabinet's CPEC (Committee on Preparations for the Commonwealth Economic Conference) on 11 September. At the Far East Committee meeting, the Treasury stated very clearly that Britain would have to come to a clear decision on whether to accept Japan into the GATT or oppose its entry, and warned against a compromise between the two. Britain was placed in a difficult position because it wished to discourage Japan from playing a 'lone hand in international trade', as in the 1930s, when Japan's economic isolation had led to the Pacific War. Britain was also aware that its rejection of Japan's membership of the GATT would be met with strong American disapproval, with a potential strain in Anglo-American relations over other economic matters. The Board of Trade explained that it would recommend a delay in Japan's entry to the GATT at present, as the current GATT rules did not provide an effective mechanism for the protection of British goods in their traditional trading areas against Japanese competition.[65]

At the Cabinet's CPEC, the Board of Trade presented a memorandum recommending that Britain table a resolution deferring Japan's application until a later session, 'on the grounds that the UK was currently reviewing its whole commercial policy and that the question of Japan's accession presented special difficulties'.[66] During the meeting, Eden opposed any action which would offend the United States and Japan. Conversely, Viscount Swinton, the Chancellor of the Duchy of Lancaster, warned that Japan's entry would lead to great pressure on the government to 'disown the GATT'.[67] R. A. Butler, the Chancellor of the Exchequer, expressed the need for extreme caution, as a wrong step either way would lead to international repercussions. Due to the sensitive nature of the issue, and the inability of the CPEC to decide whether to support Britain's domestic and Commonwealth interests over its international ones, the Committee decided to raise the discussion to Cabinet level.[68]

Two memoranda were submitted for discussion at the Cabinet meeting on 18 September. The Board of Trade's memorandum recommended that Britain defer the issue, and approach the US government for its support.

The Foreign Office's memorandum supported Japan's accession to the GATT for political and economic reasons. Politically, the Foreign Office was against any possible deterioration of relations with Japan and the United States, and moreover, felt that Japan's entry into the GATT would guarantee Japan's economic allegiance to the Western sphere. Economically, the Foreign Office argued that Japan's accession to the GATT was desirable as it contained a number of 'useful safeguards against the sort of trade malpractices which caused such bitterness between Japan and the United Kingdom before the war'.[69] The Foreign Office thought that there would be less damage to its position *vis-à-vis* Japan if it were to invite the latter to participate.[70] In discussion, however, the Board of Trade's views were accepted as the 'logical sequel to an expression of Her Majesty's Government's views', and it was agreed that Britain should approach the US government with the Board of Trade's proposal.[71]

Christopher Steel, the minister to Washington, was instructed to meet with relevant members of the State Department in order to convey the British view. On 22 September he met Willard Thorp, Assistant Secretary of State for Economic Affairs, who sympathised with the British position and explained that although the United States supported Japan's accession, it was by no means anxious or intending to 'make rapid progress in getting down to tariff negotiations with Japan'.[72] Moreover, Thorp explained that the United States did not envisage tariff negotiations with Japan for another twelve to fifteen months, and that they were thinking of putting forward the idea that the timing of Japan's tariff negotiations should be discussed at an intersessional committee of GATT after the seventh session.[73] Britain and the United States, therefore, agreed to collaborate on a text, which recognised Japan's desire to enter tariff negotiations with the contracting parties, but remained reserved in its invitation to Japan. This was distributed to the contracting parties, and as a result, Britain and the United States were able to delay Japan's tariff negotiations at the seventh session.

Japan's accession was discussed at the sixth meeting of the seventh session on 10 October, at which Thorp proposed the establishment of an intersessional committee to discuss Japan's application. The United States' proposal was supported by the British delegation, which emphasised that Britain's intention was not to be unfriendly to Japan, and explained that the United Kingdom's reservations in regard to Japan's immediate membership were due to uncertainties over Japan's future trade practices, and concern over whether Britain could extend GATT concessions to new acceders (i.e. Japan). The other contracting parties which supported the US proposal were Canada, France, Greece, Italy, Brazil and Haiti; Pakistan, India and Turkey supported Japan's early accession but also understood the need of some countries to discuss the issue at an intersessional committee. Conversely, Germany, Sweden and Indonesia supported early tariff negotiations with Japan. The only country to abstain on the formation of an intersessional committee and the start of the tariff negotiations was Czechoslovakia. In light of the fact that the majority of countries favoured the establishment of an intersessional committee meeting, an intersessional committee was established for 2 February 1953.[74]

Japan was aware that its attempts to enter tariff negotiations with GATT members through the intersessional procedure would be difficult, but felt that some action had to be initiated given the strong domestic public opinion in favour of Japan's membership. As expected, more than three countries had opposed conducting tariff negotiations through the intersessional procedure. Japan had, however, been more optimistic about its chance of discussing tariff negotiations at the seventh session, but here the two most influential GATT countries, Britain and the United States, were against conducting tariff negotiations with Japan at that time. Britain could not accept Japan's membership unless certain revisions were made to the GATT rules, in order to safeguard British trading interests. Conversely, the United States wished to avoid complications during an election year, and before the renewal of the reciprocal trade agreement in 1953. What was most interesting was that Britain did not wish to oppose Japan's application outright because of the possible repercussions for its relations with the United States and Japan respectively. The United States was also most concerned not to press for Japan's tariff negotiations at the seventh session in case of any resultant damage to its relations with Britain and the Commonwealth.[75] And so 1952 saw Anglo-American collaboration to postpone Japan's tariff negotiations at the seventh session. The United States had, however, guaranteed Japan that it would oppose any outright rejection of Japan's application; thus the US formulated a compromise whereby Japan's application would be discussed at an intersessional committee. The Anglo-American cooperation to defer Japan's application was successful. The next challenge for Britain was to formulate a government policy towards Japan in the extra months it had now been granted.

Conclusions

Japan's first year as a sovereign nation saw much progress but many obstacles in her attempt to re-integrate herself in the Western comity of nations. She made headway in her membership of international organisations. She felt protected under US aegis both on the defence and trade fronts, but the realities of the Cold War were difficult for Japan to digest, particularly in relation to China. In order to compensate for the loss of trade links with China, Japan sought to establish alternate avenues of trade. Trade relations with the Sterling Area proved to be a challenge due to the complex set of business rules attached to these. Japan's attempts to manoeuvre within the rules were frustrated by British negotiators. Japan thus felt that Britain, the banker for the Sterling Area, was intent on maintaining political leverage for its own benefit.

During this time, Britain remained opposed to Japan's GATT entry because of the possible implications it would have on the preferential intra-Commonwealth trading system. Thus Japan increasingly felt that Britain was not supporting her attempts to seek alternative trading partners in the Sterling Area.

5 Britain at the helm?

Introduction

1953 saw a continuation of Japan's reintegration into the Western comity of nations. The United States set the example by signing the Treaty of Friendship, Commerce and Navigation with Japan on 2 April 1953. The purpose of the agreement was to restore US-Japanese bilateral relations, and to set a precedent for other nations to sign similar treaties with Japan.[1] The year saw a change of US administration from Democrat to Republican with the inauguration of Dwight D. Eisenhower as President on 12 January. The new administration remained committed to Japan's economic recovery, but the rest of the decade saw constant struggle between the administration and a small but influential protectionist Republican minority over liberal economic policy, which undermined US attempts to endorse Japan's GATT membership.

In the meantime, Japan was attempting to expand her trade with the non-dollar area, since the armistice in the Korean War on 27 July 1953 signified the end to Japan's extraordinary dollar earnings through Korean War procurements. Japan could therefore no longer rely on an indefinite dollar supply. Given that procurements had not eased Japan's balance of payments deficit, she needed to place even greater emphasis on trade expansion.

The year saw a continuation of Yoshida's premiership in Japan, but he was increasingly seen as a caretaker Prime Minister. Just as Churchill lost his popularity in his postwar administration,[2] Yoshida's star lost its lustre after Japan's independence. In fact, his fourth cabinet only lasted for six months, due to an incident between the Prime Minister and a socialist legislator.[3] The last Yoshida cabinet began on 21 May and lasted a little more than a year and a half, until he was forced to step down.[4] Despite decreasing popularity at home, Yoshida did initiate important steps towards Japan's closer relations with Southeast Asia. In early 1953, the government established the round-table on the Asian economy as an advisory organ to MOFA. In May, Yoshida set up a committee on trade promotion and Southeast Asian development. Yoshida also admitted publicly that Japan could not rely on trade with China and that it would have to turn its efforts to Southeast Asian development. Thus 1953 saw Japan increase its focus on Southeast Asia as a viable trade outlet.

Britain continued to seek a solution to inconvertibility, and approached the United States and Western European countries with the so-called collective approach to convertibility, but the proposal was rejected and the plan failed.[5] The Anglo-Japanese Sterling Payments Agreement was characterised by operational frustrations and Japan's sterling depletion. The Bank of England therefore agreed to extend sterling/dollar swaps to Japan until she could rebuild her reserves. Overshadowed by these difficulties was the British decision to permit an increase in colonial imports of Japanese goods to alleviate Japan's sterling shortages. The choice of the colonies instead of the dominions was a calculated British decision to open up Sterling Area-Japan trade to markets that had the least repercussion on British domestic manufacturers. Visible progress was also made when Japan grudgingly accepted the use of third country transfers of sterling for trade. She had originally feared that the instrument would lead to an uncontrollable levels of sterling reserves, but the decision paved the way for Japan's use of sterling for multilateral trade. These positive steps were hindered, however, by Britain's inability to accept Japan as a member of the GATT. Various means were sought to enable Japan to co-exist in the same trading organisation, but each failed to meet Britain's conditions. Thus Britain's inconsistent policies towards Japan resulted in confusion and suspicion.

Talks in Tokyo

When the Sterling Payments Agreement was renewed at the end of 1952, Japan requested that talks be convened at the beginning of the following year. Britain's initial plan was to hold talks in London, but officials at an ONC meeting decided that the consultative review should be held in Tokyo, due to the political embarrassment it was likely to face in having a Japanese delegation in London while Japan's GATT accession was being discussed in Geneva. British officials in Tokyo were therefore instructed to hold a consultative review in Tokyo on Japan's trade relations with the UK and its colonies. Moreover, the British representatives were instructed to discover Japan's plans for sterling usage in 1953, and to what extent Japan was willing to implement its rights to third country transfers.

Consultative talks began on 29 January and lasted until 3 February. The Japanese officials asked for trade to be set at £230 million each way. Although the Japanese side was no longer worried about Japanese goods sold on from Hong Kong to Indonesia and Thailand, it was concerned with Hong Kong's newly placed import restrictions against Japan. Furthermore, they asked that Japanese goods be given equal treatment with goods from OEEC countries. Discussions on administrative transferability were conducted but little progress was made. The problem lay in Japan's rationale that she had to earn dollars from as many countries as possible, even if this meant sacrificing greater trade flows by using sterling as a trade medium.[6]

British negotiators in Tokyo felt that if trade relations were to improve, the Sterling Area as a whole needed to relax its import restrictions on Japan, because statistics in their possession indicated that Japan's exports were decreasing even further, while imports were increasing. The rise in imports from the Sterling Area was due to increased purchases of cotton, jute and coal from India; wool from Australia; and rice from Burma. At the conclusion of the consultations, the British negotiators were acutely aware that if trade relations were to improve, the Sterling Area as a whole needed to relax its import restrictions. This was because the rise in Japan's imports was not a result of seasonal purchases as originally thought, but rather due to Japan's decision to relax its import restrictions. They therefore emphasised that Britain should reciprocate Japan's initiative of the previous October, and also ease its import restrictions.

Thus it was up to Whitehall to come up with a counter-proposal. The agenda was first discussed at the EPC meeting on 25 February. Both the Treasury and the Board of Trade submitted memoranda, which agreed in principle that the Sterling Area should increase its imports from Japan. The differences lay in whether all Sterling Area territories should import 20 per cent more goods from Japan, as recommended by R. A. Butler of the Treasury, or whether the import increases should be limited to specific territories, as suggested by Peter Thorneycroft of the Board of Trade. The latter's memorandum supported a two-thirds increase in colonial imports[7] and an expansion in the re-export of Japanese goods to Thailand and Indonesia from the two Southeast Asian entrepôt trading centres. Thorneycroft was, however, opposed to the easing of restrictions by ISA countries such as Australia and New Zealand because they were already restricting imports from the UK and Japan due to a sterling shortage. Thus, if import restrictions were to be lifted, Thorneycroft believed that the UK should be the beneficiary, not Japan.[8]

In the ensuing discussion at an EPC meeting on the same day, the Secretary of State for Commonwealth Relations supported the Board of Trade's view and discouraged any relaxation of import restrictions by the ISA. The minutes of the meeting indicate a heated debate where attendees questioned the need to single Japan out for special import restrictions and a minimum working capital of £55 million. By the end of the meeting, it was agreed that the UK and its colonies (including Hong Kong and Singapore) would ease import restrictions, while Australia and New Zealand would be discouraged from pursuing relaxations. The Board of Trade was instructed to draft a telegram in consultation with the Foreign Office, the Colonial Office and the Treasury, and this was approved by the EPC two days later. The telegram would have been dispatched to Tokyo immediately had it not been for the conspicuous absence of Board of Trade representatives, who had in the meantime decided to reverse the EPC conclusion of February 25.

At an EPC meeting on 4 March, Thorneycroft recommended that 'in view of the politically explosive nature of the subject' no concessions should be made without Cabinet approval.[9] He went on to justify the Board of Trade's decision not to support the EPC conclusion, based on three reasons. These were: his ministry's refusal to accept £55 million as the minimum level of Japan's sterling reserves; its scepticism towards the Treasury's gloomy projection of the rate at which Japan's sterling reserves were declining; and lastly, he asked why the UK should ease its import restrictions when the amount of trade at stake with Japan was so small. The underlying reason for his protest was the Board of Trade's conviction that the earlier EPC decision was driven entirely by political concerns to improve Britain's relations with Japan, with detrimental effects on the Lancashire textiles industry. Thorneycroft argued that the Board of Trade had only recently persuaded cotton interests to reduce their cheap cloth prices to compete with Japanese products, and so he could hardly announce a sudden increase in Japanese imports without loud protests from the cotton lobby.[10] He explained that the Board of Trade could only support Japanese trade expansion if it did not affect Lancashire.

The Board of Trade's protestations could not have come at a worse time for the Foreign Office and the Treasury. Both Eden and Butler were in Washington attempting to gain US approval for a collective approach to convertibility, and were unable to exert their influence on the EPC. Thus Selwyn Lloyd and Reginald Maudling were left to represent their respective ministries.[11] In his memorandum, Lloyd emphasised the international repercussions of a reversal in British policy, ranging from the effects on Anglo-American relations on Southeast Asia's economic activity, to the damage it would have on Anglo-Japanese relations. Lloyd and Maudling were, however, overwhelmed by the combined influence of the Board of Trade and Commonwealth Relations Office, who received the committee's endorsement to draft their point of view for the Cabinet on 10 March.[12]

As soon as the EPC meeting came to a conclusion, the Treasury dispatched a note to Sir Leslie Rowan, a Treasury delegate in Washington, who communicated their anxieties over the outcome of the EPC. Rowan asked Butler and Eden to intervene to prevent Britain's policy being dictated by the Board of Trade and Lancashire. In the meantime, to the Treasury and the Foreign Office's dismay, the majority of EPC members supported the Board of Trade's position at the subsequent EPC meeting, thus elevating the Board of Trade-centred memorandum to the Cabinet meeting of March 10. This time, the Foreign Office sent a telegram to Washington reiterating the hope that Eden and Butler would endorse the respective ministerial lines, and intervene by sending a telegram to the Prime Minster, Winston Churchill, before the cabinet meeting was convened.[13] Butler and Eden's communication to Churchill had its effect. British policy towards Japan inched back in favour of the Treasury and Foreign Office line. It was decided in Cabinet that, first, the colonies should be permitted to increase their imports to 120 per cent of the amount they imported in the second half of 1952; second, that imports into Hong Kong and Singapore for re-export outside the Sterling Area were to be licensed freely; and third, that all ISA countries, except Australia and New Zealand, would be encouraged to relax their imports from Japan.[14] Although the above policy was not drastically different from the Board of Trade's proposal, Butler and Eden's intervention enabled Britain to remain flexible if Japan were to refuse the British offer.[15] In case of Japan's refusal, UK representatives in Tokyo were instructed to make every effort to dissuade Japan from imposing restrictions, and to report back to Whitehall with Japan's minimum terms.[16] British officials presented their terms to Japan five days later, and after a few days of back-and-forth, both sides agreed to trade based upon British terms. Japan held off imposing new restrictions against the Sterling Area until their next review in four months time.[17]

Once the discussion over trade was over, Tôjô Takei, the Chief of the Foreign Exchange Bureau with the Japanese Ministry of Finance, was dispatched to London to discuss methods to counteract Japan's serious sterling position with the Bank of England and the Treasury.[18] His visit, which was originally scheduled for four days, lasted a month as officials sought a solution to Japan's woes. Meetings between the two sides focused upon third country transfers and credit facilities. The first four meetings were dedicated to third country transfers. This was the one Sterling Area transactional mechanism that had been rejected by Japan in the past because of its potential for unwieldy accumulation of sterling reserves. The British side, however, argued that much of Japan's lack of sterling reserves could have been avoided if they were open to accepting third country transfers. Britain's stance seems to have had some effect on the Japanese delegates because they offered to accept sterling from all countries outside the US dollar and open account areas, with ad-hoc exceptions for the latter.[19] Tokyo approved the proposal subject to a few changes, including its request to exclude the Belgian monetary area, Switzerland and Liechtenstein from the arrangement.

The rest of the discussions revolved around the different credit facilities open to Japan. The Bank of England offered three options; usance bills, sales of dollars and sterling/dollar swaps. Japan's initial stance was against the use of usance bills because of the lag time between approval and activation. Furthermore, she opposed the outright sale of dollars to the Sterling Area, and as an extension of the principle, the Japanese government was not happy with the idea of sterling/dollar swaps because Japan would have to sell dollars at the outset.[20] Japan proposed instead that the Bank of England extend a collateral loan to MOF or to commercial banks to reduce Japan's margin on credit cover from 50 to 25 per cent.[21] Neither option was feasible. Japanese delegates were unable to persuade commercial banks to change their credit margin; while the Bank of England could not extend loans given that this ran counter to their general credit policy. Tôjô, who needed to resolve the credit issue before departing for Japan, asked for Serpell's assistance. At the seventh meeting, Serpell offered sterling/dollar swaps to Japan for a period of up to six months. If the market was unable to provide sufficient swap facilities or was unable to continue the swaps for the full six months, he stressed that the Bank of England was prepared to offer the necessary facilities on the same basis.[22]

The meetings thereafter were spent on various drafts of the agreed minute. In the meantime, the government in Japan approved Britain's sterling/dollar swaps; and Tôjô remained in London until the agreed minute was signed on 29 April.[23] The two main decisions reached in London between the Japanese representatives and Treasury and Bank of England officials were the introduction of limited third country transfers to and from Japan, and the offer of six-month sterling/dollar swap facilities of £25 million to Japan by the Hong Kong Bank, the Chartered Bank, Chase National Bank, National City Bank, Mercantile Bank and the Bank of America.[24]

American observations

During this period, the American Embassy in Tokyo was constantly keeping the State Department informed of progress in the Anglo-Japanese payments talks. The most interesting of the reports dispatched to the State Department was written by Frank A. Waring, Counselor for Economic Affairs at the Embassy. In his report, dated 6 May, he highlighted the enthusiasm expressed by the Minister of Foreign Affairs, Okazaki Katsuo, about sterling trade. Okazaki had reportedly informed a Diet committee which was monitoring the Anglo-Japanese discussions, that Japan was considering the possibility of converting its entire dollar-expressed open-account agreements with Southeast Asian countries to sterling bilateral agreements.[25] Furthermore, he identified MITI and MOFA as most attracted by the possibility of shifting Japan's trade with the dollar area to sterling-expressed payments arrangements.[26] Waring reported that there were various government officials who supported such a move because of their pessimism over Japan's future dollar position. He also noted that several business and financial groups, who were advocating the establishment of an Asian payments union with settlements in sterling and an expansion in the use of sterling to trade with the PRC, were also supporting such a move.[27] The second point of interest was Waring's scepticism about Britain's drive to wean Japan from the Dollar Area to the Sterling Area. Although he saw the inevitability of Japan moving towards regional trade (as advocated by the United States as well as Britain), he questioned Britain's motive in drawing Japan into the sterling fold. His scepticism arose from the fact that Britain was making promises of freer Sterling Area-Japan trade, but restricting imports of Japanese goods, and showing a reluctance to maximise Sterling Area exports of raw materials to Japan.[28]

Britain's policy towards the intersessional committee

In the meantime, having succeeded in postponing Japan's GATT accession until the beginning of 1953, Britain had to establish its position regarding the February intersessional committee meeting. The Foreign Office and the Board of Trade reached a compromise solution based upon Article 19 of the GATT treaty, and presented it at an informal meeting of the two departments on 9 January. The protective or emergency clause, if accepted by the contracting parties, would be inserted into Japan's protocol for accession and enable Britain, the Commonwealth and the colonies to take 'emergency action against Japan to deal with an intensification of Japanese competition in particular goods or in particular localities when they were deemed to be causing or threatening serious injury'.[29] The insertion of the clause was proposed on the basis that Britain would be unable to compete fairly with a low-cost producer that had a history of commercial malpractice such as unauthorised copying of textile designs.[30]

The use of the Article 19 emergency action clause was not only novel but controversial in that it would be aimed at Japan alone. Not knowing how the Americans would react to the clause, the Board of Trade and the Foreign Office decided to approach them informally, before taking the issue to Cabinet. On 13 January the Board of Trade set up an appointment with Winthrop Brown of the US Embassy and informed the Americans of the latest British position towards Japan and the GATT.[31] Winthrop Brown's reaction was less favourable than expected. In a telegram to Dulles, Brown expressed the reasons for his opposition to the British proposal.[32] He believed that the implementation of Article 19(b) would be acceptable if it were to 'restore previously reduced duties' in the preferential markets, but he was against 'greater or new increases as the British were intending'.[33] Second, he thought it would be better to extend preferential treatment to Britain's Commonwealth countries on a case-by-case basis, rather than see the emergency action implemented directly against Japan. Third, he thought that discriminatory action against products of a named country was contrary to the principles of the GATT, because it could establish an 'undesirable precedent' among contracting parties. Moreover, Brown thought that other contracting parties would be shocked by such a discriminatory proposal from Britain, one of the chief architects of the GATT.[34]

While waiting for the State Department's formal views on Britain's proposal, Brown and his colleagues took it upon themselves to visit the Board of Trade and the Foreign Office on consecutive days to express their concern over Britain's proposed position, perhaps with the hope that such a barrage of visits by US Embassy officials might change the views of the British government. If the US officials had such hopes they were to be disappointed, as on 22 January Eden and Thorneycroft submitted a joint memorandum to the Cabinet along the lines agreed at the meeting of 9 January.

The joint memorandum was passed by the Cabinet, in spite of Cabinet concerns over the level of US opposition to the proposal. Members felt that there could be a chance of its acceptance by other countries if the proposal was presented skillfully. It was agreed that in the first instance, the UK should seek the response of the other intersessional members and Britain's line could be altered according to the results of this preliminary consultation.[35] On the following day, telegrams were dispatched to UK embassies and consulates in the intersessional member countries, and to Japan, to seek their views on the British proposal.

In the meantime, US officials continued to express opposition to the British proposal and made further visits to the Board of Trade and the Foreign Office, while American officials requested parallel meetings with British officials in Washington. The US message at every meeting was consistent – the US opposed the British proposal for two reasons: the political difficulty of singling out Japan for special discriminatory treatment, and the legal issue of whether Article 19 was the legitimate article under which Britain should try and protect its trade in third countries. In an attempt to break the impasse, American officials decided that an Anglo-American agreement should be reached before the discussion transferred to the public arena. And so US delegates to the intersessional meeting stopped off in London to confer with Whitehall officials before the start of talks in Geneva on 2 February. The meeting, however, ended inconclusively.[36] After the US's departure, Britain decided that it would present the Article 19 proposal in Geneva and attempt to persuade the GATT officials to adopt it in spite of the lack of US support.

Meanwhile telegrams were arriving back from various UK embassies and consulates with regard to other contracting parties' views on the British proposal. Many, such as Norway, expressed sympathy with the British position;[37] some, such as Chile, gave unconditional support to Japan in its bid to accede;[38] while others, such as Cuba and Italy, remained unsure about what course they would take with regard to Japan's accession to the GATT.[39]

By the start of the intersessional committee meeting, the view in Britain was that most of the contracting parties were sympathetic to the British position, but many were unwilling to reach a decision until the American position became clearer. Therefore the British delegates to Geneva were instructed to seek informal support for the proposal. If it was rejected, they were to report back to London with the best alternative proposal. The Cabinet could then 'consider whether the solution was acceptable', and if so, take steps to canvass industry and the parliamentary committees concerned.[40]

Although the United States' intention was to play a dominant role at the intersessional committee meeting, the American position was not well defined, partly because the new administration had only recently taken office and policy towards the intersessional committee meeting was slow in forming. More importantly, although the United States was in favour of Japan's eventual GATT accession, they were unable to grant a quick accession while the RTA (Reciprocal Trade Agreements) Act was still being discussed in Congress.[41]

The RTA Act and its significance in the first year of the Eisenhower administration should be seen in light of the fact that Eisenhower had campaigned for the presidency with a programme that emphasised the need for a liberal foreign economic policy, while this position was opposed by a protectionist minority of the Republican Party who held key positions in Congress. The RTA Act had first been passed by Congress in 1934. It did not repeal the Smoot-Hawley Tariff Act of 1930, but it authorised the President to negotiate agreements with other countries for mutual reductions in tariff rates of up to 50 per cent of the Smoot-Hawley Tariff.[42] In this way the power over tariffs had passed from Congress to the President in the 1930s. Eisenhower faced opposition to the renewal of the RTA Act because a small Republican minority believed that freer trade through lower tariffs was a 'Democratic-inspired program that challenged the nation's economic interests by fostering increased foreign competition'.[43] The protectionist elements within the Republican Party held key positions in the congressional committees which the Reciprocal Trade bill had to pass through, such as the Senate Finance Committee and the Committee on Ways and Means. Moreover, a conservative Republican, Richard Simpson of Pennsylvania, introduced a bill (HR 4294), which aimed at raising existing tariff levels and import quotas. The Chairman of the Committee on Ways and Means, Daniel A. Reed of New York, who was an old-guard Republican, chose to hold hearings on the Simpson Bill while ignoring the administration's trade bill.[44] By June it was apparent that neither side of the Republican Party was going to win. The Simpson Bill was defeated, and Eisenhower realised that it was impossible to reverse the historic Republican protectionist position within the short period before the RTA Act was due to expire. Therefore Eisenhower asked Congress for a one-year extension of the RTA Act and dropped his request for additional rate cutting powers. Moreover, he promised not to negotiate new trade deals during that year, thereby preventing America from conducting tariff negotiations with Japan in 1953. Meanwhile, the administration concentrated on the study of a comprehensive economic programme, in order to rally support for freer trade policies. This study became known as the Randall Report.[45]

The intersessional committee meeting

The intersessional committee meeting to discuss Japan's accession to the GATT began on 2 February in Geneva. The fifteen members of the intersessional committee were Australia, Cuba, Italy, Belgium, Denmark, Pakistan, Brazil, France, South Africa, Canada, Germany, Chile, India, the United States and Britain.[46] Real progress took place outside of the formal session, where Wyndham White introduced an alternative to Britain's Article 19 proposal to a group of delegates from the United States, Canada, Australia and Britain. Wyndham White's proposal envisioned the inclusion of Article 23 in the protocol of accession, rather than Article 19.[47] The proposal was based on the idea that if a contracting party experienced problems in regard to another member, the matter could be brought to the attention of the GATT, and the contracting parties would promptly investigate the issue and make appropriate recommendations. The advantage of adopting Article 23 was that Japan would not be singled out as the 'only possible sinner', thus avoiding any appearance of discrimination, and this would therefore be more acceptable to Japan and the GATT members.[48] The disadvantages were in the wording of the actual text, which restricted the injured party from taking action until after consultations with the contracting parties; together with the fact that the new proposal was not targeted at any one particular country, thus there was a danger of a wider application of Article 23, including its use against Britain in the event of currency depreciation; moreover, Britain would still have to resort to Article 19 until a situation developed which clearly justified a resort to Article 23.

The British delegates were not in favour of adopting article 23, and relayed their view to the Foreign Office, which instructed them to participate in the amendment of the text, so that they could mould it to apply to confined situations that did not affect Britain or its interests. Moreover, they were instructed to support a proposal that enabled a contracting party to take action either with or without the prior approval of the other members, so that damage control would be in the hands of the contracting party that felt wronged by actions of another signatory. If the proposal were not accepted, the delegates were asked to reserve their position.

The drafting committee met between 6 and 13 February to finalise the text of the Article 23 proposal. The United States had a problem with the wording of any protocol which specified 'serious injury' in the text, because the new Eisenhower administration was attempting to tighten emergency provisions in the Reciprocal Trade Agreement in order to reduce the number of applications for tariff increases by inefficient domestic producers.[49] For this reason, the Americans were against the use of the particular words in the declaration, which could be cited by domestic producers to protect their business against foreign competition. This was acknowledged, and the words 'violent disruption of trading conditions' were inserted instead of 'serious injury'. The issue that caused great debate was the question of 'prior approval' and whether a contracting party should be able to take unilateral emergency action before seeking GATT approval. America and Canada opposed inclusion of the 'prior approval' clause in the protocol of accession because they thought it unlikely that a serious situation would arise overnight. Moreover, they thought it was against the spirit of the GATT for a member to take unilateral action.[50] The issue was resolved when the drafting committee decided that the contracting party would be able to take provisional, emergency action if the other members were unable to reach a decision within thirty days of the situation being reported.

The intersessional committee report was finalised on 13 February. The report favoured Japan's GATT admittance, but the terms of her entry included an emergency action based on Article 23, which would enable any member to take action against another signatory if it produced or threatened violent disruption of trading conditions through its export practices, so as to affect a significant sector or sectors of production of one or more contracting parties. Under this emergency action, the injured party might take unilateral interim emergency action if the contracting parties were unable to reach a decision on the issue within thirty days of filing. The report also envisioned the tariff negotiations to take place at a single general tariff conference, but the nature and the timing of the talks would be decided at a special session. A number of delegates, including those from Brazil, Denmark, Belgium, France and Italy, emphasised that they were adopting the report *ad referendum*. The United States made it known that it was unable to make a commitment to enter tariff negotiations with Japan while the RTA Act was being discussed in Congress. The next step, therefore, was for the contracting parties to endorse the report. This would be done by postal vote to the secretariat, indicating whether they were ready to open tariff negotiations with Japan on the terms outlined in the report.[51]

Japan had a group of ten representatives in Geneva.[52] After the completion of the intersessional committee meeting, Hagiwara Tôru, who headed the group, sent a telegram to MOFA, in which he reported that the group had no objections to the report because Japan did not have to fulfill any criteria to join the GATT, nor did the conditions for Japanese entry include any drawbacks. They accepted Britain's explanation that it was not against Japan's long-term trade recovery, and that safeguards were proposed in order to ensure Britain against unforeseen trade practices.

British officials had cause to be satisfied as well as relieved by the outcome of the intersessional committee meeting. Although, they were unable to persuade other members to agree to their proposal of an Article 19 escape clause, they were able to safeguard their position by retaining the right to take action in case of 'violent disruption of trading conditions'.[53] The initial British euphoria was short-lived, however, as the general feeling in the Foreign Office grew that Britain might have made too many compromises in order to reach a settlement with the Americans and the Canadians. The discomfort grew with America's proposal to suspend action by an injured party for sixty days as opposed to the agreed thirty days. The British viewed this recommendation as a further erosion of their power to act in defence of their overseas markets. They felt that in a matter of a few months, they had drifted from their declared intent not to confer MFN rights to Japan, to accepting Japan's GATT membership without strong safeguards for British industry. Thus the Foreign Office feared that the Geneva agreement would not be acceptable to the Board of Trade, who would object to the thirty-day suspension of action period. A month later, the Foreign Office was notified that, as predicted, the Board of Trade had rejected the agreement, and the issue was rescheduled for further Cabinet discussion on May 14.

The Cabinet met to discuss whether Britain should accept the Article 23 intersessional committee report. Three memoranda written by the Board of Trade, the Foreign Office and the Treasury respectively were distributed for discussion. The Board of Trade rejected the intersessional report because it made Britain far too reliant upon the GATT vote concerning violent and disruptive competition. Its recommendation was for a vote of absentia so as to postpone any decisive action on the MFN issue for as long as possible to safeguard the rights of British industries. The Foreign Office and the Treasury both recommended acceptance of the GATT intersessional report, and stressed the serious consequences of absentia on Britain's economic, trade, sterling and political policies towards Japan. The Treasury was particularly concerned with the inconsistencies in Britain's policy towards Japan, and recommended that a study similar to that carried out in 1951 be undertaken to resolve the contradictions in Britain's policy. The recommendation was supported fully by the Cabinet, which postponed a decision on the intersessional committee report until various aspects of British economic policy towards Japan had been further studied and findings became available in a government report.

The report

The Cabinet Tariff Policy Committee on Japan was designated responsible for the report. It met in early June and twice after that before the report was compiled on 16 July. The actual work was carried out by an inter-ministerial working party, which divided the work into four sub-divisions in order to manage the load. The questions they were asked to answer fell into the following four categories:

1 Japanese competition with the United Kingdom To what extent is Japan competitive with the United Kingdom, both now and potentially, in the main fields of industry (e.g. textiles, engineering, etc.)? This should include a study of the colonial markets.

To what extent, and for what reasons, is Japan to be feared more than other competing countries in these fields?

Which countries have the most reasons to fear Japanese competition?

2 Japan's economic relationship with the Sterling Area How far is Japan dependent on the Sterling Area as a source of supplies and for markets for her exports? In this connection, the prospects for United States aid and of a cessation of procurement for the war in Korea, together for a re-opening of trade with China, should be taken into account.

How far does the Sterling Area need to look to Japan as a source of supplies, and as a market for exports, including invisibles? In particular, what is the position between Japan and the United Kingdom itself?

3 Balance of payments What are the Sterling Area/Japan balance of payments prospects, and their implications for the short term (i.e. 1953/4), and the long term?

4 GATT What forms could Japanese disruptive competition, unfair practices, etc., take? What safeguards against them exist, and what safeguards would exist if Japan were in the GATT?

What are the likely reactions of the colonies, Japan, Commonwealth countries, the United States and other contracting parties, to a decision by the United Kingdom to invoke Article 35 against Japan?

What action by these countries is likely if Japan is admitted to the GATT?

What are the advantages and disadvantages of a United Kingdom-Japan treaty?[54]

The first section concerning Japanese competition with the United Kingdom specified the industries vulnerable to disruptive competition from Japan. They were cotton textiles, rayon textiles, pottery, toys, finished steel, textile- and other machinery, bicycles, cables, clocks, cameras and glassware.[55] The amount of trade at risk was considered to be £70 million a year, or 3 per cent of Britain's total exports, or 18 per cent of British exports to East Asia (excluding Australia and New Zealand). Although these figures seemed low on the whole, the threat was large to the individual industries. For example, the threat to cotton and rayon textiles industries amounted to 30 per cent respectively. The markets which were considered most vulnerable to Japanese goods were those areas where cheapness was a decisive factor. Moreover, given that China could no longer absorb Japanese exports, there were concerns that Japanese goods might spill over to South America, the Near East, the Middle East and Canada.

On Japan's economic relationship with the Sterling Area, the report indicated that neither Japan nor the Sterling Area were dependent on the other for materials, except for Japan's purchases of wool. Japan's need for Sterling Area products was less a direct supply problem and more a function of its foreign exchange position. Japan's import programme was based on the reserves and expected earnings of the different currencies, and the bargaining strength of other countries with whom it had bilateral agreements. The peculiarity of Japan's foreign exchange budget rested on the strict division between dollar, sterling and open account expenditures. Therefore, as long as Japan had ample dollar reserves, it was not expected to be over-reliant on the Sterling Area. However, the 'underdeveloped' territories of the Sterling Area looked to Japanese goods as a valuable source of cheap manufactures (especially textiles and light metal products). Japanese goods were deemed important as a means of preventing inflation in those countries. In view of the poverty of the inhabitants of the new dominions and the colonies, it was politically impracticable for them to do without Japanese goods.

With respect to the balance of payments prospects of the Sterling Area and Japan, the report was unable to offer a decisive recommendation because of fluctuations in Japan's sterling reserves. Although Britain had offered a £25 million sterling/dollar swap facility to Japan in order to restore Japan's sterling balances to £50–55 million by the end of 1953, the facility was not considered enough to enable Japan to overcome its deficit with the Sterling Area. The report identified three options open to Britain. To relax import restrictions to give Japan better access to Sterling Area markets; to force Japan to reduce its purchases from the Sterling Area generally; or to ask Japan to buy sterling using dollars or other currencies. No option was deemed ideal and so the report did not recommend any one over the other.[56]

On the GATT issue, the report attempted to identify the ways in which Japanese competition might prove to be disruptive. But it was unable to provide any specific examples except for the possible repetition of pre-war malpractices such as infringement of copyright laws and the practice of dumping. The report identified several safeguards available to Britain should Japan join the GATT. If Britain decided not to invoke Article 35, it could protect its home market by increasing tariffs on a non-discriminatory basis, raise unbound MFN rates and negotiate increases in bound duties, or implement Article 19. The problem with the above options was that they would not help colonial, Commonwealth or foreign industries to safeguard their industries in British markets, nor could they help Britain in their respective countries. Other options open to Britain included citing balance of payments as a means to restrict Japanese imports; the use of Article 23; or the implementation of Article 35. These also hampered Britain's ability to take effective action against Japanese competition. For example, the balance of payments argument would become ineffective in the long run, due to Britain's expected move towards convertibility. Article 23 would enable Britain to safeguard its home market, but any discrimination against Japan was subject to the prior approval of a majority of the contracting parties. Article 35 would limit protection to Britain's domestic industries and its export interests in its colonies. The report stressed the potential adverse impact on the Commonwealth if Britain decided to invoke Article 35, given that some member countries were expected to vote for and others against Japan's accession, leading to a division within the organisation.

Regarding what action would be taken by these countries if Japan joined the GATT without any additional safeguards, the report concluded that it would result in an overall tariff increase, with the probability that it would affect Britain's exports to the Commonwealth.

On the advantages and disadvantages of signing a commercial treaty, Britain had until mid-1956 to decide on what form of treaty it should sign with Japan, because the peace treaty of September 1951 had stipulated that Japan give MFN treatment to all goods for four years after the ratification of the treaty. Various formulas for a commercial treaty with Japan were proposed, such as a normal commercial treaty without an MFN-goods clause or a treaty with a MFN clause, which would enable Britain and the colonies to take unilateral defensive action in an emergency. The British Embassy in Tokyo had already communicated the view that the first formula would be unacceptable to the Japanese. The report indicated that it did not expect Japan to accept the second option either, but recommended that Britain 'sound out' the United States and the Commonwealth countries on the proposal.

The report outlined clearly Britain's dilemma regarding its economic and trade policies towards Japan. On the one hand, Britain wished to include safeguards in Japan's protocol for accession to the GATT to protect its domestic industries from disruptive Japanese trade competition. On the other hand, Britain was aware of the negative impact such a safeguard would have on Sterling Area-Japan relations. Britain was particularly concerned about the potential impact the GATT would have upon trade relations in light of the underdeveloped Sterling Area countries' reliance on cheap Japanese goods. Amicable relations were also important if Britain wished to continue nurturing Japan towards the Sterling Area. Moreover, Britain had to consider Commonwealth views concerning the GATT to ensure that circumstances did not lead to a split amongst the membership.

The Cabinet Committee on Trade Policy was given the task of bringing the several strands of the report together into a comprehensive recommendation. At their second meeting on 22 July, the committee members decided to focus upon the GATT portion of the report because of the immediate pressure on them to recommend a British GATT policy towards Japan before the start of the eighth GATT session in September. The UK's commercial policy towards Japan was given a lower priority. The committee, chaired by Thorneycroft, recommended that Britain defer its decision for the time being, given that the United States, the main proponent of Japan's accession, was unable to support Japan's accession in 1953. Everyone on the committee agreed in principle to the decision, but all agreed to raise the issue in the Cabinet in order to discuss an alternative option in case deferment of action was not possible.

The issue of Japan's GATT entry was discussed at a Cabinet meeting on 30 July 1953. The Cabinet supported the Committee on Trade Policy's conclusions, and decided that it would not support the Article 23 safeguard, and that Britain would not show its hand at the September session, due to the domestic, colonial, Commonwealth and foreign pressures.[57]

Towards the temporary accession of Japan to the GATT

As Britain was formulating its policy towards Japan, a parallel set of developments was taking place in Geneva. GATT's Executive Secretary, Eric Wyndham White, who was seeking ways of bringing Japan into the organisation, had begun to consider temporary accession as the most feasible solution for Japan.[58] He contacted Hagiwara in early May, and together they discussed ways of presenting the proposal to the contracting parties. They decided to bypass the usual diplomatic channels used to canvass support, which took place weeks ahead of the GATT session, and instead decided to telegraph the contracting parties immediately prior to the GATT session.[59]

Wyndham White identified two options for Japan; the Annecy formula – accession to the GATT through a minor tariff negotiation – or provisional accession, which entitled Japan to enter GATT without prior negotiations on the understanding that they would begin as soon as the freeze on tariff talks was lifted.[60] Wyndham White abandoned the first option after he learned that the United States was restricted from entering any major tariff negotiations as part of its renewed commitment to Congress. Thus Hagiwara and Wyndham White collaborated closely to prepare a proposal for Japan's provisional accession that would be the most attractive to the GATT contracting parties, in particular the United States.[61]

In mid-July, Wyndham White flew to Washington and discussed his temporary accession proposal with US officials. By the end of July, he had Dulles' support for the proposal in principle, although the US government's formal endorsement would not be forthcoming until the government had gained approval from the interdepartmental trade agreements committee and congressional leaders. Neither could be approached until the RTA act had been extended.

By early August, both Britain and Wyndham White were preparing telegrams to lay out their respective positions on Japan's GATT accession. In Britain, a Board of Trade draft telegram was being circulated to the Foreign Secretary and the Chancellor of the Exchequer for their approval when the Board of Trade received Wyndham White's airgram conveying Japan's proposal for provisional membership.[62] The letter written by the Japanese government expressed its desire to enter into the GATT as a temporary member, because it did not foresee a general round of tariff negotiations in the immediate future. As quid pro quo for this irregular procedure, the Japanese offered to bind a substantial number of its tariffs. To make its proposition attractive to the contracting parties, the Japanese government outlined the following concessions. First, that accepting Japan as a provisional member does not bind contracting parties into accepting Japan as a permanent member. Second, Japan expressed its readiness to accept the Article 23 safeguard in its protocol of accession. Third, Japan indicated its willingness to negotiate reciprocal tariff concessions with any GATT members in advance, with a view to incorporating them eventually into the GATT schedule. Lastly, the airgram highlighted the fact that the US government supported Japan's provisional GATT membership.

On receiving the airgram, the British government sent a telegram to the British Embassy in Washington to ascertain whether the US administration was indeed supporting Japan's provisional GATT membership. Moreover, it instructed the British embassy to inform the US government that Britain wished to see the issue deferred for a further period and that it hoped for

American support of British policy.[63] British Embassy officials were able to schedule a meeting with State Department officials four days later. Samuel C. Waugh, Assistant Secretary for Economic Affairs, and John M Leddy, Director of the Office of Economic Defense and Trade Policy, sympathised with Britain's position but were unable to support it. Their concern centred on the possible repercussions that a delay would have on US-Japan relations.[64] When the results of the Washington meeting was relayed to the Foreign Office, the Marquess of Salisbury, who was then the acting Foreign Secretary, wrote to Thorneycroft suggesting Britain's acceptance of Japan's provisional accession to the GATT, provided there were safeguards for Britain such as the original Article 19, the alternative Article 23 or Article 35 options. Replying, Thorneycroft rejected the suggestions on the grounds that 'any form of Japanese association, however provisional in its technical status, must almost inevitably set the pattern in practice for Japan's later association on a permanent basis'.[65] He further recommended that telegrams be sent to all Commonwealth countries in order to drum up support for Britain. In an attempt to rein Thorneycroft in, Salisbury proposed that the matter be raised at a Cabinet meeting, in the hope that the other members would agree with him that accepting Japan's provisional association would be better for Britain than standing aside to let other members decide the terms of Japan's accession.

At the Cabinet meeting of 25 August, to the Foreign Office's detriment, the majority of members expressed support for the President of the Board of Trade and the Commonwealth Secretary's views that Britain should follow its original decision to abstain from voting for Japan's temporary accession, and that it should try to persuade as many Commonwealth countries as possible, in particular Australia and New Zealand, to follow its lead. Thorneycroft, who was scheduled to attend the GATT session, was instructed to re-submit the issue to the Cabinet for further consideration if it failed to obtain Commonwealth support.[66]

While the British government was finalising its policy towards Japan's provisional accession, an intersessional GATT committee was in session to decide on an appropriate draft for Japan's provisional participation in the GATT.[67] The main points of the draft specified Japan's rights and obligations as a temporary member of the GATT, such as attendance at meetings, veto rights and subscription payments. In return, Japan would agree to treat the commerce of the other contracting parties according to a set schedule that would be submitted at the eighth session. The Foreign Office became alarmed when it received the conclusions of the GATT session, because the intersessional committee did not include any mention of safeguards in the text, not even Article 23, which had been discussed during the previous meeting in February. Therefore, Foreign Office representatives to the eighth GATT session were instructed to ensure through other delegates that the conditions for Japan's provisional membership would be acceptable to the British government when Japan applied for permanent membership.

The British delegates to the GATT session had a difficult task ahead. They were instructed to abstain from voting for Japan's temporary accession, and to rally the Commonwealth members behind Britain's lead. Although they were ordered to maintain their distance from the proceedings, they were expected to influence the wording of Japan's temporary accession through third parties. A week before the start of the GATT session, the British government was already aware that one of its three key objectives would not be feasible. A Commonwealth session organised prior to the start of the GATT session revealed the disparate views of the Commonwealth countries. Both Ceylon and India were in support of Japan's provisional accession. Southern Rhodesia, New Zealand and Australia were in opposition, while the Canadian, Pakistani and South African representatives were still unclear about their government's policy. Thus Britain was made acutely aware that its influence was diminished as a result of a lack of support from its own Commonwealth organisation.

The eighth session of the GATT

The eighth session of the GATT was convened in Geneva between 17 September and 23 October 1953. The main issue on the agenda was Japan's provisional entry into the organisation. This was also the cause of the most serious division among the contracting parties, because many opposed the basis of Japan's provisional entry, which would allow Japan to base its commercial relations upon the GATT basis. Attempts were made to placate the contracting parties who opposed the provisional formula, but all proposals came to nothing.

The contracting parties made their respective views public at the first plenary session of the GATT session on Japan. The majority of the contracting parties were supportive of Japan's entry, such as the United States, Germany, India and Sweden to name but a few. Those who were opposed were the United Kingdom, France, Australia and New Zealand.[68] The opposing countries were a minority, but there was a GATT-wide concern over the serious split on the Japan issue. The British delegation, which had initially opposed Japan's temporary accession, was by this time reconsidering its stance. The sticking point for Britain from the start had been the automatic extension of commercial obligations to Japan with the vote for temporary accession. Thus the British began to devise a recommendation whereby members could invite Japan to the GATT as a fellow of the organisation, which would resolve the obligation issue.[69]

By the end of September, the Board of Trade and the Foreign Office had managed to convince Wyndham White and the GATT working party on Japan's temporary accession to revise the draft decision regarding Japan's temporary accession. The major difference between the original (old look) and the new draft (new look) was that in the old look, all those who voted for Japan's temporary accession were also voting automatically to base their commercial relations with Japan on the GATT. In the new look, Japan's temporary accession to the GATT would require a two-thirds majority, but those who wished to normalise relations with Japan were invited to sign a separate protocol. The two-stage approach meant that all contracting parties would have to accept Japan's participation in GATT meetings, but only those countries that wished to normalise their commercial relations with Japan were invited to do so. The Foreign Office expressed satisfaction with this compromise formula, and hoped that the Board of Trade would also support it, as the initial French, Australian and New Zealand reactions were also favourable.[70]

On receiving the progress report from the GATT, Thorneycroft in London arranged an emergency meeting of Board of Trade officials. On 30 September, the Board of Trade met to discuss the compromise formula and decided that this had strayed from the original British strategy to abstain from voting and to hold together the group of countries who opposed Japan's accession. It decided that Britain should only rely on the compromise formula if it found itself alone in opposition. In that case, Britain should agree to Japan's continued observer status instead of temporary accession, with full opportunity to participate in the discussions of the contracting parties. The Board of Trade also decided that Britain should persuade other contracting parties to acknowledge rather than sign its intention to place their commercial relations with Japan on the GATT basis. Thorneycroft then delegated E.A. Cohen to fly to Geneva. The Foreign Office was not informed of Cohen's departure, perhaps because of Thorneycroft's anger at the former for derailing Britain's GATT strategy.

On 1 October Cohen flew to Geneva as the Board of Trade's representative. On arrival, he immediately set up appointments to meet the Australian and New Zealand delegates to see if they would follow Britain's lead and abstain from voting. Both delegates thought the compromise formula would be acceptable to their respective countries. Thus Cohen had the option of uniting in opposition with France or falling back on the alternative strategy. A united opposition with France seemed remote given the two countries' difficulties over the no-new-preference rule. And so Cohen launched into the back-up strategy of persuading the contracting parties to continue granting Japan observer status. Later that day he met with White and Brown, and asked them to exclude voting rights from Japan's terms of temporary accession. As difficult as the request was, White was able to concur.

Cohen returned to London after the series of meetings to report back to the Board of Trade and to prepare a memorandum for submission to the Cabinet. At a Cabinet meeting on 6 October, Thorneycroft asked for the government's authorisation to enable Japan to participate in the GATT without becoming a provisional member. The Cabinet granted Thorneycroft's request and the British line was relayed to the British delegation in Geneva and to the UK High Commissioners in Australia and New Zealand on the same day. New Zealand expressed support for the British line but the Australian delegate informed Britain that, although a decision had not been finalised, Australia would not be supporting the new proposal.

By 16 October, Australia's final decision not to support Japan either as a provisional member or as an observer had been relayed back to Britain. On receiving this news, Thorneycroft felt that there was no alternative but to revert to Britain's original standpoint and abstain from voting on Japan's accession.[71] On hearing of this, the Foreign Office's Japan and the Pacific Department refused to let the Board of Trade abandon the compromise formula without first referring the matter to Cabinet.[72] At the Cabinet meeting on 19 October, Thorneycroft asked for permission to abstain from voting. Eden warned the Cabinet that several compromises had been devised to meet British needs, and by abstaining Britain would impair its relations with Japan and cause annoyance to the US government. The Cabinet decided that a further message would be sent to the Australian government to try and get them to reconsider their decision.[73] But the Australian Prime Minister, Robert Menzies, refused to budge from his position. He thought Australia was already giving favourable treatment to Japan, on the release of prisoners of war and on import relaxations, and did not feel that he could compromise any further without being severely criticised at home.[74] Therefore the issue was brought back to Cabinet three days later, where the British government formally agreed to abstain from voting on the question of Japan's provisional association with the GATT.[75]

In Geneva, on 23 October, the plenary session was convened and votes were cast on Japan's temporary accession to the GATT based on the new look. Twenty-six contracting parties supported Japan's accession, which was enough for the requisite two-thirds majority. None voted against, and seven abstained from voting.[76] The abstainers were the UK, Australia, New Zealand, France, Southern Rhodesia, Czechoslovakia and Burma, but on the following day Burma asked that it be regarded as having voted in favour.

Japan's Declining Sterling Balance

The Sterling Payments Agreement between Britain and Japan was never far from the Bank of England and Treasury officials' radar, even while the GATT conundrum was taking centre stage. Treasury officials, in particular, wished to bolster Britain's trade relations with Japan for the benefit of the Sterling Area at large, but as in the past, Japan's lack of sterling reserves forced officials to focus upon the inherent problems of the agreement. Thus much of the period from mid-1953 to the end of that year saw British officials bogged down in operational minutiae as they attempted to provide financing for Japan.

Japan spent much of the period hoping for an upturn in colonial purchases from Japan, but the months went by without any improvement. This lack of visible trade improvement led to anxious visits by various Japanese Embassy officials to the Treasury and to the Board of Trade. The

Japanese expressed concern that colonial countries were not relaxing their import restrictions fast enough, and many started to believe that the lack of development might be tied to discrimination against Japanese manufactured goods. Ihara Takashi of the Japanese Embassy even proposed sending a mixed mission of officials and businessmen to London and the colonies to make contacts and enquiries into the marketability of Japanese goods.[77] The British officials reassured Japanese officials of the inevitable time lag between the announcement of import relaxations and the opening of letters of credit. Despite these assurances, there were no visible signs of trade increase from the colonies.

By late July, the Japanese had come to realise that the sterling/dollar swap arrangement was insufficient for Japan to meet its sterling commitments. Without an additional £10 million swaps, Japan's sterling trade would grind to a halt within two months. The Bank of England was opposed to extending further swaps to Japan in principle, because the instrument was designed for temporary relief and Japan's sterling shortage no longer seemed short-term. This forced Ihara to request an extension of the swap arrangement from Serpell.

Serpell at the Treasury was in favour of extending further swaps, as he believed there was a good chance that Japan would be able cover or repay them by the end of the year. He wrote a note of justification to the Bank of England explaining that Britain had some obligation in extending swaps to Japan until the Sterling Area's trade relaxations came into effect. He thought Britain's insistence that Japan pay dollars to resuscitate its trade might reverse the carefully nurtured relationship and turn it into a bilateral one, which was contrary to Britain's sterling policy towards Japan. Serpell subsequently learned from Washington that Japan was also exploring the possibility of borrowing $25 million worth of sterling from the IMF. Serpell felt the political pressure ease off him when he read the telegram, because Japan's reliance upon other sources meant fewer onuses on Britain to find export outlets for Japan. Serpell, therefore, proposed a further £10 million swap – £5 million in the first instance and an additional £5 million if nothing came of the IMF proposal.[78] Ministers accepted Serpell's proposal and the £5 million was extended to Japan in August. The outstanding £5 million was extended to Japan in September, when it was again unable to meet its commitments and the IMF's loans were slow in coming.[79]

By September, it was obvious to both Britain and Japan that talks on full trade and payments needed to be convened by the end of the year in order to resolve the increasing number of problems which were plaguing the signatories. For Britain, the payments talks were imperative because policymakers had been dragging their feet on a clear British policy towards Japan. In leading up to the talks, Britain had to hammer out some preparatory arrangements, such as an extension of the sterling/dollar swaps from November, when it was originally due, to 31 December, in order to prevent ill feeling between Britain and Japan prior to the talks.[80] The Treasury's request for an extension of the swaps was, however, refused by the Bank of England. The Bank's opposition was due to several reasons, but primary was the principle of the sterling/dollar swap agreement, which was temporary in nature. To extend it would invite Japan to postpone payments.[81]

In the meantime, the Japanese had finalised their agenda for the talks. On 20 October, Oda visited Roberts at the British Embassy in Tokyo to inform him of the list of discussion points. First on the list was the relaxation of colonial restrictions on Japanese goods, with particular focus on the African ban on imports of Japanese textiles. Second was the increased tariff rates in South Africa and Australia, which had affected Japanese textiles, tinplates and plywood imports to the those countries. Third was Britain's decision against extending further swaps to Japan. The Japanese side was especially indignant because it had extended credit to Sterling Area countries when they were short of sterling, and they expected reciprocal treatment. Fourth, the reasons why Britain opposed Japan's application for provisional membership of the GATT. Finally, Japan wanted to know more about how it would be treated once sterling became convertible, and whether Japan would be one of the first countries to have convertibility, and, if not, when.

Nine days later, the Foreign Office sent a telegram to Tokyo instructing its embassy officials to tell Oda that the British government was prepared to receive a Japanese delegation in late November or early December, but the British side narrowed the focus of the payments agreement and listed the topics that they were unwilling to discuss during the meeting. These included Commonwealth tariff matters, Japan's accession to the GATT, and the convertibility issues.[82]

Soon after the exchange of views on the agenda, the Japan working party was reconvened to discuss and recommend Britain's policy towards Japan once the existing Sterling Payments Agreement expired on 31 December. The findings were discussed on 6 November at a meeting of the ONC.[83] Japan was identified as a problem because it was not in any monetary bloc, but deemed an important trading partner, not so much for Britain but for the rest of the Sterling Area. In order to sustain a high level of trade between Japan and the Sterling Area, Britain had to devise a way of increasing Japan's sterling reserves. She had three options: increase reserves by lowering Sterling Area-Japan trade to a minimum; continue to extend credits to Japan, or open the Sterling Area to Japanese goods.[84] The Treasury favoured increased trade between the Sterling Area and Japan, and in particular greater colonial and British market openings to Japan. The committee supported the Treasury's recommendation. The only dissension came from the Board of Trade representative, A. E. Percival, who thought increased Japanese exports to the colonies would be at the expense of British industries.[85]

On 1 December, just days before the start of payment talks with Japan, the Cabinet Tariff Policy Committee on Japan held its third and the final meeting. Members of the Committee reiterated the importance of encouraging Japan to maintain a high level of trade with the Sterling Area. For Japan to sustain such a high trading level, two factors had to be addressed. First, future financing outlets when it faced a sterling shortage and second, greater access to the Sterling Area. As to the first issue, the committee agreed that Japan should either look to the IMF for assistance or it should be encouraged to use its own dollar reserves to finance a shortage, instead of relying upon the British government to finance a syndicated loan agreement as it had done with the sterling/dollar swaps. Concerning the second issue, it supported the ONC suggestion of opening up the colonial market to Japanese goods. However, the sticking point was how to manage the potential outcry from Lancashire, which would feel threatened by any relaxation of restrictions on Japanese textile imports to Britain's African colonies. The Board of Trade requested that increased quotas be given to goods which were not particularly in the public eye.[86] The issue was addressed but not resolved by the Committee. And so, just two days before the start of trade and payments talks with Japan, the British side still had an outstanding issue to resolve – namely the inevitable political fallout that would arise from Britain's decision to open up African trade to Japanese goods.

Conclusions

Britain's trade policy towards Japan began positively in 1953, as the Board of Trade decided against forestalling Japan's GATT accession. Although this was conditional on appropriate safeguards for British industry, it was still a step forward for Britain. The rest of the year saw Britain retreat from this position due to the inadequacy of the Article 23 proposal as a such a safeguard.

As for Britain's handling of the Sterling Payments Agreement, British officials in Japan were acutely aware of the urgency of relaxing Sterling Area import restrictions against Japan, but politics within Whitehall prevented Britain from formulating a policy to increase Japan's sterling reserves immediately. The main culprits impeding such a swift policy formulation were the Commonwealth Relations Office and the Board of Trade. The Board of Trade, in particular, did not take into account the amount of damage which would befall British and other Commonwealth interests if they were unable to sell goods to Japan. Japan's sterling shortage meant that there would be less foreign exchange allocation for sterling goods purchases; therefore traders would be unable to sell their goods due to Japan's rigid separation of her foreign exchange budget. Fortunately, it was agreed that Britain would extend credit to tide Japan over her period of sterling shortage.

1953 was supposed to have been the year when Britain took greater control of its financial and trade policy towards Japan, but Britain's handling of the above issues indicates that it was not entirely successful. In order to understand Britain's problem one has to look at Japan in a wider context. Britain was aware of the importance of Japan becoming part of the Western trading community, and knew that Japanese goods were crucial to certain sterling countries. Britain, however, realised that once sterling became convertible, it would no longer be able to use balance of payments as a reason to restrict imports of Japanese goods in its traditional areas. Thus it was not long before Britain would have no effective safeguard against a possible influx of Japanese goods such as textiles and pottery into Britain's traditional trading areas. In short, the postwar sterling and GATT policies hinged on Britain finding a suitable safeguard which would enable it to implement protective measures if Japan violated friendly trading rules. With convertibility looming on the horizon, it was only natural that both the Sterling Payments Agreement and GATT issues were elevated to Cabinet level, as the Board of Trade made certain that Lancashire's interests were represented when the government formulated its financial and trade policy towards Japan. Thus Britain's procrastination and foot-dragging in 1953 resulted from her inability to come up with a suitable safeguard acceptable to all parties.

Throughout this period, a great effort was made by both the United States and the United Kingdom to reach an agreement over Japan's GATT application. Britain realised that without US backing, none of Britain's proposals would have a chance of success with the contracting parties. The United States' motivation behind its close cooperation with Britain was its knowledge that as head of the Commonwealth, the latter could influence several dominion votes against Japan and sabotage Japan's efforts to enter the GATT.

6 Limits to Britain's policy towards Japan

Introduction

1954 saw another attempt by Eisenhower to push through his liberal economic policy. This time his policy was based on the Commission on Foreign Economic Policy, known as the Randall Commission. Although not all of the commission's work was approved by Congress, Eisenhower was able to gain the power to enter into tariff negotiations, thus opening the way for Japan's GATT entry. Furthermore, the year saw the United States release Japan gradually from its obligations under the US-Japan bilateral agreement to maintain higher controls on exports to the PRC. As a result of this decision, Japan was given permission to remove 383 items from the embargoed list at a rate of thirty items per week beginning in April. Eisenhower embarked on this policy in order to ensure Japan's continued alignment with the United States' trade control policy.[1]

The one area where the Eisenhower administration's policy was diverging from its predecessors was the economic linkage between Japan and Southeast Asia. The administration was aware of the enormity of the challenge that was associated with 'creating a coherent economic system out of a variegated region'.[2] It realised that the region could 'strain the resources and the political will of any power'.[3] Moreover, the Japan-Southeast Asia scheme was a long-term initiative, which meant that interim measures would have to be put into place while the region developed. Last, the region was considered an inadequate source of supplies for Japan. These realisations crystallised into the administration's decision to resist supporting any large capital investment into the region, and drew the US line of responsibility at military protection.

For Britain, the year was turning into a test of its relations with Japan, with the negotiations for the Sterling Payments Agreement and the problem of Japan's GATT entry. The previous year had highlighted Britain's inability to formulate a congruent policy with respect to the above issues; thus it was crucial that every effort be made to emphasise that she was not pursuing an obstructionist policy *vis-à-vis* Japan. This was to become extremely difficult because of the strong domestic opposition to Japanese competition. Despite the limitations placed on Britain's trade policy, an examination of its regional policy highlighted Japan's importance for Britain in Southeast Asia. By 1954, Britain came to appreciate Japan's role as a bulwark in a region which seemed to be in the process of being overtaken by communism. Consequently, contrary to its GATT policy, Britain supported Japan's entry into regional organisations such as the ECAFE and the Colombo Plan.

Japan continued in its quest to enter the GATT in 1954. In addition, it attempted to initiate closer relations with Southeast Asia by conducting reparations talks with its neighbouring countries. When Yoshida embarked on an overseas tour to improve his embattled image at home, he unveiled his $4 billion Marshall Plan for Asia to be endowed by the US government, the World Bank and the members of the Colombo Plan. However, given the US decision against investment in the region, Japan was unable to launch the plan.[4]

Meanwhile, in Britain, the London Gold Market was reopened on 22 March 1954. In order to reduce the amount of administrative work, a single rate was established for transferable sterling, and all bilateral account countries became transferable accounts. Thus Japan became a transferable account country by default.[5] This chapter will continue to examine Britain's sterling and GATT policies towards Japan. The above policies have been juxtaposed with Britain's policy towards Japan's integration in regional organisations in order to elucidate the overall policy towards Japan.

Balancing the Trade Flows

The overdue Sterling Payments Agreement negotiations began on 3 December 1953 and lasted for two full months until 29 January. As in previous negotiations, the aim of the talks was to agree to the expected trade flows between Japan and the Sterling Area to enable both sides to plan their currency and economic activities for the coming months. But the talks were overshadowed by Japan's sterling crisis, and pressure was placed on Britain to find a viable solution. The two key issues that Britain needed to resolve were, first, whether the Sterling Area countries should relax their import restrictions to enable a greater level of Japanese goods to enter the market. The second and less politically explosive issue was how to handle Japan's future sterling crises: whether Britain should continue to provide credit facilities during lean times or encourage Japan to seek its own solution. These issues were so contentious that Britain did not reach a Cabinet consensus in time for the arrival of the Japanese delegates to the talks. Thus the British representatives spent the first few days discussing the agenda and the past history as a stalling tactic.

The first occasion on which the Cabinet could discuss Japan was on 8 December. Butler submitted a memorandum concerning the state of the Sterling Payments Agreement. At the meeting, he steered the discussion towards Japan's sterling shortage problem, and opened up the discussion on different ways of alleviating Japan's sterling shortage crisis. He suggested that Britain propose several measures. The first and foremost was to encourage Japan to convert its own dollar reserves into sterling in order to compensate for future shortages. He also recommended that Britain make an effort to alleviate Japan's sterling shortage by lifting colonial and entrepôt import restrictions against Japanese goods. Butler was aware of the deep fears among British industries concerning Japanese goods, but stressed the necessity of cheap Japanese goods for the African colonies and in Asia.

The President of the Board of Trade, Peter Thorneycroft, agreed to Butler's proposal and was willing for all the colonies to export up to their maxima, except for Nigeria because it was one of the last three major overseas customers left for Lancashire. Thorneycroft expressed hope that Nigeria would limit its imports to £10 million. To compensate for the low increase in the Nigerian market, Thorneycroft agreed to increase the grey cloth quota by £2 million for re-export.[6, 7] In regard to an extension of credit facilities, Butler recommended that they should only be extended to Japan on political grounds, for example, if Britain or the colonies were unable to relax their import restrictions.[8] The Cabinet was unable to reach a conclusion by the end of the meeting and so the discussion continued at the EPC on the following day.[9]

At that meeting members were informed of the IMF's reluctance to allow Japan to make further drawings from the fund unless an enquiry into Japan's economy and trade was conducted. The committee realised that, faced with international bureaucratic difficulties, Japan would rely more heavily upon Britain and its colonies to relax their import quotas. They therefore decided to voluntarily agree to import relaxations. The committee members agreed to increase colonial imports to between £21 million and £33 million. Thorneycroft, again, asked for Japanese imports into Nigeria to be limited, and as a trade-off asked that Britain increase its textiles imports by £2 million. Thorneycroft's request was accepted on the condition that Nigeria acquiesced to limiting its imports from Japan. Thus the Colonial Office was instructed to dispatch a telegram immediately to Nigeria.[10]

The Anglo-Japanese meetings on the Sterling Payments Agreement proceeded in London in parallel to the British talks over Japan's imports. A third plenary meeting was held on 10 December, where Japanese delegates continued their protestations about Sterling Area trade arrangements. They were dissatisfied with the fact that Japanese exports to the entrepôt centres were prohibited from being sold-on to Sterling Area countries except for those so-called traditional destinations such as Burma, Brunei and Sarawak. Moreover, they were perturbed by import restrictions placed on Japanese goods in the African colonies, as they saw the African market as equal in importance to entrepôt trading centres. Especially disturbing were import restrictions on all Japanese cotton and textiles exports to British East Africa, which represented 77 per cent of the East African colonies' imports from Japan in 1951 and 74 per cent during the first six months of 1952.[11] The Japanese were unable to comprehend the need for the Sterling Area's implementation of administrative import restrictions on Japanese goods when, according to the official line, there was no local demand for Japanese goods.[12]

On 16 December, the EPC convened a session to update the members regarding Nigeria. Unfortunately for the British delegation, the Nigerian government was unable to respond fully to British enquiries as ministers were 'up country' and a meeting of the Council of Ministers was not possible until 22 December at the earliest. The interim reply only added to the British frustration because they could not make headway in the Sterling Area-Japan negotiations until they received Nigeria's formal reply. So the committee members agreed to inform the Japanese delegates that Britain's position on import relaxations would not be finalised until after Christmas.

Meanwhile, the Anglo-Japanese talks finally turned to the 1954 estimates at the fourth plenary session of the Sterling Payments Agreement. The two sides presented their trade figures – the Japanese had planned to sell £205 million worth of goods to the Sterling Area, whereas the British estimated a slightly larger figure of £230 million that they wished to export to Japan.[13] The discussion became contentious as the focus shifted to line items in the estimate. The key point of difference was the amount of purchase allocation given to each Sterling Area product. The UK delegation seemed particularly concerned by Japan's decision to shift £3.5 million of their oil allocation away from the Sterling Area. Oil was an important issue for Britain because it was one of the commodities that Japan needed and the Sterling Area could supply (the other being wool). Thus they wished to maintain their market share in Japan. British delegates were also disconcerted by the Japanese government's policy of extending financial incentives to the Japanese shipping industry – either encouraging its use over that of other flags or extending financial assistance – and deemed these to be unfair commercial practices.[14] The Japanese denied the allegations of unfair competition and assured Britain that Japanese vessels had only carried 48 per cent of Japan's foreign trade in 1952, which was a far lower figure than in the pre-war years.[15]

On 23 December, the Colonial Office finally received a definitive telegram from Nigeria, which relayed its government's decision to lower Japanese imports from £15 million to £10 million for 1954, thus safeguarding UK exports.[16] With this piece of information in hand, the negotiators resubmitted the Japan issue to the Cabinet. The Cabinet met to deliberate the issue six days later, where Butler gave an oral report on the progress of the negotiations and asked for Cabinet authorisation for an increase in Japanese imports to the UK by £3.35 million, bringing the total UK imports to £13.35 million as a 'trade-off' for Nigeria's decision to limit its imports from Japan. The additional £3.35 million would consist of £2 million worth of Japanese grey cloth for processing and re-export, and £1.35 million for other goods.[17] Thorneycroft objected to the increased imports to Britain for the record, but grudgingly agreed to the Cabinet recommendation 'in the general interests of Sterling Area trade'.[18]

Solving the Nigerian question cleared the allocation issue out of the British delegates' way, and the two sides were now able to buckle down to iron out other contentious issues. By the end of January, both sides were satisfied and were ready to sign the new payments agreement. The laborious negotiation process continued, however, due to an unexpected complication. On 25 January, an emergency meeting of the key British and Japanese negotiators was arranged by Percival, Kennedy and Serpell, who had received the ill timed news from East Africa that these colonies wished to reduce their Japanese textiles estimates from £5 million to £2.5 million and to increase orders from the UK. Asakai Kôichirô, Ihara Takashi and Ushiba Nobuhiko the leaders of the Japanese delegation, who were summoned to the meeting, took the news very badly and left the room.[19] The Japanese delegates were aware that Britain did not have the 'jurisdiction' to mandate East African quotas, but were unable to comprehend why the Britain could not put pressure upon the East African countries to maintain their agreed quota. The incident, again, raised Japanese suspicion over British protectionism in its colonial markets and whether this was another example of Britain's bid to protect its market share.[20] The Japanese delegates were also concerned because they had received Tokyo's approval of the Sterling Payments Agreement based on the premise that the colonies would be increasing their import relaxations toward Japan, and this latest news was contrary to what had been agreed.[21]

In order to salvage the negotiations, the two sides met on the following day to seek a face-saving solution. Asakai submitted a proposal drafted on his own initiative that asked for three revisions to the existing draft of the agreement. First, Britain would be asked to increase grey cotton cloth imports by £1 million. Japan would in exchange subtract £1.5 million from the colonial figures to balance out the accounting in the short-term with a view to restoring the colonial quota to the original figure by the time of the next review. Third, the United Kingdom was asked to accept Japan's estimates for sterling imports – despite British dissatisfaction with the quota for oil.[22] British delegates were surprised by Japan's lenient demands, but knew full well that the Japanese delegates wished to finalise the negotiations and return to Japan before another colony had the chance to revise its trade quota with Japan. The British also knew that Japan was hoping that their cooperation would induce Britain to extend its £10 million swaps, and possibly another £2.5 million if the agreement was mutually satisfactory.

The British delegates were willing to accept the Asakai proposal without any revisions, but were wary of an adverse reaction from the Board of Trade and the textiles industry. Surprisingly, the Board of Trade was in support of increased grey cloth imports into Britain if that was the price that had to be paid to settle the negotiations. On 28 January, the Cabinet gave British delegates the authority to agree to the extra £1 million grey cloth imports.[23] Later that day, the delegates met to confirm the acceptance of the Asakai proposal. At the same meeting, Serpell announced that Britain would extend three-month 'swaps' of up to £12.5 million to MOF.[24] The Sterling Payments

Agreement between the United Kingdom and Japan was signed on the following day by the Japanese Ambassador, Matsumoto Shunichi, and the Minister of State for Foreign Affairs, Selwyn Lloyd, while the agreed minute was initialled by the two leaders of the delegations, David Serpell of the Treasury and Asakai Kôichirô of the Japanese Embassy.[25]

The two-month long negotiations ended successfully with the revised Sterling Payments Agreement between the Sterling Area and Japan. It had been the first comprehensive negotiations since the original agreement was signed in 1951. Like its predecessor, the agreement would last until 31 December of that year unless extended prior to that date. Both sides were eligible to terminate the agreement with three months' notice. The target for trade in 1954 was £209.5 million both ways, and for the first time, Japan acquiesced to the practice of third party transfers. Japan was also extended £12.5 million swaps for a maximum of six months.[26]

Not long after the payments agreement was signed, the British government braced itself for a harsh wave of criticism from domestic lobbyists. It was prepared for the widespread protests that would ensue as a result of the its decision to increase Japanese grey cloth imports by £3 million. In a House of Commons debate on 1 February, Maudling came under heavy attack from opposition speakers – with the support of industrial associations[27] – who were opposed to the government's decision to inform the relevant industries after the fact.[28] Maudling's defence of the government and his insistence that Sir Raymond Streat, the Chairman of the Cotton Board, had been informed did not abate the furore.[29] It even led to a request for the adjournment of the House under standing order number nine by the former President of the Board of Trade, Harold Wilson.[30] In the end, a Commons debate was scheduled for 10 February on the basis of an opposition motion that the British government had entered into a trade agreement with Japan without first consulting the relevant industries or securing assurances that Japanese exports would not revert to previous unfair trade practices.[31]

The Commons debate on the Japanese trade agreement was a heated one, which lasted from 7.15 to 10.00 in the evening. At the end of the debate, the opposition motion was rejected by 296 votes to 265. A Conservative amendment, which supported the signing of the payments agreement, but which reassured Lancashire that it would not be at the mercy of Japanese competition if Japan broke its treaty obligation, was approved by 297 votes to 258.[32]

The emotional furore in the Commons that was ignited by the Sterling Payments Agreement underscored the deep suspicion and dislike of Japan that was ingrained among British industrialists. The government was visibly disturbed by British industry's emotional reaction and its lack of appreciation for Japan's strategic importance in the wider Cold War context. To correct this imbalance, the Cabinet felt it necessary to reach a decision on Britain's overall policy towards Japan. The Cabinet meeting of 24 March was not so much to break new ground but to agree to shift British public opinion in favour of Japan. The focus of the campaign would be to stress the strategic importance of Japan to the Western bloc and to stabilise Japan's access to Western markets to prevent her from leaning towards China. In order to reach these ends, the Cabinet agreed to commit the government to a high level of trade between Japan and the Sterling Area as was consistent with British national interests. Equally important was the agreement to change 'the climate of British opinion towards Japan so as to bring it into closer accord with the overriding requirement of our national policy and interest'.[33] Consequently the government embarked on a major campaign to shift public opinion towards Japan. It would have its first chance to test this policy later that year with Yoshida's visit to the United Kingdom.

The postponement of Yoshida's visit to the UK

In January 1954, Sir Esler Dening extended a formal invitation to Yoshida to visit the United Kingdom. Authorisation for the visit had been approved as early as September 1953, but sensitivity over multiple Anglo-Japanese negotiations prevented the British from approaching Yoshida any earlier.[34] The invitation to Yoshida was not a British initiative, but rather originated in Yoshida's desire to visit England as part of his planned European and American tour. When Yoshida was formally extended the invitation, he expressed delight but warned Dening that his visit would be subject to political stability at home. The timing of the invitation was not exactly ideal in Britain either, because it was extended at a time when the House of Commons was in an uproar over the recently signed payments agreement with Japan. The government had hoped to keep the invitation quiet until firm plans were finalised, but rumours of it had already reached the press, and so it became important for the government to substantiate it publicly.[35]

Once the invitation was extended to Yoshida, the focus shifted to the probable discussion points between the two prime ministers. One of the main issues that was expected to be raised was the question of a treaty of commerce and navigation, because Japan had been enquiring on and off about Britain's intentions for the past two years. It was a growing concern for Britain, because Article 12 of the peace treaty obliged Japan to extend MFN treatment to the treaty's signatories for a limit of four years. Thus Japan's MFN treatment towards Britain would terminate in April 1956 – which was only two years away. In that time, Britain would have to devise a way of protecting its markets as well as making inroads into Japan.

By the middle of April, Yoshida's itinerary was taking shape, and the Foreign Office was informed by Japan that the Prime Minister would be visiting Britain from 21–30 June.[36] A British policy on a commercial treaty with Japan therefore became urgent enough for the Foreign Office and the Board of Trade to propose presenting different options to the Cabinet. A draft brief was completed by the Board of Trade in late May and distributed to the Foreign Office for comment. The brief supported a commercial treaty between Britain and Japan as long as provisions and safeguards remained in place to protect British, Commonwealth and Colonial industries from 'disruptive' or 'injurious' Japanese competition. Furthermore, the Board of Trade saw the utmost importance in stressing Hong Kong, Singapore and Malaya's desire not to extend MFN and national rights to Japanese business people.[37] On the following day, Thorneycroft convened an internal meeting to discuss the draft brief. He opposed a commercial treaty with Japan as premature, for two reasons. First, the mounting evidence of excessive Japanese copying of British textile designs directly affecting sales of British fabrics abroad,[38] and second, adverse public opinion as a result of the recent Commons uproar. He thus recommended postponement of any commercial treaty.[39] The amended version of the memorandum was approved by Thorneycroft and was submitted to the Cabinet for discussion.[40]

Before further policy work could be undertaken, the Foreign Office received a telegram from Japan on 5 June, informing it of Yoshida's decision to postpone his visit to Britain indefinitely due to domestic political problems. Yoshida, however, authorised Mukai Tadaharu, former Finance Minister in the Yoshida Cabinet, to represent Japan in trade talks with the United States and Britain respectively. This shifted Anglo-Japanese talks from strategic to existing trade issues.

On 24 June, the Board of Trade's memorandum was discussed at the Cabinet's EPC meeting, in spite of Yoshida's decision to cancel his visit to the UK. Thorneycroft gave his reasons why Britain should postpone signing a commercial treaty with Japan. The basis of his argument was the recent evidence of Japanese malpractices as well as other forms of unfair Japanese competition known to the UK, such as the existence of Japanese apparatus to stimulate exports by means of incentives and tax allowances, which raised questions about the future and whether Japan might revert to these malpractices again, given its long history of reliance on unfair forms of competition.[41] This underlying fear and uncertainty was the reason why the Board of Trade could not commit Britain and the colonies to a commercial treaty. Several points were raised during the ensuing discussion, such as the importance of keeping Japan within the Western bloc and the importance of negotiating a treaty to safeguard Britain's banking, insurance, oil and shipping interests in Japan before the expiry of the peace treaty in 1956. In spite of such counter-argument, the Economic Policy Committee supported the Board of Trade's recommendation that a commercial treaty should not be signed at the present time. Furthermore, it was agreed that Britain should make a strong protest to Mukai about Japanese malpractices. The committee also endorsed an official study on the question of a commercial treaty with Japan in the context of Britain's policy towards the GATT.[42]

Mukai arrived in the last week of June and met with Butler, Thorneycroft and the Minister of Transport and Civil Aviation, Alan Lennox-Boyd. The meetings were on day-to-day trade issues. The reason for raising these with Mukai was to resolve the question of Japanese trade malpractice before Japan acceded to the GATT. Thorneycroft went through a list of Japanese trade practices deemed unfair by Britain. They varied from export subsidisation programmes such as currency retention schemes, tax relief and link systems;[43] barter arrangements, which were against the spirit of multilateral trade; and Japan's blatant copying of British textile designs. Mukai reassured Thorneycroft that he would attempt to curb export subsidies. He was less willing to reign in barter arrangements because it was sometimes the only recourse open to Japan when it was unable to pay for goods through normal exchange. With regard to copying of designs, Mukai had heard of such practice but had seen little evidence to substantiate British complaints. Mukai was later shown samples of Japanese copying, and he expressed his desire to stamp out the malpractice.[44] Mukai's agenda with Thorneycroft was, as expected, his hope that Britain would support Japan's GATT entry and also sign a commercial treaty with Japan in the near future. Thorneycroft explained that a commercial treaty would not be possible as long as Japan's commercial malpractices existed.

Lennox-Boyd, who had asked to meet with Mukai, asked him about the state of the Japanese shipping industry and whether it was being financed or assisted by the Japanese government. He suspected some form of underwriting or financial assistance because Japanese shipping lines were expanding their operations and fleets in spite of financial losses. Mukai emphatically denied all such allegations and explained that Japanese shipping companies would go bankrupt if they continued to record losses in the long run.[45]

Japan's GATT application

In the United States the first half of 1954 saw the Commission on Foreign Economic Policy headed by Clarence Randall produce a tepid report for Congress. The commission was intended to empower the Eisenhower administration with bargaining power against the protectionist minority in its own party, but the compromises built into the report to ensure Congressional endorsement limited Eisenhower's options. Thus the administration began the second round of the reciprocal trade agreement renewal process with little support in Congress. What saved Eisenhower's hopes for a renewal of the RTA bill was a series of crises in Asia, starting with Japan's record trade deficit for 1953, followed by the French defeat at the hands of Vietnamese communists in May 1954 at Dien Bien Phu, which made 'lawmakers wary of appearing to undermine the administration's policies in Asia'.[46] Consequently, when Eisenhower decided to seek a one-year renewal of the RTA bill, both houses of Congress passed it with the explicit understanding that the RTA was being renewed to enable the United States to carry out tariff negotiations with Japan.

Now with Congressional support, the US government could embark on its acceptance of Japan into the GATT. In late June, Winthrop Brown informed the Board of Trade of the official American position towards Japan. To ensure Japan's smooth entry into the GATT, this went so far as to provide compensation to any third country willing to extend concessions to Japan prior to the tariff negotiations. The offer was extended to Britain as well as other third parties until 1 September, to enable the United States to process all concessions prior to the expiration of the Reciprocal Trade Act on 12 June of the following year.[47] Frank Lee of the Board of Trade, who met with Brown, was not so much opposed to tariff negotiations, but he expressed discomfort at Japan's early entry into the GATT. More worrisome for Britain was the possible backlash from a unified anti-GATT and anti-Japanese faction in Parliament and business which would influence public opinion. So Lee sought to find a solution whereby Britain could conduct tariff negotiations independently of Japan's GATT accession. The meeting ended inconclusively but both sides agreed to reach an amicable solution on the matter. A similar meeting took place on 29 June between Eden and Dulles, where both sides acknowledged the difficulties of Japan's GATT entry but Dulles felt compelled to go forwards in preparing for Japan's admission.[48]

On 16 July, the Board of Trade found a solution to the stalemate. They proposed an amendment to Article 35 whereby a contracting party could invite an acceder into the GATT but base its trade relations on a separate bilateral treaty. If the proposal were accepted, the UK would be able to take emergency action to protect itself from severe trade disruption and potential injury to its domestic industries. The proposed amendment was presented to the Assistant Secretary of Economic Affairs, Samuel C. Waugh. Waugh who expressed his reservations because the proposal set a precedent for other contracting parties to adopt the article when faced with potential competition. The Board of Trade was prepared for this initial opposition, and asked the United States to take some time to reconsider the proposal. In the meantime the Board of Trade asked for American confidentiality because the proposal had not been approved at Cabinet level. Japan was discussed on 29 July, the third day of the *ad hoc* committee meeting. The presiding committee agreed to commence Japanese tariff negotiations from 1 February 1955. All contracting parties who wished to enter tariff negotiations with Japan were asked to inform the Executive Secretary by 15 September. Britain, which had not reached an official government position on Japan's GATT entry, reserved its position.

The report on a commercial treaty with Japan

As Japan was inching closer to becoming a GATT member, Britain was finally establishing a working party under the ONC to examine the pros and cons of a commercial treaty with Japan, with possible alternatives in case this was not a viable option for Britain. At a meeting on 14 July, the Treasury was delegated the chairmanship of the working party and representatives of the Colonial Office, the Commonwealth Relations Office, the Foreign Office, the Ministry of Supply, the Board of Trade and the Ministry of Transport were designated as members.[49] Each ministry was given responsibility for sections of the report, in the interest of time and resources. The Board of Trade was given the task of establishing the overall strategic framework of the report by assessing the advantages and disadvantages of the treaty in light of Britain's needs as well as Japan's wants. The Treasury was asked to examine Japan's general economic position, its competitive power and the extent to which Japanese exports could be regarded as a danger to British interests. The Foreign Office, in consultation with the Commonwealth Relations Office, was asked to prepare and circulate a paper dealing with the possible complications that might arise from Britain's policy position.

Nine days later, an informal meeting of the ONC was held to discuss the completed sections of the study as well as the overall recommendations of the report. After a lengthy discussion, F. F. Turnbull, Treasury chair, concluded that the group had identified three possibilities. The first was to sign a full MFN commercial treaty with Japan and to invite the latter into the GATT. The second approach was the Board of Trade's proposal for a revised version of Article 35, which would enable contracting parties to discriminate against products deemed to have been imported on an injurious or unfair basis. The third option was for the signing of a commercial treaty which excluded MFN treatment for goods, otherwise known as an establishment treaty, which was unlikely to have Japan's support. The ONC was aware that none of the three options would be palatable to all the countries involved, and so the working party was instructed to explore alternative possibilities, such as revisiting Article 19 or approaching Japan's full or qualified MFN treatment gradually.

While the working party was searching for a viable commercial treaty, a parallel session of the Cabinet's External Economic Policy Committee (EEPC) began to meet to discuss Britain's GATT policy. The issue of the Commercial and the GATT policies were tackled by two different committees because the EEPC was deemed the more appropriate committee to discuss Britain's policy towards international meetings. Moreover, it was made up of Cabinet ministers. There must have been some internal bureaucratic logic behind the division of the two interlinking topics, but the outcome was less than productive given the EEPC's penchant to ignore the recommendations of the ONC. The EEPC had asked the Board of Trade to draft a memorandum addressing Japan's GATT accession, including the problem of the 'no new preference' rule in relation to Japan.[50] The Board of Trade drafted its Article 35 recommendation whereby contracting parties would be permitted to override the GATT with a separate bilateral treaty. Thorneycroft envisioned a carefully drafted 'escape clause' in the treaty, which would give Britain and the colonies absolute discretion to place discriminatory tariff or quantitative restrictions on Japanese goods if their trade caused serious injury to UK or Commonwealth industries, if they were sold under unfair conditions or if they were dumped abroad with the help of government subsidies.[51] Thorneycroft was aware that the recommendation had little chance of success with the Americans, but he remained optimistic as long as he had a slight chance of winning them over.

The Foreign Office, which received the draft memorandum prior to the committee meeting, was disturbed by the Board of Trade's proposal because it did not account for the international or long-term implications of such a recommendation, let alone reflect the views of the other ministries. Most disturbing was the clear absence of any reference to the combined efforts of the ONC's working party on an Anglo-Japanese commercial policy. Thus, the Foreign Office decided to reserve its position if a discussion took place.[52]

The Board of Trade's proposal was discussed at an EEPC meeting on 27 July. The Colonial and Commonwealth Secretaries dominated the meeting. The Colonial Secretary expressed scepticism towards the proposal and thought that Uganda or Kenya would be the only countries to take advantage of the proposal. Conversely, the Commonwealth Secretary was appreciative of the proposal because it would enable Australia, New Zealand and South Africa to continue discriminating against Japan using tariff controls as the excuse. The Minister of State, the Marquess of Reading, who was representing the Foreign Secretary, asked that a final decision on the Board of Trade's recommendation be delayed until ministers had the chance to read and react to the ONC report. His hope was for the GATT policy to originate from the working party's report instead of the Board of Trade's recommendation. Thus the Board of Trade's proposal was accepted provisionally, subject to the cabinet's receptivity towards the ONC report.[53]

On the following day an informal ONC meeting was held to discuss the proceedings of the previous day's EEPC. A.D. Wilson, of the Foreign Office, attempted to widen Britain's options by initiating a discussion on alternatives to the Board of Trade's Article 35 proposal. He wanted to find a different solution because he saw little likelihood of the United States and Japan acquiescing to the proposal. He mentioned the ill-fated Article 19 amendment as an example of a possible option, which only invited the Board of Trade's wrath. So Wilson proposed a delay in adopting the Board of Trade's proposals until Washington and Tokyo's replies reached Whitehall. The Board of Trade counteracted the Foreign Office's delaying tactic by persuading the committee that the United States would approve the proposal if they were forced to decide between the Board of Trade's proposal and Britain's decision to invoke the existing Article 35. The negotiating tactic worked with the committee, which adopted the two options as Britain's GATT policy, but in reality, the options severely limited Britain's policy towards Japan.[54]

Immediately after the meeting, Wilson wrote of the disaster that had taken place at the ONC. He was particularly angry at the Board of Trade presenting two restrictive choices, and he attempted to rectify the committee's decision through informal meetings of the Board of Trade, Treasury and Foreign Office, but his attempts were to no avail.[55]

On 3 August, Britain's commercial policy towards Japan was discussed at the ONC. The revised report was circulated to the ONC, the EEPC and the EPC. The working party was hoping for the blessings of all the interested committees before the recommendation was put to Cabinet. The report was comprehensive in that it referred to the possible content of the commercial treaty, the pros and cons of more liberalised trade with Japan and the options open to Britain. The section on the content of the commercial treaty was factual in that it listed the usual components of a commercial treaty. They were the reciprocal rights and treatment of individuals and firms as well as provisions about the reciprocal treatment of goods. The pros and cons of a commercial treaty were summaries of the Foreign Office and the Board of Trade's respective views. The reasons for a more liberal trade with Japan were prepared by the Foreign Office. It underscored the importance of winning Japan over to the West in the context of the Cold War, as well as dealing with the regional Asian context. The Foreign Office highlighted the latter in particular because Japan's turning communist could pose a direct danger to Britain's colonial interests in Hong Kong and Malaya, which were Britain's main economic assets in Asia. From a financial angle, the Foreign Office highlighted Britain's hypocrisy of advocating multilateral trade and the elimination of quantitative restrictions upon imports on one hand, while excluding Japan from the Western multilateral trading system on the other.

The arguments against a more liberal trade policy towards Japan were a reiteration of the Board of Trade's position. They were based on defensive measures to protect British industries from Japan's injurious or unfair trade practices. There was concrete evidence to support this argument in the form of illegal Japanese copies of British fabric designs. Thus measures were proposed that would enable Britain and the Commonwealth to react unilaterally to Japan's injurious actions.

There were several recommendations open to Britain, but the report deemed the Board of Trade's the most appropriate because it satisfied Japan's desire to enter the GATT while also ensuring preferential treatment for British products in its southern dominions. The Cabinet approved the recommendation and the Board of Trade's proposal was adopted as Britain's official policy towards Japan's GATT membership.[56] Fortunately for Britain, officials had already approached the United States regarding the matter and were awaiting their reply. British officials were instructed to broach the subject at the Anglo-American talks on the GATT review in Washington if there was no reply prior to that meeting. The Commonwealth countries were to be approached at the October meeting of Commonwealth officials in London.[57]

As Britain had feared, the United States did not respond to Britain's proposal before the Anglo-American GATT review. Consequently it was raised at the end of September in Washington. The United States' reaction remained unchanged. They were unable to embrace the British proposal, because they felt it was against the whole GATT concept. The three-day session ended with the State Department agreeing to consider the matter further, but in reality it remained sceptical that it would be adopted by the GATT members.[58] In spite of this lukewarm reception, the Board of Trade decided that the best course of action was to allow time for the British arguments to sink in, and for Roger Makins, the British Ambassador to Washington, to follow up the question with Dulles a week later.[59]

A few days later the matter was proposed to the representatives of the Commonwealth countries. The members were far from unified in their outlook. Canada, for example, remained distant because it had already signed a commerce agreement with Japan on 1 April and supported its GATT accession. Australia, New Zealand, South Africa and the Federation of Rhodesia were the only countries to overtly support Britain's proposal. The South Asian representatives saw the advantages of including safeguards but were unable to support a discriminatory policy against a fellow Asian country. Britain was unable to obtain full support for its policy during the Commonwealth meeting, but it relayed an optimistic version of the outcome to the State Department in the hope that the message would persuade the United States to rally behind the British position.[60] Unfortunately for Britain, C. Thayer White, Acting Officer in Charge of Economic Affairs of the Office of Northeast Asian Affairs, was already predicting the inevitable erosion of the Commonwealth's united front under a hammering from other countries.[61]

The Board of Trade seemed undaunted by the overseas scepticism towards its proposal, and sought the Cabinet's authority to hand an *aide-mémoire* to Japan either before or during Prime Minister Yoshida's rescheduled visit in October. Before the Board of Trade could place the item before Cabinet, Oda of the Japanese Embassy requested a meeting with Percival on 9 October to ascertain whether the rumours about a bilateral treaty were in fact true. When Percival substantiated the rumours, Oda 'stressed the undesirability of any action which formally singled out Japan'. Two days later, Oda met with W.D. Allen of the Foreign office to reiterate Japan's opposition to the British proposal because of the real possibility that other countries would clamour for the same rights, stripping Japan of everything that it hoped to gain by becoming a GATT member.

In spite of the doubts voiced by various countries, the Board of Trade went forward with the proposal. On 23 October – despite the misgivings of all sides – the *aide-mémoire* was handed simultaneously to MOFA's Acting Director of Economic Affairs and the Japanese Ambassador to Britain in the hope that it could be discussed with Yoshida during his UK visit.[62]

Unfortunately for the ministers who had hoped to discuss the *aide-mémoire* with Yoshida in an intimate setting, the latter, who was in Britain for seven days between 21 and 28 October, expressed no interest in discussing the issue. In fact, Yoshida had his mind set on discussing only two topics. The first was China and his vision of weaning it away from the communist bloc. The second was his attempt to appeal the sentences of ninety-five Japanese war criminals convicted by the British and still incarcerated in Sugamo Prison.[63] And so the British representatives were forced to seek other channels for initial feedback on the *aide-mémoire*.

In the meantime, Treasury, Foreign Office and Board of Trade representatives were beginning to consider alternative measures in case Japan rejected the Board of Trade's proposal. At a meeting on 28 October, the group reviewed all the possible scenarios open to Britain, including Articles 19 and 23.[64] In conclusion, the group decided that all the alternatives were second best to Britain's *aide-mémoire*, but that America's proposal of permitting Britain to invoke Article 35 at any time after Japan joined the GATT was the least objectionable.[65]

Back in Geneva, the contracting parties met on 29 October to vote on the recommendation that tariff negotiations with Japan should start on 21 February 1955. The vote did not commit any member to enter into tariff negotiations, but all the contracting parties voted in favour except for Britain, Australia, South Africa, the Federation of Rhodesia and Nyasaland; France, who abstained; and Uruguay, Peru and Nicaragua, who were absent.[66]

The informal discussion that Britain had been hoping for was finally arranged on 1 November between Percival and Asakai. At the meeting, the latter expressed Japan's opposition to the *aide-mémoire* and asked that Britain invoke Article 35 rather than resort to the British proposal. Thus the Board of Trade's strategy, which hinged on the likelihood that Japan would opt for its proposal rather than watch a contracting party invoke Article 35 against its GATT application, backfired.

By mid-November, it was obvious that Japan was against the proposal and that therefore it was only a matter of time before Britain received an official Japanese reply to this effect. On 1 December, Japan handed an *aide-mémoire* to Britain which indicated her inability to accept the British proposal. No alternative proposal was mentioned, but the document did indicate Japan's wish to see the two countries conclude a treaty of friendship, commerce and navigation in the near future. The Japanese *aide-mémoire* confirmed the death of the Board of Trade's proposal. On 14 December, the Cabinet met to decide on Britain's next strategy, given that it was left without a guiding policy two months before Japan was scheduled to start tariff negotiations.

Japan's membership of ECAFE and the Colombo Plan

In spite of the Board of Trade's overwhelming dominance over Britain's policy towards the GATT, the fruits of the Foreign Office's influence were apparent in more Asia-centric regional organisations. This was most evident in Britain's support for Japan's membership of ECAFE and the Colombo Plan in 1954.

ECAFE (the Economic Commission for Asia and the Far East) was an organisation established under the umbrella of the United Nation's ECOSOC (Economic and Social Council) in March 1947. The original UN aim behind

ECAFE was to 'give effective aid to the countries devastated by war'. ECOSOC further detailed the functions of ECAFE and directed the organisation to assist in the reconstruction of Asia, and to maintain and strengthen the economic relations of the countries of the region 'both among themselves and with other countries of the world'.[67] Initially, ECAFE membership was limited to Asian and non-Asian UN members with interests in the region. The charter members were China, India, Thailand, the Philippines, Australia, France, the Netherlands, the Soviet Union, the United States and the United Kingdom. At the subsequent general assembly, membership was opened up to non-self-governing Asian countries.[68] Japan's first observer to ECAFE was a Japanese technical adviser who attended the sub-committee on the seel industry in August 1949 as a SCAP member. Japan began sending observers from the eighth session of ECAFE in January 1952, and it was then that Pakistan proposed to extend ECAFE's scope to include Japan. The proposal was adopted by the general assembly, with the Philippines the only dissenting voice. In April 1953, the United States and France jointly proposed the full admission of Cambodia, Ceylon, Japan, Laos, Nepal, South Korea and South Vietnam at an ECOSOC meeting. This was opposed by half the ECOSOC members. A year later, the above countries were given full membership, due to their eligibility for UN membership.

Initially, the Asian ECAFE members had hoped that the non-Asian members would help the region industrialise, and they especially set their hopes on ECAFE becoming an organisation capable of arranging an Asian economic recovery plan similar to the Marshall Plan, but they were to be disappointed.

The Colombo Plan for Cooperative Economic Development in South and Southeast Asia fared better than ECAFE. It was formally launched on 1 July 1951.[69] The idea behind the plan was proposed by the then Australian Foreign Minister, Percy Spender, at the first postwar meeting of Commonwealth foreign ministers in Colombo. The aim of the plan was to promote economic assistance to the non-communist countries in South and Southeast Asia. Although it was named the Colombo Plan, there was no single integrated plan for the region, and in fact it was made up of a series of bilateral arrangements between donor and recipient countries. The bilateral framework of the plan was established partly due to American insistence that it continue to maintain control over the assistance rendered and to retain freedom of action over US-funded projects. The plan was originally established for a six-year period, and it was made up of Ceylon, India, Pakistan, Malaya, British Borneo, Britain, Canada, Australia and New Zealand. Representatives of the IBRD and ECAFE attended the meetings. From the beginning, the members' intention was not to restrict it to a 'Commonwealth club', and by 1954 the United States, Cambodia, Laos, Vietnam, Burma, Nepal and Indonesia had also become members.[70]

Aid supplied through the Colombo Plan was made up of capital assistance. This was divided into assistance not described as Colombo aid because it was channelled through other international organisations such as the World Bank and the Export-Import Bank, and capital assistance provided by the donor countries. Furthermore, capital was also supplied through the release of India, Pakistan and Ceylon's sterling balances, and later through Japan's reparation payments to Burma, Indonesia, the Philippines and Vietnam. The other function of the Colombo Plan was the Technical Cooperation Scheme, which consisted of 'the supply of experts to assist in training, research or development in the requesting country; the provision of training places in institutions; and the provision of equipment for training and research purposes'.[71]

Japan originally requested to join the Colombo Plan in late 1951, but Britain was against Japan's affiliation at that point, although it was not opposed to the strong Asiatic support for Japan's entry in the future.[72] In 1953 Japan asked to send an observer to the fifth consultative committee of the Colombo Plan. Japan's request was supported by India, but it was rejected formally due to Australia and New Zealand's opposition. It was not until the sixth session of the consultative committee meeting in Ottawa in October 1954 that Japan became a member of the Colombo Plan as a donor country.[73]

Japan's aim behind her entry into the Colombo Plan was both economic and political. On the economic front, it was a better way of establishing economic relations with the countries of South and Southeast Asia than the earlier policy of exploitation of Southeast Asian raw materials for her own ends. In 1951, for example, Japan tried to wean herelf from her over-reliance on American iron ore imports by shifting the emphasis to iron ore deposits in Southeast Asia. The MITI initiative envisaged investing in iron ore mining in Southeast Asia with Japanese private and public finances, and if Japan became short of capital, she planned to rely on US capital. Japan expected to develop iron ore mining in India, Goa, Malaya and the Philippines, and many missions were dispatched to South and Southeast Asia, but with very little result.[74] Japan's mistake lay in the fact that she sought raw materials out of pure self-interest, without emphasising the possible gains for the countries of South and Southeast Asia. Second, she relied on US economic assistance, which was not forthcoming. Thus from 1953 Japan decided to place more emphasis on the countries in question by actively cooperating in plans sponsored by the United Nations and other institutions, including ECAFE and the Colombo Plan. Furthermore, future projects would be limited to those that were financed almost entirely by private firms, with some government assistance. Third, Japan was to settle her reparation payments to Southeast Asian countries as soon as possible.[75] There was also, however, a political incentive, namely that of diluting Britain, Australia and New Zealand's fear of a repetition of Japan's 'unfair trade practices' of the pre-war period.[76]

Japan's entry into the Colombo Plan was made possible by three factors. The reversal of Britain's opposition to her membership, American support, and the Asian members' desire to see Japan cooperate in Asian economic development. Britain's position was discussed at the working party on Economic Development in South and Southeast Asia on 25 August and 8 September respectively. On both occasions there was almost no debate on Japan's membership, as it had become an accepted fact that Japan could serve a useful role in the 'underdeveloped' British colonies.[77] British support for Japan's membership of the Colombo Plan coincided with America's search for a viable economic organisation which would facilitate economic development in South and Southeast Asia. The organisation was to parallel the functions of the newly established Manila Treaty or SEATO (SouthEast Asia Treaty Organisation) in the aftermath of the disastrous French defeat at Dien Bien Phu in May 1954.[78] The United States had the option of creating a new economic organisation or expanding one of the regional organisations. The issue was discussed at an Asian Economic Working Group set up by the State Department and the Foreign Operations Administration in the spring of 1954.[79] ECAFE and SEATO were ruled out as the bases for a Southeast Asian economic organisation; ECAFE for the obvious reason that its membership included the Soviet Union and the PRC, and SEATO because the regional members were restricted to the Philippines, Thailand and Pakistan. The Colombo Plan was considered the most appropriate because of its bilateral nature, which meant that Congress would approve any foreign aid to the region, and it would enable the United States to maintain strict control over its expenditure. More important was the fact that it represented almost all the non-communist Asian nations in the region, except Japan, the Philippines and Thailand. Therefore, by the second half of 1954, the United States had begun to focus on the Colombo Plan as the most viable regional organisation, and campaigned for Japan's inclusion.

Conclusions

1954 saw an expansion of Sterling Area-Japan relations, but this came at a price. It opened up fears of Japanese competition and it also reflected badly on the British government, which was portrayed as insensitive to Lancashire's plight. The industrial outcry and extensive press coverage high-lighted the political clout of the Lancashire textiles industry. Moreover, evidence of Japan's copyright infringements was further proof that Japan could not be trusted. The two factors restricted Britain's policy towards Japan's GATT membership, thus the government had to support a policy with definite safeguards for Britain. The best option was the amendment of Article 35 of the GATT and the conclusion of a bilateral agreement, which overrode the GATT. The government's policy, however, received little inter-national support, and by the end of the year Britain was without a policy. This series of events highlighted not only the extent of political influence held by Lancashire's representatives, but also the underlying national anti-Japanese sentiment, which was experienced by Yoshida on certain occasions during his UK visit.

Although Britain was willing to see Japan incorporated in regional organ-isations to help the 'underdeveloped' countries in Asia, it became a different matter when Japan's trade expansion infringed on the lives of Lancashire workers. To understand why Britain opted for a policy in defence of Lancashire, one has to understand the fact that Lancashire symbolised British exports and British survival, while Japan was seen as the sinister and unfair rival. Thus, despite the Foreign Office's attempts to highlight Japan's geopolitical importance, the British public could only comprehended the issue in terms of British prestige and livelihood.

7   Britain and Japan's GATT entry

Introduction

1955 saw a distinct shift in Japan's foreign policy as Hatoyama Ichirô took over as Prime Minister. He veered away from Yoshida's diplomatic platform and called for a more independent Japanese foreign policy, which culminated in the normalisation of relations with the Soviet Union in the following year.[1] It was also during his time in office that the Liberal and Democratic parties converged in November to form the Liberal Democratic Party to counter the formation of a unified socialist challenge in the Diet. But these political shifts had little effect upon Japan's determination to return to the Western comity of nations and her focus on successful entry to the GATT.

The Eisenhower administration remained committed to its foreign economic policy, but the administration's efforts met resistance from protectionist elements at home. A particularly vocal group were the domestic textiles manufacturers, who felt threatened by the increase in Japan's textiles exports to the United States. Thus Eisenhower's attempts to ensure a safe passage of the RTA renewal bill in the first session of the 84th Congress became entangled in domestic politics when an amendment to the RTA renewal bill was made by Senator Walter George (D-Georgia) due to pressures from his rival, Governor Herman Talmadge, who accused him of his apparent lack of sympathy towards textiles workers in his state. The amendment was designed to curtail a provision within 1954 RTA bill that enabled the President to cut tariffs by 50 per cent of the base rate of 1 January 1945 to 15 per cent. The bill passed through the Senate on 4 May with a 75–13 vote, thus limiting the United States' tariff negotiating powers. By the time it became the Trade Agreements Extension Act, further restrictions had been applied to ensure that any items that received a 15 per cent tariff reduction would be automatically excluded from the 1956 round of tariff negotiations.[2] Pressure from the textiles industry did not abate with the RTA renewal bill, and the mounting calls for the Eisenhower administration to introduce quota restrictions upon Japanese textiles imports eventually led Japan to impose voluntary export restrictions on textiles exports by the end of the year.[3]

In Britain, the year saw Churchill's resignation and the formation of a new Cabinet under Anthony Eden in April. Eden took over from Churchill at an important juncture, when British policy towards Japan's GATT entry had just been formulated and Britain was embarking on a damage limitation exercise to ensure that its decision to invoke Article 35 would not have an adverse effect on Japan's GATT entry. This chapter will illustrate that Britain did its best not to be seen as the leader of an anti-Japan bloc in the GATT. Deliberations in various Cabinet committees underscore the politically sensitive nature of Japan's GATT entry. Domestic pressure was without doubt omnipresent, but Britain was equally concerned with the effects of invoking Article 35 upon its relations with the United States and Japan respectively. With the invocation of the article, Britain saw an urgency in exchanging drafts of the Anglo-Japanese commercial treaty to ensure that official relations existed between the two countries once the obligations under the 1951 peace treaty lapsed the following April. The urgency of the situation, however, did not translate into decisive action on the British part, as delays in the completion of a draft commercial treaty and the long-winded sterling payments negotiations left Japan with the impression that Britain was disinterested in pursuing expanded trade relations.

Britain and Japan's GATT entry

The Cabinet meeting of 14 December 1954 culminated in another round of studies on Britain's GATT policy towards Japan. This time, a single committee, the Official Committee on the Review of the GATT, compiled the report on the studies' findings to ensure a coherent recommendation to Cabinet. The aim of the report was to tackle two fundamental questions. First, 'whether and under what conditions should the British Goverment assume GATT obligations towards Japan', with equal weight given to Britain's foreign policy as well as the domestic industrial impact of any recommendation. The second related concern was the potential adverse impact that Britain's continued denial of GATT rights to Japan would have on the impending Anglo-Japanese commercial treaty, the contents of which would serve to safeguard British interests in Japan.[4]

The report underscored the fact that extending GATT obligations towards Japan would mean that Britain would have to grant the same trade privileges afforded to the OEEC countries.[5] In real terms, it meant that Britain would have to open import gates to light Japanese manufactured goods such as textiles, pottery, toys, sewing machines and clocks that were presently restricted due to licenses and quotas. The report predicted that British industries would be severely affected, with limited government options for protection. This was especially true once Japan became a GATT signatory, because of the rules prohibiting one member from discriminating against another.

The minimal condition that Britain sought was its freedom to take discriminatory action in the form of tariffs or quotas in the United Kingdom or the colonies against dumping, counterfeiting or mass imports that would 'threaten serious injury to United Kingdom or Colonial or Commonwealth industries'.[6] Safeguard articles that had been identified in earlier discussions, such as Article 19 and Article 23, were reconsidered, but none was deemed to provide immediate protection. Even Britain's small victory gained through the waiver of the no-new-preference rule in 1953 was so limiting that it was not considered an adequate protection.[7]

Conversely, the report identified several advantages for Britain in entering GATT relations with Japan. For example, it predicted a small but definite opportunity for increased British exports of machinery and quality consumer goods if it were positioned to take advantage of the reduction in Japan's quantitative restrictions, which were bound to occur within a reasonable time after its entry. GATT relations were also expected to afford a better negotiating position for Britain in the upcoming talks over the commercial treaty, where it was seeking safeguards for British nationals, companies and shipping in Japan.

The report highlighted the foreign policy consequences for Britain's GATT decision. It reminded its readers of the major adverse impact that a GATT rejection would have on Japan, given that the Japanese government had raised GATT entry to a 'symbol of Japan's rehabilitation as a responsible member of international society'.[8] The report also cautioned Britain from contributing to what seemed like a build-up of destabilising influences in Japan, starting with the new apparently anti-American Prime Minister, Hatoyama, who seemed, intent on taking Japan out of the Western camp. Moreover, by rejecting GATT relations with Japan, Britain would be injecting an element of doubt into Sterling Area-Japan relations by its refusal to grant *de jure* MFN rights.

The other foreign policy consequence concerned the United States, which had a 'major interest in the economic stability and prosperity of Japan' for political, strategic and economic reasons, and would resent Britain's exacerbation of the sensitive situation. Moreover, the repeated British calls for protection against Japanese manufactures were liable to complicate Eisenhower's foreign economic policy platform, because domestic political opponents could cite British protectionism as a legitimate excuse to oppose US tariff concessions towards Japan.

Having explored all the conflicting objectives that Britain deemed important, the report identified three broad choices open to Britain. The first choice was for Britain to accord GATT rights to Japan with safeguard provisions that protected British industries, such as variations of Article 19 or 23, which had been discussed as early as 1953. The second choice proposed withholding GATT obligations to Japan 'at least for a transitional period', with the aim of solving Britain's tariff problems in the interim period.[9] Britain would grant immediate import quotas, and in addition agree to extend GATT obligations in three years' time. The extension would provide select industries time to adapt themselves to Japanese competition. In the interim period, Britain would expedite a commercial treaty with Japan whereby Britain would extend near-GATT rights to the latter in exchange for satisfactory shipping and establishment provisions. The disadvantage of this option was that no matter how many years elapsed, the time lag would only serve as a delay and no adequate safeguards would protect British industries against the so-called unfair Japanese competition.

The final option was for Britain to invoke Article 35 but accompany it with a declaration of intent to give near-GATT rights through a commercial treaty, where in return for a satisfactory shipping and establishment provisions, Japan would receive MFN rights subject to minimum quota or tariff safeguards that would protect British and colonial territories from disruptive Japanese competition.[10]

The period between 7 and 18 January 1955 saw a series of meetings held by various Cabinet committees to discuss the report and the three distinct options open to Britain. The first two meetings on 7 and 10 January were *ad hoc* gatherings of senior Cabinet committee officials chaired by Sir Bernard Gilbert. At the 18 January EPC meeting, ministers had the opportunity to voice their views prior to the item's escalation to Cabinet level on 24 January. The ministerial representations at the meeting were somewhat predictable, with the Foreign Office backing the option to support Japan's entry with safeguards. The Economic Secretary of the Treasury wished to see a postponement until British industries adjusted to Japanese competition. The President of the Board of Trade wished to invoke Article 35, but if that option was deemed to have an adverse effect upon Britain's relations with Japan and the United States, he was open to immediate support of Japan's GATT entry instead of the intermediate option. He thought that taking the unpopular decision of admitting Japan to the GATT and defending it would be preferable to the alternative option of committing to it in the future only to suffer the disadvantages that would flow from it in the present.[11] There was strong insistence from the Commonwealth Relations Office that no decision should be made without first consulting with the Commonwealth countries.

The disparate views and the inconclusive discussion were carried over to the 24 January Cabinet meeting, where ministry heads differed over the three available options. This forced Churchill to insist that the Foreign Secretary, Chancellor of the Exchequer, Chancellor of the Duchy of Lancaster, Commonwealth Secretary, President of the Board of Trade and Minister of Agriculture examine the options open to Britain, in light of the discussion, and report back to the Cabinet in ten days' time.[12] The core group of ministers met three days later and discussed Britain's policy options. The Board of Trade remained convinced that Britain should opt for the Article 35 solution. The Foreign Secretary and the Chancellor of the Exchequer grudgingly agreed to the protectionist option on the condition that foreign policy and external economic policy considerations were reflected in any decision concerning the GATT.[13] On 31 January, the core group of ministers returned with their final decision on the GATT issue and announced that they would go with the middle course, whereby Britain would invoke Article

35 on the mutual Anglo-Japanese understanding that GATT rights would eventually be accorded to the latter. The interim period would provide Britain with not only time to bolster its vulnerable industries against Japanese competition, but would empower Britain 'to impose countervailing duties against dumped goods if necessary', without affecting Britain's right to extend most-favoured-nation tariff treatment to Japan.[14] It was agreed that any decision reached in Cabinet would not be relayed to the Japanese government until after Japan's general election of 27 February.[15]

The next two months saw the British government debate the appropriate date to announce its decision to invoke Article 35 against Japan. It became a damage limitation exercise, whereby Britain had to choose a date that did not overlap with any events in Japan or Washington that could have an adverse impact on Anglo-Japanese or Anglo-American relations, and more specifically on Japanese public opinion. Sensitivity towards Japanese opinion was of utmost importance, given the weight Japan placed upon its GATT membership as a symbol of its return to the Western comity of nations. On the one hand, a delay would prevent other countries following Britain's lead to invoke Article 35. Conversely, the announcement had to be early enough for Japanese officials to have adequate time to register Britain's decision before the start of the payments talks in June, so as to prevent any adverse impact on Britain's negotiating position.[16]

Dening in Tokyo ruled out late March as a desirable time for the announcement due to the arrival of Soviet and Chinese delegates to the ECAFE conference in Tokyo, thus an announcement then could play into the communists' hands.[17] Makins in Washington requested that Whitehall avoid mid-March because Dulles was scheduled to give evidence before the Senate Finance Committee as part of the administration's attempts to renew the reciprocal trade act through Congress.[18]

The government therefore decided to make its announcement on 19 April, to coincide with the release of the Board of Trade's White Paper stating general conclusions of the British government towards the new amendments to the GATT and the advantages that it would have for Britain.[19] With this date in mind, MOFA and the State Department were informed confidentially of Britain's decision to invoke Article 35 of the GATT against Japan. Last minute attempts by Washington to delay the announcement were made due to the overlap with the final and critical stage of the HR1 through the Senate Finance Committee. The request was denied due to the Board of Trade's inability to revise its schedule.[20]

On the day, the British government released a statement in which it was announced that 'before they could accept the obligations of the General Agreement towards Japan they must see how the pattern of trade will develop'.[21] The statement underscored the fact that Britain was not attempting to injure 'Japan's legitimate efforts to expand her exports in fair competition with other countries'.[22] In support of this statement, Britain expressed its wish 'to negotiate a treaty of friendship, commerce and navigation' and that a more formal approach would be taken with the first draft of the treaty in the near future.[23]

The Japanese reaction to the British decision was controlled. MOFA expressed regret, but the hardliners in MITI questioned the value of membership 'on such humiliating terms'.[24] The major Japanese newspapers printed the entire British statement, the Japanese government's reaction, and various commentaries and analyses. The views of the newspapers ranged from disappointment to dissatisfaction, and some thought that Britain's action ran counter to global steps towards free trade and lower tariffs, while others wondered why the 'country of gentlemen' was so opposed to Japan joining the international club.[25] Japan was faced with another blow a few days later when it was informed that the George amendment to HR1 would apply the new stricter tariff reduction rules of 15 per cent on all new tariff negotiations conducted during the period 1 January–1 July 1955. It was obvious to all that the new amendment was directed at Japan, which was the only country negotiating tariffs with the United States during the specified period.[26]

After Britain announced its decision, it became a bystander to Japan's tariff negotiations in Geneva, which were completed on 7 June.[27] Japan conducted bilateral tariff negotiations with seventeen countries. During this period, the United States and Japan conducted 'triangular negotiations in which the United States offered concessions to third countries for compensatory concessions from Japan'.[28] This was followed by a protocol of accession, which had to be signed by Japan and needed the endorsement of two thirds of the contracting parties. Last, a vote had to be taken on the decision of accession, which also needed a two-thirds majority of the contracting parties' votes. The vote was more important than the first in that Japan could not formally become a GATT member without it; therefore the United States and Japan asked Britain to consider voting in support of Japan's accession. The issue increased in importance as a result of Japan's concerns that some countries that had promised to vote in Japan's favour would not be able to post their ballot before the 11 August deadline due to 'legislative procedures or administrative incompetence'.[29]

The question was raised in Cabinet on 30 June, where the Foreign Office recommended a positive vote for fear of a number of political repercussions should Britain vote against, such as, first, that Britain would be held responsible for Japan's failure to gain the two-thirds majority, given the perception that it was the ringleader of all those opposed to Japan's admission; and second, that Japan's deep disillusionment would cause her to turn her back on the West and ally herself more closely with the Soviet Union and China. Lastly, a positive vote was seen as mitigating the worsening of Anglo-Japanese relations as a result of Britain's earlier decision to invoke Article 35 against Japan.[30]

The Board of Trade, on the other hand, was opposed to voting for Japan because it saw such a decision as a mere political gesture which would have little substantive effect on the issue. Thorneycroft thought that Britain's prior decision only highlighted the inconsistencies in her policy towards Japan. Furthermore, he felt unable to support a decision that did not uphold Britain's commercial interests.[31]

The discussion of 30 June ended inconclusively. Subsequent Cabinet meetings were held on 14 and 19 July, while the Foreign Office and the Board of Trade kept what seemed like a constant vigil on the contracting parties voting intentions. Uncertainty arose from the fact that five of the seventeen countries that entered tariff negotiations with Japan would be unable to register their positive vote in time. Unexpected complications from Germany's textile industry, which sought protection from Japanese competition, also threw what seemed like another solid vote into question.[32] Thus a last minute scramble ensued to find a solution for Germany's problems within the confines of the GATT.[33] On 26 July, Britain decided to vote in Japan's favour in spite of the strong likelihood that the latter would have more than the minimum votes. The final decision was driven by Britain's attempts to offset the guilt that arose from the fact that a surprisingly large number of contracting parties had decided to avail themselves of Article 35.[34]

By August, all thirty-four contracting parties had voted unanimously for Japan's accession to the GATT. On 10 September, Japan became the thirty-fifth contracting party to the GATT. Surprisingly, fourteen contracting members decided to invoke Article 35 against Japan, which was unprecedented in the GATT's history.[35] The article had never previously been used as an escape clause by such a large group of its contracting parties; it had only ever been invoked by India and Cuba. Moreover, Japanese officials did not fail to notice that many of the fourteen were British Commonwealth countries.

At the tenth GATT session, Hagiwara expressed his deep disappointment with the invoking of Article 35 and expressed hope that all those countries would one day be able to overcome trade problems within the framework of the GATT. He spent the following weeks interviewing GATT representatives of the fourteen countries concerned and attempted to seek a face-saving resolution that he could take back to Tokyo. Japan's frustration and humiliation was understandable, given that the those countries who had invoked Article 35 accounted for 40 per cent of Japan's overseas trade.[36]

Britain's decision to invoke Article 35 of the GATT against Japan after a long and tortured debate in Cabinet, ended foreign speculation about Britain's position towards Japan's GATT entry. The British decision may have seemed like a foregone conclusion from the outside, but the minutes of Cabinet meetings underscore the dilemma that stemmed from conflicting objectives. Once it announced its decision, the government placed priority on limiting its impact on Anglo-American and Anglo-Japanese relations respectively. In order to illustrate the sincerity of its statement, the British government placed emphasis upon completing the first draft of the Anglo-Japanese commercial treaty. Unfortunately, the document lingered in the hands of officials for most of 1955, which sent mixed signals to Japan about Britain's commercial interests there.

Towards a commercial treaty

Britain's initial strategy had been to present a draft commercial treaty to Japan by January 1955. To that end, a flurry of activity took place at the end of the previous year. Correspondence over specific clauses in articles was exchanged with Dening in Tokyo, who was familiar with corresponding Japanese laws, and a sub-committee under the chairmanship of the Board of Trade drafted the commercial treaty. British officials were acutely aware of the fact that their Japanese counterparts would scrutinise every word of the treaty, and that a comparison would be made with the US-Japan commercial treaty of 1953. In spite of the early effort at submitting the treaty's first draft to Cabinet, the commercial treaty did not reach a Cabinet committee until July, months after Britain had announced its decision to invoke Article 35 of the GATT against Japan. What hindered the presentation of the treaty were shipping and balance of payments issues. The problem was not about Japanese shipping practices *per se*, an issue which was also brewing simultaneously. It was more to do with the wording of the shipping clause and the consequences of this for Britain's dollar reserves.

The issue at hand was the proposed navigation article with Japan, which provided for the 'complete freedom of access for nationals of each country to the shipping services provided by the other' except in time of war or the termination of the treaty.[37] By including this clause in the treaty, Britain was setting a precedent for its future obligations in bilateral commercial treaties. There were two core problems with the shipping clause. First, British nationals and companies could potentially use shipping carriers registered in dollar countries to transport their freight, which could lead to an invisible dollar drain from the Sterling Area. The inclusion of a balance of payments clause, on the other hand, could be harmful for a global shipping country like Britain, which may find other countries resorting to the clause to block hiring and earning by Britain in its waters. As a result, in July the draft commercial treaty was brought to the Economic Policy Committee for resolution.[38]

It was discussed again at the subsequent EPC meeting on 28 September. During the one-month lapse between the meetings, Cabinet members discussed whether to include the clause in the Sterling Payments Agreement, but eventually decided against it because the annual payments agreements were considered too short-lived to have any influence upon the bilateral shipping policy. Thus the Cabinet had to decide whether to remain with the present draft clause in the model commercial treaty, or whether an escape clause should be inserted to enable Britain to 'restrict shipping payments in times of balance of payments difficulties'.[39] At the end of the discussion, it was clear that most members were against the inclusion of an escape clause, especially as 'such a provision might open the way to discrimination against our shipping to the detriment of our balance of payments'.[40] Butler then concluded the meeting and expressed his desire to consider the matter further. In the meantime, without a conclusive solution to the shipping clause, Britain decided to submit its first draft of the commercial treaty to Japan in October, in the hope that the two sides would be well on the way to signing such an agreement by the time the peace treaty lapsed in April 1956.

Britain's decision to invoke Article 35 of the GATT, together with its time-consuming efforts at compiling a draft Anglo-Japanese commercial treaty, meant that only one agreement governed mutual commercial relations: the Sterling Payments Agreement. Even these relations were less than satisfactory to both sides, as each suffered from excessive discrimination in the other's market. But the restrictive nature of Anglo-Japanese commercial relations seemed destined to remain in place for the foreseeable future.

The Sterling Payments Agreement

By early January 1955 the Cabinet had begun to consider a renewal of the payments agreement, which was due to expire in March. The Sterling Payments Agreement was at this point overshadowed by Britain's attempts to formulate a GATT policy towards Japan. Given the inevitable repercussions of Britain's final decision both at home and abroad, the ONC was wary of overlapping the payments negotiations with the GATT issue. Therefore the ONC voted for a three-month extension of the payments agreement. The Japanese government concurred with the proposal because Japan was equally keen to postpone negotiations until after its general election.[41] So the interim Japanese government proposed that a meeting be held at the end of February in Tokyo to extend the payments agreement and to discuss any pertinent issues relating to the extension.

The ONC met on 26 January to deliberate the agenda for Tokyo. The committee members were aware that Japan wished to confine talks to administrative issues relating to the extension, and to exclude all matters concerning shipping and copyright infringement. The ONC agreed to limit the talks to the issue of Japanese import estimates because the latter's actual imports from the Sterling Area had not achieved the original projection established in September. The overall result was not only the accumulation of Japan's sterling reserves, but also her failure to fulfill her obligations to purchase sterling goods such as oil. Thus there was a growing British view that Japan was somehow discriminating against Sterling Area goods and that there was an urgent need for Japanese assurance that this was indeed not the case.[42] At a minimum, British negotiators wished to see a balance in Japan's sterling receipts and payments in the future. In the ensuing discussion, the Board of Trade proposed to implement a retaliatory British action to limit Japanese exports to the colonies if Anglo-Japanese trade relations remained imbalanced. The idea was vetoed for various reasons, including the fact that many of the colonies had already made licensing arrangements for the whole year. Any changes to the colonial import policy took an average of four months to take effect, and finally, the West African colonies, which imported a large amount of Japanese textiles, were unlikely to heed British advice on the matter.[43] Thus the ONC's instructions were to investigate the reasons for Japan's decreased purchases from the Sterling Area in contrast to her increased purchases from the dollar and the open account areas; to press the Japanese to improve their sterling allocation during the summer budget to £95 million or £100 million; to make up the backlog in Japanese payments; and finally to implement the previous year's agreed minute to purchase sterling oil.[44]

Once the negotiations began in Tokyo, Britain made very little headway in obtaining Japan's assurance that she would increase sterling purchases during the three-month extension, or increase her sterling quota in the summer budget. With only minor concessions to the agreement, the issue reverted to the ONC, where policymakers discussed whether Britain should, in fact, extend its payments agreement for a further three months. The proponents of the extension felt that Britain would not receive improved concessions by postponing the negotiations. They felt that, on the contrary, Britain might find itself with a lower allocation in Japan's summer budget and also find that its representatives had spent the time in Japan without arranging for the extension of trade commitments, most of which were due to expire by the end of June. The arguments against signing on Japan's terms were based on the principle of accomplishing the defined objectives of the Tokyo meeting.[45] In the end, the ONC agreed to the extension because it wished to avoid an overlap of the review and Britain's announcement on Japan's GATT entry. British negotiators were, nevertheless, instructed to 'strongly express [the British government's] deep dissatisfaction with the Japanese concessions and its refusal to make definite commitments to its summer budget or that if allocated, these commitments will be used'.[46] The negotiators were also instructed to explain that if Japan's sterling balances continued to accumulate 'as a result of Japanese restrictive policy, we may find it necessary, before the next negotiations to take certain precautionary measures, on balance of payments grounds, to control the level of imports from Japan during the second half of 1955'.[47]

On 31 March the two sides exchanged notes and agreed to a three-month extension of the payments agreement. In the meantime, Asakai approached J.E. Chadwick of the British Embassy with an invitation to begin the annual payments negotiations from 25 May in Tokyo. The date of the negotiations was delayed by a month to June at the Treasury's request. In the meantime, the ONC set to work to compile a brief on the direction of the payments agreement, and the final version was approved on 17 June.[48]

The overall policy for the negotiation rested on Britain's hope that trade relations could develop to the point where it could extend GATT obligations to Japan. The negotiators wished to work in the spirit of Britain's April GATT declaration, which stressed fair and reasonable opportunities for Japanese trade, and the maintenance of a high level of trade between the Sterling Area and Japan.[49] Another policy objective was sterling convertibility, which was bound to come up in the negotiations. Britain was prepared to abolish the Sterling Payments Agreement as soon as sterling became convertible, but trade arrangements based upon the existing objectives would continue to define British Commonwealth and Japanese trade. A particularly long section of the document dealt with the chronic imbalance provision and the need to emphasise its existence in the upcoming negotiations. The rationale behind this request was in part due to Britain's frustration over what it saw as Japanese discrimination against Sterling Area goods, but the main reason was Britain's anxiety over Japan's sterling surplus and the possible effect that this would have on Britain's dollar reserves once sterling became convertible. Britain wished to see Japan maintain only enough reserves to conduct uninterrupted trade.[50]

The rest of the instructions concerned increasing Japan's payments to the Sterling Area to £210 million in order to correct the trade imbalance. They hoped for the elimination of discriminatory trade practices such as the larger deposit requirements for purchases from the sterling versus the dollar area (i.e. 25 or 35 per cent of the value versus 3 or 1 per cent for the dollar area) and for a greater inclusion of the Sterling Area goods in the AA list. Furthermore, specific desiderata in the visibles included increased Japanese imports of British machinery, including the creation of a specific quota for British motor vehicles and spare parts sales. Other requests for increases included wool textiles. The key invisibles requests were sterling oil, films, facilities for foreign banks in Japan and foreign capital investment. In all cases, Britain expressed frustration over licensing limitations and administrative restrictions, which prevented British companies from expanding their business activities in Japan.[51] Due to the severe fluctuations in Sterling Area-Japan trade and the uncertainty of future relations, the President of the Board of Trade was asked to arrange a study of the long-term prospects for Japan's trade and payments with the Sterling Area.[52]

Negotiations began on 23 June in Tokyo, and updates were sent back to Whitehall primarily via the Foreign Office. The ONC scheduled a meeting to update its members on the progress in Tokyo one month into the negotiations. It became apparent on this occasion that many of Britain's desiderata were not being fulfilled. For example, Japan was unwilling to increase her visible payments to the Sterling Area to £210 million. Britain was having equally limited success in persuading Japan to increase her invisible purchases from the Sterling Area in areas such as motor cars, machinery and light engineering products. The British side suspected that Japanese disinterest was motivated by the wish to protect her domestic markets. They were equally pessimistic about their chances of lifting Japanese discrimination against all Sterling Area goods when the Sterling Area itself did not extend favourable trade quotas, nor base Anglo-Japanese relations upon the GATT. Thus the British decided to concentrate their efforts on lifting discrimination in certain key areas rather than attempt an overarching improvement in trade relations. Of all the negotiating positions, the only positive feedback Britain received was over colonial purchases, which Japan was willing to increase.[53]

In the meantime, a final version of the study on trade and payments was completed by an inter-departmental working party and distributed by the Treasury to all interested departments. The five-page report was useful in contextualising and providing a historical perspective on the payments relations to date, but it did not forecast future relations between the Sterling Area and Japan. The two sections that referred to the future were conservative assessments based on Britain's hopes for liberal and expanded trade relations after sterling convertibility, in spite of its decision to invoke Article 35 against Japan.[54]

The rest of July saw continued negotiations in Japan. A subsequent ONC meeting was convened on 27 July to update the committee members on further developments. The central issue was, again, the level of Japan's commitment to sterling spending. Outstanding items included non-discrimination and the invisibles. The British negotiators had by this time decided that they would only push for the removal of non-discrimination in 'collateral deposits for import licences, the merit system for oil imports and a formula about wool merchanting'.[55] For invisibles, they decided to obtain the best assurances overall for miscellaneous invisibles other than oil, which they decided to negotiate separately.

On 2 August, however, the British negotiators adjourned their talks in Tokyo and flew back to London to receive further instructions from Whitehall. The negotiators sought a persuasive bargaining position in order to complete the three outstanding British objectives in the talks, which were designed to increase Japan's commitment to sterling spending. They wanted:

(a) A general statement of intention by Japan to facilitate imports, visible and invisible, from the Sterling Area to the amount of Japan's total earnings from the Area.
(b) A more specific commitment that Japan would make available for spending in the Sterling Area in the coming year – preferably in the year beginning July 1955, but failing that, October 1955 – as much sterling as she had earned in the Sterling Area in the preceding twelve months.
(c) Finally, a concrete undertaking that the winter budget would provide not less than £105 million for visible Sterling Area imports, i.e. excluding oil and imports from third (i.e. non-sterling) countries.[56]

The three objectives were discussed at length by the ONC, but the committee was unable to find a persuasive negotiating position. Thus they decided to re-consider the Board of Trade's colonial bargaining proposal that had been raised and rejected earlier in the year. The ONC decided on a revised version of the original proposal, which would reward Japan with the freedom to export up to the maximum required level if she agreed to point (a) and a combination of (b) or (c). If Japan failed to commit to any of the three points, Britain would penalise Japan by reducing its exports to the non-entrepôt colonies. A majority of the committee was in agreement over this proposal, but the Board of Trade refused to endorse the recommendation. The Board of Trade's opposition was, as in the past, driven by fears that any increase in Japanese exports to non-entrepôt colonies in Africa as a reward for favourable performance would cut into Lancashire's textiles market share. Thorneycroft was particularly concerned at the prospect of a repeat of the 1954 Parliamentary outcry, and proposed a ceiling on Japanese exports to the colonies regardless of the outcome of the negotiations.[57]

A majority of the ONC disagreed with the Board of Trade's view and argued that a restrictive policy was against the entire British strategy towards a trade and payments agreement with Japan. Lowering Japanese exports to the colonies would act as a disincentive and lessen Japan's likelihood of cooperation. Furthermore, Britain could not ask the colonies to restrict their imports from Japan unless this was related to balance of payments issues; and finally, a restrictive import policy could only be implemented temporarily for balance of payments reasons.[58]

The impasse over negotiating instructions was so serious that the discussion was elevated from the ONC to the Cabinet. It was debated over three sessions from 15 August to 5 September, until the Board of Trade finally submitted to the majority view that these colonial exports should be increased as quid pro quo for a more balanced Sterling Area-Japan trade.[59]

The final outstanding question that remained was whether to insert a shipping clause in the existing payments agreement. Shipping was a particularly sensitive subject because of Britain's increased concerns about the anti-competitive practices of the Japanese shipping industry, which included government subsidies to new shipbuilding and shipping operations. In the long run, these practices guaranteed distress for foreign shipping companies, which would lose out to Japan's cutthroat freight and shipping prices. The shipping clause was raised within the context of the trade and payments agreement because Cabinet members thought that they could use colonial purchases as a lever against Japan's shipping practices. Therefore the Foreign Secretary, Harold Macmillan, was asked to consider linking shipping and colonial purchases at the 15 August session of the Cabinet.[60] The Foreign Office examined the dilemma and the results were submitted to the ONC and the Cabinet for distribution and discussion. The Foreign Office discouraged any linkage between the two because the payments negotiation was a short-term instrument that did not have the weight to impact long-term Japanese shipping policies, which were of vital Japanese national interest. Furthermore, the Foreign Office was convinced that if negotiations were stalled, Britain was more likely to suffer from the inevitable accumulation of Japan's sterling reserves. Given that it was Britain's policy to bring 'Japan into the community of western powers and to get her to participate in the Colombo Plan', the Foreign Office considered the plan imprudent.[61] Lastly, the Foreign Office could not justify using colonial import restrictions as a bargaining position, because there was no legitimate reason for such a decision except to anger the Japanese and start a trade war between the two countries.[62] At the twenty-ninth Cabinet session, the Cabinet agreed that the shipping issue would be pursued separately 'through diplomatic channels and on other suitable occasions'.[63]

By 5 September, British negotiators felt that they had clear instructions to continue with the payments negotiations, and the talks were resumed on 8 September. The bargaining strategy – the restriction of colonial purchases if Japan did not agree to Britain's desiderata – had a positive impact on the British position. They were able to make headway regarding the three most important British wishes concerning Japan's sterling expenditures. Japan agreed to 'facilitate imports, visible and invisible, from the Sterling Area to the amount of Japan's earnings from the area';[64] she also agreed to 'provide in the winter budget not less than £127.5 million for visible and invisible exports from the Sterling Area'.[65] Lastly, the Japanese agreed to break down their £105 million into commodities and values that represented real trade opportunities for Britain.[66] The Japanese negotiators also expressed readiness to provide assurances on non-discrimination as requested by Britain, with exceptions over machinery and exclusive import quotas for their exports to the independent Sterling Area.

Regarding invisibles, Japan offered to increase sterling oil imports from 25 per cent to 27 per cent, in addition to abolishing discriminatory practices such as the merit system, which obstructed importers' attempts to sell oil to Japan. They also assured British negotiators that oil allocation would be based upon each importer's allocation for the years 1952–4, with the exception of a Shell subsidiary, which would see imports increase by £164,000. Unfortunately, Britain was unable to accept Japan's offer because it feared losing the goodwill of US oil companies and the State Department, which already thought that Britain and Japan were involved in market sharing. Given the importance of US oil companies to the British economy, Britain thought the resultant damage would far outweigh its 2 per cent increase in Japan's foreign oil market. Lastly, Japan agreed to 'release the accumulated blocked sterling on films' and 'to maintain import licences at the present level'.[67]

On 17 October the two sides signed an exchange of notes prolonging the Sterling Payments Agreement until 30 September 1956, thereby extending the agreement for a further twelve months.[68] Two days after completion of the negotiations, an article appeared in Japan's business newspaper *Sangyô Keizai* in the form of interviews with Asakai, Japan's chief negotiations, and Ihara, a former civil servant with extensive experience of the payments agreement who now worked for the Bank of Tokyo. The piece shed light on Japanese views of trade relations with the United Kingdom. Particularly illuminating was their belief that Britain lacked an adequate understanding of Japan's needs. Asakai and Ihara disclosed that Japan's limited orders from Britain were due to low local demand rather than state intervention. They believed that efforts towards bilateral trade expansion could not remain solely a government affair, and felt that British businessmen had to take greater initiatives to penetrate the Japanese market by 'displaying salesmanship to sell their goods to Japan'.[69] They emphasised Britain's lack of salesmanship as the one major factor that was hampering sales of British manufactured goods such as motor vehicles and spare parts. Finally, they were against the British use of import restrictions or exchange restrictions to protect domestic trade, and believed the use of these regulations only damaged the growth of overall trade between the Sterling Area and Japan.[70]

Conclusions

1955 brought an end to the British conundrum concerning its GATT policy towards Japan. Britain had spent the previous three years seeking safeguards within the GATT framework, but all had failed to gain the support of the contracting parties. Thus, left without an adequate safeguard proposal, Britain only had one option left: to invoke Article 35 of the GATT against Japan and base its commercial activities on a bilateral basis. Contrary to the previous years, however, the indecision at Cabinet level highlighted Britain's sensitivity to the Article 35 recourse. Britain's main goal after its announcement was to lessen any long-term impact of its decision on Anglo-American and Anglo-Japanese relations.

The period after the GATT announcement saw British attempts to negotiate a commercial treaty with Japan. Delays in presenting a draft treaty left Japan wondering about Britain's level of sincerity. The annual Sterling Payments Agreement had by this time been confined to Britain and its colonies, therefore responsibility for it had all but devolved to the Board of Trade. As such, the dynamics of the talks had become strictly bilateral with little reference to the rest of the Sterling Area. Thus the previous importance placed on the Japan account began to recede as Sterling Area-Japan relations shrunk in relative importance.

8   A period of lull

Introduction

The period between 1956 and 1959 saw three different leaders of the Liberal Democratic Party head the Japanese government. Hatoyama's resignation in December 1956 led to Ishibashi Tanzan's short term in office, followed by Kishi Nobusuke's leadership of the LDP in February of 1957.[1] Kishi's background in the pre-war Ministry of Commerce and Agriculture and his belief in dirigisme – the close cooperation between government and business – lent him well to the postwar focus upon economic and trade issues. Politically, his belief in greater Japanese military responsibility was out of step with the Japanese public at large, and the US-Japan security treaty revisions led to public protests and his eventual resignation.[2] His foreign economic policy reaped mixed results. His period in office saw the successful conclusion of bilateral commercial agreements with Australia and New Zealand in 1957 and 1958 respectively. The cornerstone of both agreements was MFN treatment with safeguards. Neither agreement went as far as the revocation of Article 35 of the GATT, but they were steps in the right direction.[3] The year 1957 also saw a glimmer of hope in Japan's efforts to expand trade relations with mainland China when she followed Britain's unilateral announcement of 27 May to terminate the China differential.[4] Japan's relaxation of export controls to communist China heralded expanded trade opportunities, but diplomatic bungling over the PRC's flag-flying rights in the fourth private Sino-Japanese trade agreement, and the subsequent destruction of a Chinese communist flag at a postage stamp exhibition led to the termination of Sino-Japanese trade until the early 1960s. Kishi's hopes of resurrecting the idea of an Asian payments union with US and Japanese funding was rejected not only by the United States, but also by countries in Southeast Asia, who still viewed any overarching Japanese regional investments with suspicion.

In the United States, the Eisenhower administration pursued its foreign economic policy towards its Western trading partners, but mounting domestic protectionism led to the signing of a five-year Voluntary Export Restrictions (VER) on 16 January 1957, which restricted Japanese exports of cotton manufactures to 235 million square yards per annum or 0.5 per cent of US production.[5] Ironically, Japanese voluntary restrictions did not protect US textile manufactures from overseas competition, because Hong Kong's textile exports filled the void. The period also saw continued US resistance to Japanese proposals for a Southeast Asian economic development fund of any kind, due to Eisenhower's reluctance to invest more capital in the underdeveloped and fragmented region. Thus the Eisenhower administration expressed little interest in Japanese overtures for more aid and rejected the Kishi plan.[6]

In Britain, the period began with the Suez crisis of 1956, which underscored Britain's limits in overseas military operations, together with sterling's problems in functioning as an international reserve currency, and tested the definition of Britain's 'special' relationship with the United States.[7] The crisis emphatically ended Eden's eighteen months as Prime Minister, and Harold Macmillan took over as leader of the Conservative Party. The period also saw a shift of emphasis in Britain's commercial policy, from the Commonwealth to Europe. Britain proposed a free trade area of sixteen countries as an alternative to the customs union envisioned by the 'Six' (France, Germany, Italy, Belgium, the Netherlands and Luxemburg). Britain's proposal, also known as Plan G, had little impact on the original Six, who signed the Treaty of Rome on 27 March 1957. Britain thus embarked on an alternative strategy of a free trade area of seven European countries (Norway, Sweden, Denmark, Austria, Portugal and Switzerland) in order to build a bargaining position against the Six, but this was also doomed to failure.[8]

Japan was not mentioned once in Cabinet during this period. This is not surprising given the political and economic challenges that Britain faced – Japan was simply not important enough to be on the policymakers' radar. This is not to suggest, however, that business as usual did not take place for the middle-ranking officials in charge of Japanese affairs. The period between 1956 and 1958 saw Board of Trade officials kept busy drafting and negotiating a commercial treaty with Japan. There was little progress towards a conclusion, because ministers of state deemed Japan of secondary importance compared to the other political and economic issues that preoccupied them. Moreover, given Britain's retreat from the Asian Sterling Area, they saw little economic gain in investing ministerial work hours towards concluding the treaty. The momentum of Anglo-Japanese relations swung from inactivity to hastened activity, however, as a direct result of European currency convertibility in 1958. Convertibility, which took effect on 27 December, ended the postwar dollar gap.[9] With convertibility in place, America's trading partners could no longer use balance of payments as a justifiable excuse to discriminate against dollar imports. The United States pushed for its trading partners to liberalise their import policies, which opened markets to new opportunities. The significance of these changes was not lost on Japan or on the United Kingdom, who saw each other's markets open up to goods that had been restricted or prohibited. And so 1959 saw a slow but definite turning point in Anglo-Japanese relations. This chapter has been divided broadly into two sections, dealing with the periods prior to and after 1959, to emphasise the significance of currency convertibility in Anglo-Japanese trade relations.

Trade and payments negotiations, 1956–8

Early in February 1956, the ONC met to assess the major agreements reached in the October negotiations and the subsequent state of Anglo-Japanese bilateral relations, in preparation for the mid-year review. In the previous year Britain had asked for and received Japan's commitment to balance its imports with its earnings. Britain became privy to Japan's provisional summer budget ahead of its release to ensure that the latter's announcement did not come as a surprise. Japan also promised not to discriminate against Sterling Area imports; and finally, Japan agreed to relax its restrictions on invisible trade.[10] In return, the United Kingdom agreed to maintain the 1954 quotas for all items imported from Japan, with the exception of an increase in canned salmon imports by £2.5 million. At Japan's insistence, no restrictions were to be placed on Japanese imports to Hong Kong, Singapore, Aden and the Federation of Malaya. It was also agreed that no ISA countries would lower their trade with Japan except for balance of payments reasons.[11]

On the whole, the ONC committee on Japan was satisfied with trade relations at the six-month point. Sterling balances at the end of December were close to agreed projections, and all evidence indicated that Japan had kept to her side of the agreement. The committee concluded that there was no substantive issue that needed to be brought to Japan's attention immediately. The only desideratum that the committee had was for a revision in the exchange allocation for Shell in Japan. The issue at hand was a processing contract that Shell had with Mitsubishi and Maruzen, whereby the two companies refined a quarter of all Shell's crude oil imports into Japan. The two companies processed the oil but did not have final ownership or sales responsibility in Japan. In spite of this, the exchange allocation for Shell's crude oil was in Mitsubishi and Maruzen's name. Shell felt vulnerable because the termination clause in the processing contract obliged the signatories to only a three-month period of notice for disengagement. The situation caused discomfort for Shell, which wished to transfer the exchange allocation in its name to retain its import allocation into Japan.[12]

The review was conducted in Tokyo in March and April, where certain minor quotas were agreed by the two sides. True to their word, the Japananese 'stated their intention of providing not less than £127.5 million in their summer budget'.[13] Shell's case remained unanswered, and Japan was unable to provide any improved treatment for UK oil companies operating in the Japanese market. In spite of the mixed results, the British were satisfied with the smooth running of the agreement, and thus decided against pursuing the outstanding Shell issue.[14]

As the year's end approached, the ONC braced itself for a renewal of the payments agreement. In August, the committee agreed to the continuation of the trade and quota arrangements and planned to apply for an increase in the UK-Japan trade level. The Shell issue was postponed from government discussion until Shell's own investigations were completed. This decision, however, did not preclude the government from applying for an increase in sterling oil imports into Japan.

The ONC agreed that two important issues should be raised during the payments negotiations: the lapse of the Sterling Payments Agreement and Japan's continued assurance of non-discrimination for sterling products. The Board of Trade and the Treasury's joint recommendation to terminate the Sterling Payments Agreement was in line with Britain's overall policy to phase it out because it was anachronistic and unnecessarily restrictive. The most restrictive element of the agreement, which fixed the yen price for sterling, had already been suspended, thus the instrument had little substantive impact upon actual Anglo-Japanese trade relations.[15] The Board of Trade and the Treasury's decision towards Japan was relatively late in coming, as Britain's only remaining sterling payments agreements were with Austria, Italy, Russia, Hungary, Poland and Czechoslovakia, and Britan's intention was to phase these out as they came up for renewal.[16]

The other instrument that governed Anglo-Japanese relations was the exchange of letters. This too was recommended for termination because it was no longer applicable to the countries' bilateral trade relations. The exchange of letters was a unique component of the agreement, which allowed either Britain or Japan to initiate talks to rectify any chronic imbalance in trade between the Sterling Area and Japan. It was drawn up in 1951 when Japan was still a bilateral account country and both sides were anxious about it's over-accumulation of sterling. Japan had in the meantime evolved into a transferable account country, and was using sterling for multilateral trade purposes. Other factors that were cited by the Board of Trade and the Treasury in favour of termination included the awkward wording of the letter. It implied distrust on Britain's part, and sent erroneous signals that 'the Japanese are not prepared to hold large sterling balances, or alternatively that we are afraid to allow them to do so'.[17] Moreover, the annual Sterling Payments Agreement and half-yearly reviews had become time-consuming. There was general consensus that the arrangement was far too taxing for what seemed like very small amount of trade for short periods of time.

The ONC's other mandate for negotiators was to ensure Japan's continued assurances of non-discrimination against British imports in the Japanese market. Japan had extended the guarantee in the previous year to treat all goods on the AA list fairly regardless of their origin. In addition, Britain wanted confirmation that Japan would not interfere administratively in importers' choice of goods, regardless of their origin (i.e. global quota or non-dollar quota). The final component of the desideratum was for Japan to relax the 'criteria used in applications for import licences for machinery'.[18]

Anglo-Japanese negotiations began in October. The trade portion of the talks progressed smoothly. Both sides were satisfied with the respective concessions. The only exception was Japan's inability to increase import allo-cations for Shell due to the creation of other instruments for oil licensing; thus the demand for Shell's facility was reduced. Japan also decided to reduce imports of British cars in order to protect Japan's expanding domestic automobile industry.[19]

By late December, the majority of the issues had been ironed out, except for Japan's concerns about its continued deficit with the Sterling Area. Japanese negotiators asked for trade concessions to correct the imbalance in line with the exchange of letters. Britain refused to relax its import restric-tions, citing balance of payments as the reason. It could only agree to reciprocal concessions aimed at trade expansion. It was at this point that British negotiators, who had waited for the opportune moment to raise the termination of the Sterling Payments Agreement and exchange of letters, brought up the matter. But Britain's announcement was poorly timed and raised fears among Japanese negotiators, who were surprised that such an important issue should be raised at what appeared to be the end of the nego-tiations. They wished to know the purpose of the abrogation, and if it would have an adverse impact upon Japan's international financial arrangement, 'so far as the holding or transfer of sterling was concerned'.[20] There were concerns that upon the termination of the Sterling Payments Agreement, Britain would impose restrictions 'on the transferability of sterling to the detriment of Japanese exports to certain regions – notably Argentina and Brazil'.[21] The Japanese therefore asked for time to consider the abrogation in some detail before giving their reply.

If Japan found the termination difficult to digest, the non-discrimination assurance proved even more so. Japan was unwilling to extend the assur-ances, explaining that these had been offered back in 1955 when she had large sterling surpluses. Given the reversal in the trade balance between the two countries, and continued trade discrimination by Britain and its colonies through OGL and import licences, Japan saw no reason why she should enter into a one-sided MFN treatment. In search for a compromise solution, British negotiators raised the issue at the ONC on 28 January during the end-of-year recess from negotiation. The ONC concluded that some form of compromise settlement should be reached, including Britain's retreat on ster-ling import inclusion on the AA list, and amendments to the text of the non-discriminating assurances to make it more reciprocal.[22]

When negotiations resumed in February, a compromise solution was reached whereby Japan could include Brazilian cotton in the AA list in return for Japan's continued level of imports from East Africa. Japan also confirmed that she would provide Britain with opportunities to negotiate import quotas for goods that were exclusive to third countries. Britain agreed to provide similar opportunities for Japan.[23] The Japanese side, finally, acquiesced to the termination of the Sterling Payments Agreement and the exchange of letters, after confirmation that Britain had no ulterior motive for abrogating them. At Japan's insistence, a formal letter was exchanged on 29 March, which read that the lapse was made 'in order to promote multilateral trade and payments in conformity with the principles of the International Monetary Fund', and that 'the lapse of the Sterling Payments Agreement does not affect Japan's position in the transferable account area in respect of the use of sterling as a means of international payment or the holding of sterling'.[24]

Once trade agreements had replaced the Sterling Payments Agreement, the operating of the trade negotiations was relegated to the Board of Trade, which wanted the termination of annual negotiations, but these were continued at Japan's request. The content of the negotiations was limited to Anglo-Japanese trade relations, with sporadic discussion on the colonies. Trade discussions were administrative in nature, concerning visible and invisible trade. Much of the focus was upon import quotas because of the sensitivity of the items on that list, but the majority of Anglo-Japanese trade took place outside of the quota arrangements.[25] The 1958 negotiations, which began on 17 February and ended on 25 April, differed very little from the previous years' agreements.[26] The Japanese side continued its relentless request to have its imports into Britain relaxed to the OEEC level. Unfortunately, with the MFN rights issue unresolved, Britain was unable to grant Japan this request.

The only significant change in relations was Britain's decision to increase canned salmon imports by £1 million in order to help Japan pay for a British atomic reactor, which was purchased in April 1959,[27] 'when Britain's General Electric Company, in conjunction with Fuji Denki, made a successful tender to build Japan's first nuclear reactor at Tokai Mura, Ibaragi Prefecture'.[28] The purchase of the atomic powered reactor was part of Japan's attempt to find an alternative source of energy that would replace hydroelectric resources and coal.[29] Britain's chances of making headway in this industry were limited from the start, due to the dominance of American companies such as Westinghouse and General Electric in the energy industry, but any chance of incremental business disappeared when the Tokai Mura project turned into a nightmare due to poor management, defective parts and bad workmanship.[30]

The period between 1956 and 1958 saw the administrative changes that led to the termination of the Sterling Payments Agreement. The financial aspect of the agreement had lost all relevance, given that Anglo-Japanese relations were primarily trade-driven. Responsibility for the annual agreements had shifted to the Board of Trade, and many of the bilateral issues that were buried under larger Commonwealth or colonial issues became magnified. The fact was that both countries were extremely restrictive in their trade, which prevented much opportunity for growth.

Negotiations towards a treaty of commerce and navigation, 1956–8

At the end of 1955, the Board of Trade had planned for an early beginning to the first round of treaty negotiations. They hoped that all the issues of clarification raised by the Foreign Ministry would be resolved by February. But this hope was unrealised, because directors of all Japanese government departments were attending the Diet and none could focus on the commercial treaty until April at the earliest.[31] Another reason for the delay was the backlog of work in the Board of Trade as a result of the list of questions sent by the Japanese government on aspects of Britain's version of the draft treaty, as well as on laws regulating foreign commercial activity in the United Kingdom.

Initial questions that were raised and resolved during this period included the issue of who would sign the treaty. That heads of state should do so was rejected by Japan because the Emperor was its head of state and did not have treaty-signing powers. An inter-state treaty was out of the question for Britain because of the difficulties associated with territorial limits for Britain.[32] Thus the two reached a compromise and acquiesced to an intergovernmental treaty instead.[33]

Two of the questions that were unanswered during the clarification period were the status of the colonies and which draft articles would be applied to them,[34] and the absence of most-favoured-nation treatment for Japanese imports.[35] Neither could be addressed fully to Japan's satisfaction during this period.

The multiple delays inevitably raised the issue of a *modus vivendi* to bridge the period between the lapse of the peace treaty and the enforcement of a commercial treaty. Officials at the Foreign Office, the Board of Trade and the Tokyo embassy began discussing the form and the content of an interim arrangement as early as December and the debate continued throughout the first half of 1956. The challenge lay in drafting a document that reflected the existing laws and regulations applied to the bilateral relations without it prejudicing Britain's future negotiating position. Furthermore, the drafting of the *modus vivendi* could not involve lengthy discussion that took time and energy away from the primary focus of negotiating a commercial treaty. British officials were also well aware of the many controversial issues that could lead to a bureaucratic quagmire, such as MFN treatment and colonial questions. Lastly, the *modus vivendi* had to be born out of a mutual desire for a written document stating the two countries' desire to respect each other in their commercial treatment.[36] After much consultation, Britain decided against concluding a *modus vivendi*, and the two sides agreed to accept each other's good faith.[37]

The first round of negotiations took place in London at Britain's insistence, because the relevant officials from the Home Office, Colonial Office and the Ministry of Labour wished to be present at the meetings to provide a full explanation of the provisions of the draft. Negotiations began on 24 July and lasted until 21 December 1957, with recesses in between.[38] MOFA was in charge of the Japanese team and the Board of Trade took charge of the British side, in spite of attempts by the Foreign Office to replace the Board of Trade on a number of occasions. Both sides brought their respective drafts of the treaty to the meeting, although Britain was determined to conduct the discussion around its draft. The talks enabled each side to better understand the reasons why their drafts differed and the reasons for these differences.[39] The subsequent meetings in 1958 and 1959 were a continuation of talks that were cordial but made little progress towards a final signing of the treaty.

From the beginning, MFN rights were a major point of contention. The issue was also the most challenging because it had become politically charged for both sides. Japan, on the one hand, had designated the revocation of Article 35 a major economic priority. She canvassed US support and raised the matter at every GATT session to remind the contracting parties of her displeasure.[40] Britain, on the other hand, was unable to grant MFN rights to Japan until its industries changed their attitude towards Japanese competition. But these changes were gradually occurring, and by early 1959 Sir Frank Lee, the Secretary of the Board of Trade, had informed the Economic Steering Committee that it was 'quietly studying the possibility of putting our commercial and economic relations with Japan on the same basis as that of most other countries'.[41]

What contributed to this change of heart in the Board of Trade was a combination of Japan's adherence to copyright laws, Commonwealth disinterest in protecting the preferential system, Britain's decision to apply for entry to the European Common Market, and Britain's duty-free imports of cheap textiles from Pakistan, India and Hong Kong, which were seen as more of a threat than Japanese textiles competition in the latter half of the 1950s.

As stated above, one reason for the softening of attitudes was the decline of Japanese infringements of copyright laws. The 1954 uproar over that country's blatant copies of British textiles designs represented the peak of anti-Japanese sentiment in Britain, when emotions ran so high that the government felt obliged to run a public relations campaign to improve Japan's image. Examples of unfair Japanese trade practices were now less frequent, due to Japan's concerted effort at creating internal patent and design protection systems.[42]

Another reason for Britain's lenient attitude towards Japan was that protecting Britain's trade with the Commonwealth against Japanese products was no longer a priority. When Japan had initially applied for GATT entry, Britain felt compelled to oppose this due to the no-new-preference-rule, which prevented discriminatory tariff hikes against one country without it applying increases across the board, thus, preventing Britain from protecting its Commonwealth preferential trade. By 1956, however, many of the Commonwealth countries were no longer interested in maintaining the preferential system, and even the most loyal Commonwealth members such as Australia and New Zealand were hoping to make 'deep cuts in contractual British preferential margins in order to facilitate trade negotiations with other countries' – such as Japan.[43]

The divergence in Commonwealth commercial policy provided Britain with an opportunity to review its commercial treaty.[44] The results of this review concluded that Britain would reap greater commercial benefits from Europe in the long run, and so the focus began to shift to Europe. Britain outlined a plan for a European Free Trade Area (EFTA), which would integrate Britain's economy with that of the Western European countries. The strategy, known as Plan G, envisioned a free trade area instead of the customs union proposed by the original six. Although Plan G would ultimately fail as a policy, Britain continued its diplomatic initiative and made steps towards its first application to join the European Economic Community.

And so, by the end of 1958, many of the original reasons for British opposition to Japan's GATT entry had become non-issues. The only valid reason which remained was the protection of domestic industries against disruptive Japanese competition. But even this excuse began to wear thin when Britain was faced with the immediate problem of large quantities of duty-free imports of cotton cloths from cheap textiles from manufacturers within the Commonwealth.

Britain's problem had begun in 1955 with a large influx of grey cotton cloths from India, followed by imports from Pakistan and Hong Kong.[45] By 1957, Commonwealth cotton textiles' combined share of the British market had risen from 11 per cent to 14.5 per cent.[46] Thus a mission from Lancashire under Sir Cuthbert Clegg, Vice President of the Cotton Spinners' and Manufacturers' Association, visited all three sources in an attempt to gain their approval for a voluntary restriction of exports to the United Kingdom.

The visits to India and Pakistan were successful, with both countries agreeing in principle to restrict exports to the United Kingdom to the 1956 level for three years. Hong Kong, however, refused to adhere to such an arrangement. The issue was raised both at the EPC and in Cabinet. As expected, the Colonial Secretary, representing Hong Kong, expressed strong opposition to voluntary export restrictions, citing the enormous difficulties faced by the colony due to its size and its forced switch from an entrepôt trading centre to a manufacturing centre due to Britain's imposed strategic controls on trade with China.[47]

An alternative suggestion, that of import licensing, was proposed by the Chancellor of the Exchequer, but this drew even more opposition because the solution would no longer be voluntary on the part of the Commonwealth, and would set a precedent for other domestic industries to protect themselves from Commonwealth competition. It was also considered that such a decision would send erroneous signals to the rest of the Commonwealth about Britain's intentions on the eve of Britain's entry into the European Free Trade Area.[48] The Hong Kong issue, which had been debated throughout the first seven months of 1957, escalated to prime ministerial level when Macmillan expressed his willingness to inform Hong Kong himself that it was in her interest to enter into a voluntary export agreement in order to avoid endangering the principle of free entry of Commonwealth goods into the United Kingdom.[49] From that point on, the Hong Kong impasse remained under Macmillan's direct supervision until it was resolved.

The following year saw the establishment of a temporary Cabinet committee on cotton imports chaired by Macmillan. The committee was established to expedite the cotton issue by limiting the debate to a group of ministry heads including the Chancellor of the Exchequer, the Secretary of State for the Colonies, the Secretary of State for Commonwealth Relations and the President of the Board of Trade. The committee revisited the two alternatives open to them: to renew the effort to persuade Hong Kong to accept a voluntary export restriction, or to inform Lancashire that changing patterns of world trade had made its industry uncompetitive and that it would have to adapt itself to new conditions. The committee agreed to support the former option, given the cotton industry trade unions' readiness to revamp their practices, among other factors. And so further overtures to Hong Kong were attempted. In the meantime, the Lancashire cotton industry was successful in concluding voluntary export agreements with India and Pakistan, subject to Britain's successful conclusion of a similar agreement with Hong Kong.[50] The British government made overtures to Hong Kong from the middle of 1958, and by December, Hong Kong had agreed to a voluntary export restriction. The rest of the month was spent negotiating the terms of the restriction, and by early 1959 Hong Kong had signed a voluntary export agreement with the United Kingdom.[51]

Thus, by the end of 1958, an accumulation of factors such as fewer blatant Japanese imitations of British textiles designs, Britain's shift towards Europe, and the problem of Commonwealth textiles competition, served to put the Japanese issue into perspective and enable the Board of Trade to inch closer to the idea of liberalising Japanese imports. The most influential factor was, however, the prospect of expanded trade relations that arose as a result of the convertibility of currencies.

When the European currencies became convertible in December 1958, this ended the postwar phenomenon of the dollar gap, whereby countries did not have adequate dollar reserves to exchange their currencies to dollars. Convertibility meant that European and Sterling Area countries could convert their currencies into dollars and vice-versa. Moreover, they could no longer claim that they had balance of payments problems or that non-convertibility of their currencies prevented them from trading with the dollar area, as they had done in the past.[52] As a result, the United States began pressuring its trading partners to liberalise their dollar restrictions through the IMF and the GATT frameworks. At the GATT, a committee on balance-of-payments restrictions was established to discuss with key US trading partners their readiness and their timetables for terminating their balance of payments discrimination against the dollar area.[53] The first countries to take part in such consultations were France, the Netherlands, New Zealand, the United Kingdom and South Africa, at the fourteenth GATT session in May.[54]

For Britain, dollar liberalisation meant aligning US import restrictions to the OEEC level. In percentage terms, it meant freeing up to 95 per cent of US imports from restrictions, as opposed to the existing 73 per cent.[55] The total cost of such an endeavour was likely to amount to £17 million. This included a switch from the Sterling Area to other sources of supply, which was expected to amount to £500,000. Furthermore, implementation of similar relaxations in the colonies was expected to affect the balance of payments by £5 million per annum.[56]

The Board of Trade and the Treasury were committed to trade liberalisation, and sought the approval of the Cabinet. The two departments realised that they had no other option but to liberalise, given the severe admonishment that France had received from the IMF for failing to liberalise her imports soon enough. The British government's problem was not so much the economic impact of liberalisation. It was the political aspect that was of concern, due to considerable public criticism of a recent US decision to double the *ad valorem* value on woollen imports, which had a substantial impact on the British woollen industry. A British announcement so soon after the debacle was thought to be likely to exacerbate anti-American feelings in Britain unless this could be accompanied by 'some tangible evidence that the United States were adopting more helpful attitude'.[57] Therefore great sensitivity and consideration was invested in considering the manner in which the government should go public with its dollar liberalisation decision.[58]

Not long after Britain underwent US scrutiny over its import restrictions, Japan faced an equally critical analysis of her existing trade practices. Japan's restrictive import policy was discussed at the IMF consultation in September, and later, on 23 October, the IMF called upon member countries 'whose current receipts were largely in inconvertible currencies to proceed with all in eliminating discrimination against member countries, including that arising from bilateralism'.[59] Further pressure was imposed upon Japan at the fifteenth session of the GATT in October, where she was criticised for her anti-competitive import regulations such as the automatic approval and fund allocation systems.[60] As a first priority, the United States recommended the immediate lifting of ten US commodities that were restricted from the automatic approval list.[61] Another list of commodities was also marked for eventual liberalisation.[62] By April of the following year, Japan was expected to have 42 per cent of her trade liberalised, and 70 per cent by April 1961.[63]

As import restrictions across Western economies began to tumble, trading partners began to eye each others' markets, and found opportunities for growth where import restrictions had previously been an insurmountable barrier to market penetration. For both Britain and Japan, who had spent the better part of the 1950s complaining about the barriers to each other's markets, dollar liberalisation was an unforeseen opportunity. The effects of currency convertibility and the subsequent dollar liberalisation had a more profound liberalising impact on Japan's import licensing system, but dollar liberalisation, in combination with Japan's exponential economic growth, had an equally powerful impact on the Board of Trade's perceptions of Japan. Dollar liberalisation redirected Britain's trade policy towards Japan.

Dollar liberalisation and its impact on Anglo-Japanese trade

In Japan, January saw a flurry of activity as convertibility led to discussions in MOFA, MITI and MOF about foreign exchange allocations, which were separated into the rigid dollar, sterling and open account areas. The three ministries were divided into two camps over future financial regulations governing currencies. MOF saw a post-convertibility world divided into two currency areas: dollars and convertible currencies versus the open account area. Thus it wished to align all financial regulations governing the two combined currencies. MOFA, with the 'ambiguous support of the MITI', was of the view that the Dollar and Sterling Areas should, in practice, remain separate because the existing arrangement decreased the margin of error and that the origination of goods would be easily traceable to the correct currency blocs.[64] Second, and more importantly, if the two currency areas were combined, Japan would have greater difficulty justifying to the IMF, the United States and Canada its continued discrimination against the dollar area.[65] The debate ensued for the rest of January, but MOFA's argument prevailed. On 30 January, the British Embassy in Tokyo was informed by MITI that discrimination between the dollar and the convertible currencies would end on the following day. As a result, items on the automatic list could be imported from any source, with the exception of the thirteen sensitive items, which were still restricted from the non-dollar sources.[66]

The change meant the gradual opening of Japan's markets to foreign imports. With the impending renewal of the Anglo-Japanese trade arrangement, however, both MITI and MOFA discouraged Britain from conducting negotiations, and instead proposed a one-year extension because of the difficulties MITI would have in granting or increasing the existing bilateral quotas, which discriminated against the dollar countries.[67] Britain was reluctant to see an automatic extension of the agreement because it wished to negotiate fairer treatment for British exports to Japan. The Japanese side had only recently submitted a reduced list of import quotas for Britain, which left the latter with £738,000 less earnings per annum.[68] Britan was not pleased with the Japanese request, but agreed to an extension on 1 April on the understanding that either government could discuss with the other 'any matter concerning the trade relations between Japan and the United Kingdom and colonial territories or to review the operation of the trade arrangements' at any time.[69]

At the time of the extension, Japan had hoped that dollar liberalisation would benefit her trade relations with Britain, and approached Britain about Japanese import relaxations, hoping that she would at last receive OEEC treatment. Britain expressed its inability to relax import restrictions against Japan unless the British government was able 'to demonstrate that they had earned additional facilities for British trade by doing so'.[70] Later, the Board of Trade confirmed its inability to extend import relaxations. It explained that Britain was unable to extend the same relaxations to Japan because the core problem underlying the two trading partners' relationship was one of finance, not trade.[71]

As trade relaxations were being imposed on the United States' trading partners, another round of Anglo-Japanese commercial treaty negotiations took place from March to June. The negotiations were friendly, and both sides were able to resolve minor conflicts and redrafts. They were, however, unable to make any headway on the issue of MFN rights. The Japanese expressed their inability to sign a commercial treaty with Britain unless the document incorporated both MFN rights and the revocation of Article 35. Anything less could not be ratified by the Diet. Conversely, Britain could not grant both MFN rights and the revocation of Article 35 without some form of safeguard, much like that incorporated in the Australia-Japan commercial agreement of July 1957.[72] In subsequent discussions, the Japanese delegates admitted that the official Japanese line was not set in stone and that Japan was open to pursuing a bilateral safeguard compromise. Thus the negotiations adjourned on the understanding that both sides would explore a safeguard solution before talks resumed.[73]

The key to progress was a safeguard solution, which was proposed by Kishi during his three-day goodwill tour to the United Kingdom. In a meeting with Macmillan on 13 July, Kishi 'recognised the apprehension felt in the United Kingdom over the possible flooding of the market by Japanese products', and suggested that Japan would impose voluntary export restrictions to ensure that it did not happen'.[74] He extended this compromise solution in exchange for MFN treatment and the revocation of Article 35.[75] Ten days later, Hughes held a meeting of the key officials in charge of the Japanese commercial question and agreed that Britain should take the opportunity presented by Kishi to formulate a viable safeguard solution acceptable to both Britain and Japan. Inaction was deemed to have an adverse effect upon Anglo-Japanese relations and lead to mounting international criticism of Britain's discriminatory policy. The plan was to establish a framework by the fifteenth session of the GATT in Tokyo, so that British delegates could continue informal talks based on a loose framework. The Board of Trade thus embarked on a feasibility study to determine the likely consequences of MFN treatment on British items, and to classify the items according to the degree of disruption these items would cause.[76]

Ahead of the GATT session in Tokyo, the British delegates were instructed to ascertain Japan's position concerning the commercial treaty, specifically, whether the Japanese were still attached to the principle of MFN treatment without qualification and the revocation of Article 35; what form of safeguards they envisaged, if it were a voluntary export restriction or import controls; and if they expected to see immediate relaxations in import controls ahead of the establishment of the safeguard proposal. British delegates were expected to sound out the Japanese position and assess its feasibility based upon the key British safeguard requirements.[77] These requirements were that any safeguard solution needed to be a public document accessible to all industries; the safeguards would have to be in effect indefinitely; and they should allow Britain to re-impose restrictions 'on any class of goods if imports threatened to disrupt any UK industry'.[78] The wording and regulations governing the safeguard would have to be drawn up by Britain. Finally, as quid pro quo for opening its markets to Japanese imports, Britain expected Japan to relax many of its import restrictions that were hindering British penetration of the Japanese market.[79] Since these British requirements were yet to be approved by ministers, delegates were told to refrain from mentioning them in any discussion.

Opportunity was taken during the GATT session in Tokyo for talks between the British delegates and Japanese representatives to discuss the safeguard solution. The Japanese side was resigned to the fact that Britain would wish to have the unilateral power to take action against Japanese imports indefinitely, and that some degree of continued restriction would have to be in place. The Japanese expressed a strong desire to ensure that any export restrictions were administered by Japan, and they had to appear to be voluntary. The British delegates were informed that Japan was divided over the Article 35 issue and sought British preference on the two schools of thought that existed in Japan. One school of thought favoured a revocation of Article 35 subject to a bilateral understanding that neither side would invoke the provisions of the GATT against each other 'in regard to MFN treatment in respect of quotas'.[80] The other school of thought was inclined to believe that a treaty, which provided for 'MFN treatment in respect of quantitative restrictions with satisfactory understandings about the qualifications to be applied in practice', would be sufficient for the time being and that the revocation of Article 35 could be revisited in three years' time.[81]

The other development at the GATT session was Britain's announcement of further liberalisation of items from the dollar countries on 5 November. Japan was excluded from this round of liberalisation.[82] The delegates to the meeting hoped that Japan would understand the reasons for this exclusion, and did not explain their position in their statement to the GATT. The delegates in Tokyo were not approached on the issue, but Ohno Katsumi, the Japanese Ambassador to Britain, met with Reginald Maudling, the new President of the Board of Trade, on 9 November to present an *aide-mémoire* protesting the unfairness of the new discrimination, which left Japan as the only country outside the communist bloc to be excluded from Britain's new liberalisation measures. Furthermore, in order avoid damaging relations, Britain was asked to re-examine the existing import restrictions against Japan ahead of, and separate from, the negotiations on the commercial treaty.[83] At the meeting, Ohno asked that immediate restrictions should be lifted on goods that would not cause embarrassment to British industries, such as cameras, optical equipment, electrical equipment, paper products and smokers' requisites, to prevent any long-term damage to bilateral relations.[84]

A discussion on Ohno's request ensued between the Far Eastern and Economic Relations departments of the Foreign Office in conjunction with the Board of Trade. The British Embassy in Tokyo was inclined to believe that some form of relaxation should be extended to Japan immediately, because the Japanese side tended to see the liberalisation and commercial policy issues as separate and thus capable of resolution independently. There was also urgency about the matter because of growing public and government opinion in Japan that she should discriminate against Britain when she was finally prepared to liberalise her import restrictions in April 1960.[85]

In the end, Britain decided against granting a separate import relaxation, because Maudling viewed the two issues as inseparable and firmly believed that a solution could only be found through a commercial treaty. He was, however, aware that indefinite discrimination would lead to a deterioration in relations; thus he recommended that a new liberal approach should be taken during the next Anglo-Japanese trade talks the following year.[86] Furthermore, he expected definite progress in the commercial treaty negotiations, scheduled for February 1960 due to the positive outcome of October's discussion on safeguards.[87]

Conclusions

Little progress was made in Anglo-Japanese trade relations between 1956 and 1959. The one change that took place was the transition of trade from the outdated Sterling Payments Agreement to the annual trade arrangement. The official change merely aligned official agreement to what had being going on in practice, but the way in which the termination was introduced surprised Japan, and she suspected an ulterior motive behind Britain's decision. This Japanese distrust and uncertainty reflected the nature of the bilateral relations, which was based upon very strict quantitative import restrictions on both sides that limited any expansion in trade. The transfer to the annual trade arrangements, in fact, magnified the limited nature of the agreement, as both sides vied for trade relaxations from the other without much success. The period also saw little progress in negotiations towards an Anglo-Japanese commercial treaty. This was in part because the two sides wished to sign a full treaty of commerce, establishment and navigation instead of a limited commercial agreement such as was signed with Australia and New Zealand respectively. Thus the negotiations were bound to take longer. That alone cannot be the reason for the delay, however, and all factors point to the undeniable truth that the British felt little urgency to complete the negotiations. As 1959 approached, however, multiple factors were converging to favour their successful completion. These ranged from the decreasing number of infringements on British copyrights, to increasing Commonwealth interest in expanding their trade relations with Japan, to Britain's focus on Europe regarding its long-term commercial relations. The event that had the biggest impact upon Anglo-Japanese trade relations was, ironically, the European currency convertibility and the subsequent American-led market liberalisation. Many of the import restrictions that governed British and Japanese trade were forcibly removed by the United States, and thus led to market opportunities that had not previously existed.

Britain was initially unwilling to extend these dollar relaxations towards Japan, but by the end of 1959 it realised the imprudence of such a decision and the negative impact it would have on Britain's future trade relations with Japan.

9   The Anglo-Japanese Commercial Treaty

Introduction

Relations between the United States and Japan underwent an upheaval in 1960, with a Japanese backlash resulting from the renewal of the US-Japan Security Treaty, which shook the foundation of their bilateral relations. It underscored the fragility of these relations when it came to security and rearmament issues. The year ushered in a new Prime Minister, Ikeda Hayato, who prudently accepted the US-Japan alliance system and focused his attention on economic development. The United States also saw a changing of the guard with the inauguration of a Democratic President, John F. Kennedy, in 1961. These changes of leadership had no immediate effect on US foreign economic policy towards Japan, which continued to emphasise trade liberalisation and domestic protection.

In Britain, much of the diplomatic focus was on that country's first application to the European Economic Community. The Macmillan government announced its decision to apply in 1961, with the full support of the Six, but by 1963 its first bid had all but failed due to three major weaknesses in Britain's diplomatic efforts. The first was the conditionality of the application, whereby Britain was reluctant to commit to its membership until all negotiations were completed and the final terms were deemed advantageous to Britain. Second was Macmillan's reluctance to confront domestic reticence about European integration, which weakened Britain's application in the eyes of the Six. The third weakness was Britain's flawed bilateral diplomacy, with France in particular, which led to De Gaulle's veto in January 1963 and the failure of Britain's initial bid to become an EEC member.[1]

In terms of the Anglo-Japanese Commercial Treaty, there were several reasons why Britain felt it should expedite its negotiations. The EEC application obviously had an impact because if Britain were to become an EEC member its bilateral relations with Japan would have to conform to those of the EEC. Further postponement of the agreement was deemed to complicate the terms of the bilateral treaty, thus there was a definite incentive for Britain to complete the negotiations before it became an EEC member. More importantly, it was to Britain's advantage to complete negotiations with Japan if it wished to reap benefits from the fastest growing economy in the world. Britain wanted to guarantee itself an equal opportunity to enter and thrive in the expanding Japanese economy, and so the Board of Trade, which was traditionally very apprehensive of Japanese competition, placed Britain's export opportunities above the protectionist interests of domestic manufacturers. As a result, traditionally protected industries now found that their protestations fell on deaf ears.

The period between 1960 and 1962 was thus marked by Britain's aggressive effort to improve its overall relations with Japan. She was successful in signing a cultural agreement with Japan in 1960, and a Double Taxation Convention in 1961. Most important of all was the completion of the commercial treaty negotiations, which would ensure that British industries received equal opportunities in penetrating the Japanese market.

The Anglo-Japanese trade arrangement

The trade liberalisation process in Japan had a more immediate impact on the annual Anglo-Japanese trade negotiations, because Japan requested for increased British relaxation of Japanese import restrictions to counterbalance the rapid opening-up of her own market. Accordingly Maudling raised the Japanese trade issue at the EPC, on 8 January 1960, ahead of the Anglo-Japanese trade talks that were due to start that week. He sought authority from the committee to offer import liberalisations for a number of Japanese goods. These liberalisations were a direct response to Ohno's complaints about Britain's reluctance to extend dollar relaxations to Japanese goods, which left Japan as the only country outside the communist bloc to suffer harsh import restrictions. The softening of the Board of Trade's attitude was to a large extent due to its concern that without these measures, Japan would consider counter-discriminating against British goods when Britain was ready to liberalise its own import controls. For the Board of Trade, the possibility of restricted access to a booming Japanese economy that could offer opportunities for British industry, was serious enough to make it willing to reverse its initial decision to maintain import controls against Japan.

Maudling circulated two lists drawn up by the Board of Trade's Import Licensing Committee in July of the previous year. The first list was made up of items which could be liberalised without causing any disruption of British domestic industries, such as clothing, fish and fish products, sporting goods and vehicle parts. The other list consisted of items such as clocks, ships, linen goods and fresh fruits, that were deemed negotiable based upon how importantly Japan viewed those items for export to the UK and what concessions she was willing to make in exchange.[2] The committee approved the content of the two lists, as well as Britain's strategy for the trade talks.

The Japan issue was raised twice at the EPC in the course of the talks. Both occasions were in conjunction with Japanese requests for greater liberalisation of British imports. The first instance dealt with increased quotas of cotton textiles for domestic consumption as well as for re-export. The requests ranged from an incremental increase of 20 per cent for cotton and rayon pieces and 250 per cent in imports of apparel.[3] Maudling revised Japan's application down before submitting the request to the EPC, but even the modest £100,000 increase in apparel was predicted to arouse hostility in Lancashire. Concern also stemmed from the adverse impact that increased overseas imports would have on Lancashire's confidence so soon after the introduction of the 1959 Cotton Industry Act, aimed at subsidising the re-organisation and re-equipment of the cotton textiles industry.[4] Moreover, Hong Kong, which had reluctantly agreed to voluntary export controls in the previous year, was unlikely to receive the news well, especially as it feared future requests for voluntary export restrictions from countries such as the United States.[5]

Maudling was willing to extend these concessions to Japan in spite of the expected complaints from Hong Kong and Lancashire, because the degree of relaxation was too modest to impact either plaintiff. Furthermore, an increase in Japanese grey cloths for re-export was justified on the ground that re-finished textiles exports were still cheaper than British products and more competitive in overseas markets.

The Board of Trade requested additional import relaxations in response to Japan's announcement that she would exclude Britain from her first round of import liberalisation in April as a counter-measure to Britain's import restrictions against Japanese goods. Discrimination was applied across all of Japan's trading partners who were applying restrictions. Maudling requested the EPC's authority for an additional £500,000 increase in quotas of real interest to Japan such as 'cameras, toys, plastic materials, binoculars and radios'.[6] Again, Maudling expected a backlash from domestic industries, but the gains were thought to outweigh the losses.[7] When Japan accepted these concessions, the annual trade arrangement was signed for the period 1 April 1960 to 31 March 1961, and extended for a further six-month period until September.

The concessions paid off handsomely for Britain. The eighteen months that ensued saw spectacular increases in Britain's exports to Japan – a 60 per cent increase in exports in the first eight months of the year – whereas the Japanese saw only had a modest 20 per cent gain in the same period.[8] Britain's export performance underscored just how much Britain was bene-fiting from Japan's trade liberalisation. Japan's economy was the fastest growing economy in the world, and the Board of Trade was convinced that there was an opportunity for Britain to export its goods to this 'large and growing potential market'.[9]

In October, Maudling again applied to remove import barriers prior to the upcoming trade talks with Japan. He justified this request because of the recent Japanese announcement on the liberalisation of further items for import by the end of the year, from which Britain was expected to benefit.

Given Britain's unforeseen gains in Japan, there was a great Japanese antici-
pation for reciprocity in the British market. Most importantly, such
authorisation was crucial if Britain did not wish to lose the opportunity for
trade, or give its competitors, the United States and Germany, whose goods
were being exported without restriction, 'the chance to establish themselves
ahead of us'.[10] Maudling's request was approved, but two months later he
was again back at the EPC for authorisation to lift restrictions on all photographic equipment as well as offer an improved quota for transistorised
radio equipment. The restrictions on photographic equipment were lifted,
but the quota for radio equipment proved a more difficult matter, and this
class of goods eventually wound up on Japan's voluntary export restriction
list for gradual liberalisation. The annual trade agreement was signed on 22
December 1961, and renewed retroactively from September to the following
September.

As the date of the expiry of the agreement approached at the end of
1961, Japanese officials began to debate about whether to extend their
dollar relaxations to Britain and the EEC.[11] Japan eventually agreed to
apply liberalised import figures to British goods, but applied enormous
pressure on Britain to reciprocate by including as many Japanese items on
the OGL as possible at the signing of, instead of the ratification of, the
treaty, which was not expected to take place until the following year.[12] Thus
the last two years of annual trade negotiations fell into a predictable
pattern of Japanese requests for British trade liberalisation to counterbalance the pace of relaxation in Japan in order to maintain reciprocity in
market penetration.

The commercial treaty

The commercial treaty negotiations, which took place parallel to the trade
negotiations, proved to be far more complex than initially anticipated. The
many unresolved aspects of the negotiations, ranging from the safeguard
proposal and the sensitive list to the actual treaty articles, forced the negotiators, in July 1962, to divide the talks in two: one half would take place in
Japan and the other in London.

The Board of Trade, which spent the latter half of 1959 building a case
for ministerial acceptance of Kishi's safeguard proposal, raised the issue
at the EPC in February. At the meeting, Maudling gave an update of
developments dating back to the previous July and the Japanese offer of
voluntary export restrictions as a solution to Britain's concerns. He
explained that the Board of Trade was not opposed to a Japanese-admin-
istered system, but reiterated the minimum requirements. Safeguards
would comprise of a sensitive list of items that were restricted indefinitely
to protect domestic industries from disruptive trade. Another list would
comprise of items that could be liberalised over time (see Table 9.1 for the
original sensitive lists). Lastly, Britain would reserve the right to 'impose

Table 9.1   Goods to be protected or liberalised on the conclusion of a
            commercial treaty with Japan

Goods on which Britain proposed to retain discriminatory import controls

---

Cameras of all types, cinematograph equipment and optical photographic
equipment, and parts

Cigarette lighters

Cutlery

Domestic sewing machines

Certain kinds of sports goods

Nets and netting

Optical instruments (including binoculars) and lenses, prisms and other optical
elements and parts

Pottery

Textiles and textile manufactures

Toys and games

Transistors and transistorised radio and television apparatus,
radiogramophones, gramophones and parts

---

*Goods already subject to discriminatory import controls, to be liberalised on the
conclusion of a commercial treaty*

*I. Goods considered but not offered for liberalisation in connection with the existing
trade arrangements*

Canned pilchards

Clocks, mechanical timing devices, and parts

Fruit pulp and fruit preserved in sulphur dioxide solution

Fruits and hams

Oleyl-Cetyl alcohol

Rubber manufactures

Screws

Ships and boats and parts

Wire cloth, fencing, netting and mesh less than half inch mesh

Table 9.1 contd.

II. Other goods

Artificial flowers, foliage and fruit

Bicycle, motor cycle, tri-car and tri-van parts and accessories

Covered rubber thread

Decorated glassware

Dowels

Glass fibres, yarns and fabrics

Imitation jewellery

Jewellery

Leather gloves

Mopeds, scooters, parts and accessories

Non-transistorised radio and television parts, radio gramophones and gramophones

Other leather clothing: rubber and plastic clothing

Pencils

Plastic materials and manufactures

Rubber and plastic footwear

Scientific and precision instruments, other than "process-control" and optical instruments

Sports goods, other than: fishing tackle and golf balls

Umbrellas and sunshades

Wires and cables

Wool or felt headgear

Source: Note from the President of the Board of Trade to the EPC, 2 May 1960, EA(60)45, CAB134/1687, PRO.

or re-impose quantitative restrictions on any import from Japan if damage were threatened or caused to our domestic industry'.[13]

As a quid pro quo for Japan's agreement to voluntarily limit her exports, Maudling wished to gain ministers' authorisation to revoke Article 35 in conjunction with the signing of the commercial treaty. Maudling was well aware of just how sensitive industries were to accepting Japan into the GATT, so he proposed that Britain and Japan sign a bilateral agreement that excluded GATT rules from any quantitatively restricted items on the safeguard list. At the 17 February meeting of the EPC, committee members asked a range of questions with the intention of weighing the opportunities versus the risks of granting MFN rights and revoking Article 35 of the GATT against Japan. These ranged from the pattern of Commonwealth-Japanese trade, the size of the Japanese market, the expected British opportunities in Japan, and the likely effects of Japanese competition on domestic industries. Maudling's and the Board of Trade's subsequent answers were as objective as they could be, given that department's desire to enter the rapidly expanding Japanese market at the earliest opportunity.[14] The EPC approved the memorandum and the request sailed through the Cabinet on 10 March.[15]

After the memorandum's approval, two other studies were undertaken by the Board of Trade at the request of the EPC. One was on the likely growth of industrial competition from the Commonwealth and the colonial territories, and the other on the prospects of increasing UK exports to Japan. Regarding the former, the scope of the report was limited to competition from low-cost Commonwealth countries because the Cabinet had been concerned about the combined threat of Japanese and low-cost Commonwealth goods to British manufactures both at home and abroad. The report focused on a five-year projected growth in the economies of Hong Kong, India and Pakistan, and the possible competitive impact that these three countries combined would have on British manufactures. The report dedicated most of its effort to examining competition from Hong Kong. This was due to the remarkable growth on the island due to the exodus of the commercial community from the mainland. In a five-year period, Hong Kong's worldwide exports of manufactured goods had increased from £42.6 million in 1954 to £140 million in 1959. In spite of these gains, the Board of Trade did not believe that Hong Kong would represent the same degree of threat as Japan, due to differences in population size, demands of the home market and complexity of industrial systems. These factors, combined with the slow-down in Hong Kong's population growth, the increasing wage costs and geographical limitations, eased any major concerns that Britain had of unabated exponential growth in the Hong Kong export market.[16]

The other low-cost countries, such as Nigeria, India, Pakistan and Malaya, were all considered together in a shorter section of the report. The limited focus was based upon the conviction that the rest of the low-cost Commonwealth countries would not pose a collective threat to British manufactures because these countries devoted much of their energy towards supplying their own domestic industrial needs, such as fertiliser, paper, cement, clothing, iron and steel.[17] Two possibilities were considered in regard to these countries: first, whether the larger countries would develop new lines of products in the next five years and become a threat to UK industry; and second, whether the smaller territories might 'acquire the psychological and economic climate that has produced the export successes of Hong Kong'.[18] The Board of Trade thought neither possibility was likely because, in the first instance, it did not foresee great incentives for the local manufacturers to develop new product lines, and there was little encouragement on the part of their governments to encourage such development. As for the second question, the requirements needed to emulate Hong Kong's miraculous economic growth were skilled labour, capital and enterprising management, and none of the smaller territories had such a combination of skills that would enable them to emulate Hong Kong within five years. Thus the concluding tone of the report was reassuring, given that, in the short term, the Board of Trade did not envisage any serious problems stemming from exports from the low-cost Commonwealth countries and territories.[19]

The Board of Trade's report on the prospects of increasing UK exports to Japan assessed British export performance to date and supplied a projection for the future. The report highlighted the fact that UK exports had not fared well in comparison to their competitors. Britain's market share in machinery, chemicals and other manufactured goods totalled an average of 4.9 per cent in 1959. This was poor market penetration compared to that of the United States, which averaged 70 per cent, and Germany, with a 10 per cent average (see Table 9.2). The report acknowledged the many reasons that impeded Britain's performance in this area, such as the strict Japanese import licensing system; the advantages accrued by the United States due to its early entry into the Japanese market; and Britain's delayed interest in technological transfer to Japan. The report, however, saw other factors as being equally important for Britain's market penetration. These included the distance between the two markets and the lingering prejudice from the inter-war and war-time periods.

The Board of Trade believed that the rapid liberalisation of Japan's trade afforded Britain a chance of breaking into a market dominated by the United States. It cited some recent commercial successes as predictors, such

Table 9.2   Percentage of total imports into Japan in 1959 from selected countries

Product	UK	USA	W. Germany
Machinery and transport equipment	5	67	12
Electrical equipment and machinery	4	82	5
Metalworking machinery	2	54	29
Office machinery	2	84	4
Motor vehicles and parts	5	88	7
Aircraft and parts	2	90	n/a
Other manufactured goods	15	36	8
Chemicals	4	55	16

Source: Note from the President of the Board of Trade to the EPC, 28 November 1960, EA(60)96, CAB134/1688, PRO.

as the sale of a power reactor, the supply of a large telescope for the University of Tokyo's observatory, the chance of supplying two major electricity generators to Tokyo, and increased orders for machine tools. The Board of Trade's overarching view was that the British share of exports to Japan would not improve without the signing of a commercial treaty. In the absence of a firm framework, exporters would be reluctant to 'invest time and money in cultivating the Japanese market'.[20]

The two reports drew a reassuring picture of adequate safeguards for British industries, greater opportunities for British manufacturers in Japan, and the added comfort of knowing that the low-cost Commonwealth countries and territories were not of immediate threat to British manufacturing concerns.

The resumption of talks

With a definite negotiating position approved by the EPC, Britain was ready to resume the commercial treaty negotiations which recommenced on 9 May. British officials planned to offer MFN rights and the revocation of Article 35 of the GATT, on the condition that the two sides drew up two sensitive lists made up of indefinite and definite safeguards, which would be excluded from GATT arbitration. The negotiations lasted for two months. By their conclusion, the Japanese negotiators had proposed two counter-proposals against disruptive Japanese imports. Alternative A envisioned the British revocation of Article 35 and the full establishment of GATT relations in principle. The arrangement would be qualified by a bilateral arrangement, which would remain in force until a solution on market disruption could be reached within the GATT framework.[21] In the interim period, any dispute that arose between the two countries would be referred to the GATT and the resultant ruling would override any provision in the bilateral arrangement. Alternative B saw Britain maintaining Article 35 against Japan, but for bilateral safeguards to be activated for three years with one-year renewals thereafter until Japan could resolve her concerns regarding market disruption.[22]

The Board of Trade studied the two counter-proposals. It concluded that the former, with modifications, was in principle more advantageous to Britain. The rationale behind this assessment was that granting permanent MFN rights to Japan at the present stage would set the stage for Britain's entry into the Japanese market ahead of the full opportunities which were expected to arise in the next ten-to-fifteen years. Alternative A was also expected to remove the constant irritation experienced by the two countries due to the lack of formal commercial relations.[23] The only modification that the Board of Trade wished to see made to alternative A was the exclusion of GATT arbitrational power over any disputes that arose in regard to the list of safeguards.[24] The recommendation was discussed in Cabinet ahead of the resumption of the treaty negotiations on 14 December, and it was approved as Britain's formal negotiating position.[25] Britain's position was communicated to Japan on the same day. The Japanese negotiators expressed surprise at Britain's willingness to revoke Article 35 of the GATT, but were concerned that indefinite safeguards might cause difficulties because this ran counter to the general trend towards market liberalisation. The Japanese also expressed uncertainty about the exclusion of GATT arbitration from the safeguards.[26] The negotiations were adjourned at the end of the year but did not resume immediately in 1961. British negotiators, who were keen to see further progress in the talks, were concerned that for the first half of 1961 no formal Japanese reply was forthcoming.

The deadlock in the talks was lifted as a result of a visit by the Japanese Foreign Minister, Kosaka Zentarô, in early July. His visit had been scheduled as a reciprocal gesture to Macmillan's tour of Japan, but the latter's postponement of his trip heightened the significance of the former.[27] A range of issues was up for discussion, including Japan's trade with China, the possibility of a closer political and economic cooperation on Africa, and Japanese membership of the OECD.[28] The most important item, in terms of the commercial treaty, was to seek the official Japanese response to Britain's proposal and ensure continued progress in the talks.

Kosaka's position was more positive than had been expected. He was willing to accept the proposal to waive GATT arbitration from the proposed sensitive list on condition that a time limit was applied. He argued that a timeless safeguard would 'perpetuate discrimination against them and would detract' from the revocation of Article 35.[29] Kosaka then proposed that a safeguard be included as a provision of the treaty, which would be valid for five years with the possibility of annual automatic renewals.[30]

The proposal was raised for discussion at the end of July in the EPC. There were obvious concerns about the consequences of a safeguard with a time limit, especially as it concerned Japanese competition. The President of the Board of Trade reassured concerned committee members that Britain would be eligible to re-impose quantitative import restrictions, or to introduce some form of voluntary export restrictions, if Japanese imports proved to be causing serious injury to British domestic manufacturers. The committee approved the proposal on the condition that the vulnerable industries concurred with the revised limitation of the safeguards.[31] The Cabinet endorsed the conclusions of the EPC in early August.[32]

The government's efforts to win industry over to its policy came to fruition with Sir Norman Kipping's trip to Japan in October. Kipping, Director-General of the Federation of British Industries (FBI), felt compelled to visit Japan and witness its economic development for himself, because of the increasing number of reports he was receiving from industrialists who had seen the rapid pace of Japanese industrial advancement. He also wanted to assess what lay ahead for Britain as a result of the reciprocal opening of markets that would follow the successful negotiation of a commercial treaty.[33] Kipping returned to Britain with a positive impression of Japan, and believed that the prevailing Japanese image in the United

Kingdom, as a manufacturer of cheap textiles and a country that had a propensity to make copyright infringements, was outdated by twenty years.[34] He published an account of his visit in a report entitled *A Look at Japan*, which was read widely in Britain and underscored the fact that Japan was 'no longer a low-wage country'.[35] Kipping thus became a strong supporter of government policy, and helped ease the industrial obstacles in the way of trade liberalisation with Japan.

When Anglo-Japanese commercial negotiations were resumed in November, the negotiators concentrated their efforts almost entirely on the sensitive list of goods and the safeguard proposal. The talks progressed slowly because of difficulties over the wording of the safeguard proposal. The problem lay not so much in that this was modelled after Article 19 of the GATT, where either signatory could resort to action if consultation did not lead to a settlement.[36] The difficulty lay in Japan's desire to insert a phrase that alluded to the possibility of the transfer of the issue to the GATT, in order to maintain some linkage with the organisation 'if only for reasons of presentation'.[37] Thus both sides struggled to link action arising from the protocol that could be referenced to the GATT, and also to find an article of the GATT that would accept such reference. The Japanese Embassy in London had no GATT experts on its staff, which compounded British frustrations. In the end, the two sides decided to adjourn for the year and to resume the negotiations early in 1962.[38] Once the talks recommenced in February, a solution was reached whereby Japan would drop her reference to the GATT if Britain, in exchange, gave up its insistence that the GATT should not apply to the safeguards. In place of the GATT reference, the two sides would exchange secret notes, which would reinforce the mutual agreement not to rely on the GATT as arbiter in any difficulties that arose in regard to the items of the sensitive list.[39]

The negotiations adjourned again in mid-May to enable British negotiators to prepare for Anglo-Russian talks. This was followed by further interruption due to the holidays planned by the two key British negotiators, Hughes and Taylor. Thus negotiations were not expected to recommence until June at the earliest. The negotiations were far from complete, with outstanding issues concerning the sensitive list, the safeguard proposal and the treaty articles. Japanese negotiators realised that their window of opportunity was narrowing, given that British ministers were expected to be fully occupied from September with European Economic Community matters. Japan wanted negotiations completed in time for Ikeda to attend the treaty signing ceremony during his UK visit in November.

These concerns were broached during the President of the Board of Trade's visit to Japan in late April and early May. The Japanese felt that transferring the sensitive list negotiations to Tokyo might expedite the completion of the treaty. Ohno repeated this view again in June. Britain resisted his overtures, but as a compromise decided that Hughes, Taylor and Russell should go to Tokyo and complete all outstanding general article questions between 16 July and 16 August. The discussion on the sensitive list and the safeguard protocol remained in London.[40]

Outstanding articles discussed in Tokyo

The key outstanding issues in the general articles that were discussed during the British negotiators' one-month stay in Tokyo were also the most difficult. They were, as expected, shipping, national treatment of foreign firms, and the colonies. Shipping had been an ongoing problem since the preliminary stage of the negotiations. Britain was particularly concerned with evidence of Japanese government shipping subsidies, which made equitable competition impossible. British shipping concerns pressed the Ministry of Transport to stem such practices in conjunction with the treaty negotiations. By 1961, however, the British government had revised its position on shipping subsidies because it saw merit in ensuring future protection for British shipping against flag- and other forms of discrimination.[41] Negotiators discussed the possibility of a secret agreed minute, but decided against it and later resisted Japanese pressure to have the treaty define what constituted reasonable government financial assistance, in order to discourage Japan's use of such assistance.[42] Another point of difference concerned Japan's insistence on controlling shipping remittance for balance of payment reasons. The Japanese argument reflected a view that had been voiced in Britain in 1956, when the British had been grappling with the same issue, but Britain remained adamant that exceptions could not be made to Japanese remittance.[43]

The other bone of contention concerned Japan's intention to protect her seas from competition and Britain's wish for 'free trade in ocean shipping'.[44] Japan was not concerned with British competition but with competitors in Southeast Asia, when she expressed her intention to protect her seas from other flags. In the end, the two sides agreed to an unpublished agreed minute, which ran as follows:

> The Contracting Parties affirm the principle that there should be complete freedom of opportunity for ships of all flags and regard the general acceptance of this principle as a common objective. They recognise, however, that the need to negotiate arrangements with certain countries pursuing discriminatory policies may make it very difficult to observe this principle in all circumstances.[45]

National treatment was another difficult issue for the two sides. National treatment obliged the signatories of a treaty to treat any goods or services that entered the other signatory's country equal to or no worse than domestic products. The underlying premise of this regulation was to prevent the importing country from using 'domestic tax and regulatory policies' as protectionist measures against the imported product once it had cleared customs or border procedures. In the same way, if national treatment was granted to companies in a commercial treaty, as it was extended to the United States in Article 7 of the Friendship, Commerce and Navigation (FCN) treaty of 1953, foreign companies were to be treated equally to domestic companies with 'respect to engaging in all types of commercial, industrial, financial and other business activities within the territories of the other party'.[46] In reality, however, foreign direct investment into Japan was restricted by the foreign investment law (FIL) of 1950, which limited foreign investment in three key areas: 'corporate stocks and proprietary interests; validation of all technological assistance contracts covering a period in excess of one year and finally all loans between foreign investors and Japanese persons where foreign exchange was a consideration'.[47] The contradiction between the two documents led to annual rows between America and Japan over limits to foreign direct investment.[48]

By the time Britain was ready to negotiate its treaty with Japan, the latter had misgivings about Article 7 of the US-Japan FCN treaty, viewing it as a 'mistake', and was not prepared to extend 'national treatment' to UK companies.[49] Japan was reluctant to even provide MFN treatment for British companies, but finally acquiesced on the condition that most-favoured-nation treatment was explicitly stated in Article 13 of the treaty pertaining to the introduction of foreign capital and technology.[50] Thus Article 6 of the treaty was to read that Japan would 'accord treatment not less favourable than that accorded to the companies of *any other foreign country*' in ' matters relative to the carrying on all of kinds of business' and in terms of personnel hired 'for the operation of any company' (see Appendix 4). Lastly, the term 'fair and equitable treatment' was dropped from the British version of the Article at MITI and MOF's insistence, because they were not willing to commit themselves to a vague and ill defined term, which could involve them in 'needless friction' with the United Kingdom. As a compromise, however, the Japanese side agreed to the inclusion of the phrase in the treaty's preamble.[51]

Another difficult issue concerned extension of the treaty's provisions to the colonies. Japan's objections were for both political and economic reasons. Politically, Japan was worried that the PRC might use the freedom of entry granted to Hong Kong citizens to send subversive political activists to Japan via the British colony.[52] No amount of assurances from British negotiators could lessen this anxiety. Economically, difficulties arose because the Board of Trade and the Colonial Office presumed that all agreed provisions of the commercial treaty would apply to Britain's colonies. As an extension of this view, they naturally expected that any safeguards that were extended to Britain would be extended to the colonies. For example, if a colony relied on exports of rubber sandals to Britain for its livelihood, Japan should voluntarily limit its exports of that product. Japanese negotiators held out on the issue until they decided that colonial safeguards were permissible subject to two limitations. They insisted that all safeguards should be confined to goods traditionally sold in the market concerned, and that the safeguards would only be applicable if the colonies acceded to the treaty.[53] Later, Japan caused further headaches for the British negotiators by insisting that safeguards could only be extended to colonies that revoked Article 35 of the GATT.[54]

The sensitive list

Of the two topics that remained in London, the one that caused protracted negotiations was the sensitive list. The sensitive list became a tricky issue for both sides because of differences in perspective. Britain envisioned the sensitive list as one of items that could be harmed by Japanese competition in the future as well as those that were in immediate danger. Japan was only willing to accept a list of products that would most definitely suffer from Japanese competition. By May 1962, the ongoing Japanese liberalisation, and pressure on Britain for reciprocity through the annual trade arrangements, had led to reductions in the scope of the British sensitive list. But these reductions were not satisfactory to the Japanese, and proposals and counterproposals were exchanged about which items would remain on the final list. In April, Japan submitted a revised proposal, which was another drastically reduced list of items. The new President of the Board of Trade, Frederick Erroll, who replaced Maudling in April, raised the issue at the EPC, where he recommended his counter-proposal to the Japanese list.

In his memorandum, Erroll listed his recommendations on the Japanese counter-proposals. He recommended immediate liberalisation of photographic equipment, clocks and golf balls. A liberalisation date was set for cigarette lighters, sewing machines and fishing tackle. Items without liberalisation dates included cutlery and netting.[55] The most difficult items on the sensitive list were textiles. The Board of Trade had hoped to include all textiles and textiles manufactures on the sensitive list without discrimination, but Japanese opposition to blanket protection led to an enforced culling of textiles items. Thus various items such as woollen textiles, cotton and rayon pieces, and silk and linen yarns were excluded from the sensitive list.[56] The one vocal industry which refused to accept liberalisation was the woollen textiles industry, which cited misleading labelling and Japanese government subsidies such as the export link system as some of the reasons why woollen textiles should be protected from Japanese competition. This led, on the one hand, to the Board of Trade's exchange with the Japanese, who refused to liberalise their woollen cloth import restrictions without British reciprocity, and to meetings with woollen textiles representatives on the other. The Board of Trade's insistence that the woollen textiles industry was not in immediate danger from Japan caused anger, and a delegation from the industry requested a meeting with Macmillan on 11 July.[57] The wool delegation's argument convinced Macmillan that the industry should be protected from Japanese competition. The issue was therefore discussed in Cabinet, where ministers agreed that woven woollen cloths would be included in the sensitive list but that 'wool tops, yarns and garments of woven cloth would be excluded from it'.[58] On hearing Britain's decision on woollen cloths, Japan decided to exclude woollen cloths from their 1964 liberalisation list.[59]

The final safeguard and the commercial treaty

The final safeguard agreement between Britain and Japan was valid for six years, the same duration as the commercial treaty. It consisted of two lists of sensitive items: the first was restricted under voluntary export controls and the other was under British import control supervision. Sensitive items under voluntary export control consisted of items that were deemed to cause serious injury to British domestic industries if imports were not restrained by voluntary export controls. The list consisted of sensitive items and their respective import quotas for three years following the signing of the treaty. A liberalisation date of 1 January 1966 was set for woven and knitted silk fabrics and radio and television apparatus. Other items without a set date were to be freed from import restrictions by 1968. Japan became the administrator of these voluntary export controls (see Appendix 5). Sensitive items under import controls were items that were deemed less sensitive, thus corresponding liberalisation dates of 1964 to 1968 were attached to all the items.

Since both sides agreed to settle any disputes outside of the GATT framework, general rules of safeguard were stipulated in the final document. The wording of the rules was based upon Article 19 of the GATT, whereby either government could notify the other of competition that caused or threatened serious injury to producers of 'like or competitive products'. The two governments would enter into consultation 'with a view to finding a mutually acceptable solution, not later than seven days after notice is given'. Both governments agreed that restrictions could be imposed upon the product in question if no settlement could be reached 'after thirty days of consultation'. Counter-action was permissible under the agreement, but the overall spirit of the clause was to encourage both sides to remedy the injury and to 'discontinue it when the situation has been rectified'.[60]

The Anglo-Japanese Commercial Treaty was signed on 14 November 1962. Both Macmillan and Ikeda were present at the signing ceremony in London. Ohno signed the agreement on behalf of Japan while Lord Home and Erroll signed for Britain. The treaty was signed with great expectations of expanded commercial and trade relations. On the same day, the two prime ministers released a joint communiqué expressing the 'hope that as well as expanding trade between the two countries, the Treaty would mark the opening of closer relations in all fields including political and economic'.[61]

An assessment of the commercial treaty and the revocation of Article 35

Britain's decisions to extend *de jure* MFN rights to Japan and to revoke Article 35 of the GATT were based on the Board of Trade's premise that

Britain would be better prepared to enter the Japanese market and take advantage of Japan's extraordinary economic growth under a formal commercial treaty. However, an analysis of British exports to Japan in the period after the signing of the treaty shows that the presence of a formal treaty did not affect Britain's penetration of the Japanese market. Britain's share of Japan's total imports hovered between 1 and 3 per cent between 1961 and 1998.[62] Furthermore, the Board of Trade's hopes of penetrating the Japanese market through technology transfers did not lead to incremental results. Prior to 1970, there were only sixteen wholly owned British companies in Japan and thirty-one joint ventures.[63] Britain's share of cumulative FDI between 1950 and 1995 was a low 4.3 per cent of the total.[64]

There are many reasons why Britain was never able to take advantage of the so-called Japanese economic miracle. Most scholars agree that several factors were concerned, such as the stringent screening of all direct investment into Japan with a strong preference for projects that involved technology that Japan needed but could not obtain. All too often, Britain did not necessarily have the technology that Japan sought. There were some successes by British firms in the 1950s in the automotive, pharmaceutical and petroleum industries, but these were few and far between.[65] Another major factor was the United States' early dominance in the postwar Japanese market. Not only did the US industries have deeper pockets, but government-industry ties ensured American dominance. A good example of US government-corporate relations would be the World Bank loan fostered by the US government to three electric power companies in 1953. The loan 'gave an unusually favourable position to Westinghouse and General Electric and assured them an early position in the postwar Japanese market'.[66] This sort of thing made British market penetration extremely difficult. Such obvious disadvantages, however, do not tell the whole story. Attempts were made in the 1960s by government officials to stimulate greater British export activity to Japan, with the organisation of trade fairs in Tokyo, but these produced only short-term gains.[67] The fact was that British firms were simply not interested enough to persevere and break into the Japanese market. This lack of interest was apparent in the paucity of senior British businessmen actively exploring the Japanese market, a lack of follow-through after overtures to Japanese industries, and ineffective FBI representation in Japan due to a part-time incumbent who was not only inexpensive but also ineffective.[68] There was some legitimacy in the lack of follow-through, which was a result of fears that the Japanese would infringe copyright laws and implement cut-throat business practices, as well as the simple fact that British manufacturers were simply committed to orders from elsewhere. When opportunities for extensive trade with Japan did arise, however, not enough was done to guarantee continued relations and bring such opportunities to fruition. Some of the fault lay in poor preparation and an inability to understand the workings and customs of Japanese business. But there was also just plain 'poor marketing and low quality of goods'.[69]

Those who did manage to penetrate the Japanese market were eventually worn down by the difficulties of doing business in Japan, and tended to lose enthusiasm. In the final analysis, the British failure to penetrate the Japanese market was due not to external factors, but to British firms' lack of competitiveness compared to their American, Swiss and West German counterparts.[70]

Conclusions

The period between 1960 and 1962 saw Britain's aggressive efforts at normalising commercial relations with Japan. The combined effect of Japan's rapid economic growth and trade liberalisation was mesmerising to the British government, which saw great market potential for British manufactured goods in Japan. To that end, great efforts were made to ensure that Britain had equal opportunity for trade. Throughout the negotiating process, the Board of Trade requested piecemeal British liberalisation measures in order to keep up with the rapid pace of Japan's trade liberalisation.

The drastic shift in the Board of Trade's policy towards Japan meant that many of the industries that had traditionally received support and protection no longer received the same level of support. In weighing the balance between opportunity and threat, the Board of Trade realised that supporting market opportunities was the better course of action. The unfortunate fact behind the Board of Trade's shift of policy was that in its eagerness to embrace the economic opportunities offered by trade with Japan, the Board failed to carry the key industries along with it, thus Britain's policy remained directed from above and did not establish a firm foundation at grassroots level.

10 Conclusions

The aim of this study has been to illustrate the fact that Britain's role in Japan's economic recovery was not entirely obstructionist, as has often been thought. It argues that Britain contributed subtly to Japan's economic recovery through its insistence that Japan terminate its dollar convertibility and base its trade and payments with the Sterling Area in inconvertible sterling. By succeeding in this, Britain was able to convert Japan from a marginal hard currency country to a soft currency country, thus establishing a solid foundation for expanded trade relations between Japan and the rest of the Sterling Area.

Britain's contribution to Japan's economic recovery has been obscured for the most part by its discriminatory tariff and commercial policies towards Japan in the 1950s. This book has argued that in order to understand Britain's contribution to Japan's economic recovery, the two strands of Britain's intertwined policies towards Japan – the sterling and the commercial – must be separated and understood in their independent contexts in order to appreciate Britain's policy objectives as they related to Japan.

Throughout this book it has been argued that Anglo-Japanese trade relations took on a greater significance because of Britain's role as head of the Sterling Area. Britain was not only responsible for negotiating the annual Sterling Payments Agreement on behalf of its members, but was also in charge of administering the smooth running of the agreement. Management of the Sterling Payments Agreement was conducted by denizens of mid-ranking officials and administrators from the Board of Trade, the Treasury, the Foreign Office and the Bank of England. Together they ensured that the payments agreement ran according to its annual projections and expectations. But the time and investment that went into the management of the Sterling Payments Agreement on behalf of the countries and territories that wished to trade with Japan, far outstripped the actual value of Japanese trade to Britain.

From the beginning, managing the agreement meant that a hierarchy of objectives existed in which the most important were those that related to the Sterling Area at large, followed by those that were specific to the Japanese account, and last were those that related to Anglo-Japanese trade relations.

The overarching objectives of the Sterling Area were to conduct orderly trade that did not lead to a dollar drain from the central reserves in London. British officials remained cautious about the Japanese account because of concerns that Japan would opt to re-insert dollar convertibility into the agreement; thus there was a strict adherence to balanced trade.

In terms of Sterling Area-Japan relations, the key objective was to encourage expanded trade relations between the Asian Sterling Area countries and Japan. From the beginning, British officials were aware that the payments agreement benefited sterling countries and territories in the Asia-Pacific region more than it did Britain, because of Japan's demand for raw materials and the Sterling Area's need for inexpensive manufactured goods. As a result, attempts were made within the limits of the agreement to expand trade relations between Japan and Sterling Area countries in Asia, which led to visible trade relaxations by the mid-1950s.

The second British objective was to familiarise Japan with the 'rules of engagement' associated with the Sterling Payments Agreement. The first two years of the agreement were peppered with misunderstandings and miscommunications which tested the patience of both British and Japanese officials. Moreover, Japan approached many of the rules with caution and was tentative about the use of administrative transferability because she feared that third country transfers would lead to excessive sterling accumulation. These problems aside, Britain was able to promote Japan to a transferable account country by 1954, and by 1955 Japan was using sterling for third country transfers.

Anglo-Japanese trade represented only a small percentage of overall Sterling Area trade. As such, it received less attention during the formative years of the agreement. Britain imported cotton cloths for re-export, canned salmon and other foodstuffs from Japan, while Japan imported machinery, machine parts, automobiles, oil and chemicals from the United Kingdom. Bilateral trade levels remained flat, with little increase in market share over the course of the decade due to quantitative restrictions, which limited the maximum level of imports that could enter the respective countries. Britain exercised import controls through a licensing system, and Japan had a reciprocal system of controls known as automatic approvals and fund allocations. These restrictions were justified on balance of payments reasons while the respective currencies remained inconvertible. In reality, these were thinly disguised attempts to protect each country's markets from foreign competition.

Had the Sterling Payments Agreement been the only nexus that governed Anglo-Japanese relations during the decade under review, Britain's contribution towards Japan's economic recovery would have been more obvious. What complicated the relationship was Britain's commercial policy towards Japan during the 1950s. Britain, like any other trading nation, wished to guarantee fair tariff treatment for its products so that high duties would not price them out of foreign markets. Britain had joined the GATT to ensure this basic principle. Britain realised that every trading nation deserved the same tariff advantages, but was unable to grant this basic trade principle to Japan in the postwar period. This was because of pressure from vocal domestic industries, particularly the Lancashire cotton industry, who feared a repetition of pre-war Japanese trade competition, which had seriously injured these industries by way of government subsidies, the dumping of goods and the use of cheap labour. British industry therefore exerted enormous pressure on the Board of Trade to ensure that Japan did not receive *de jure* MFN treatment.

This discriminatory policy was particularly evident in Britain's stance towards Japan's GATT entry. From the beginning, Britain attempted to prevent Japanese affiliation with the organisation because it wished to protect its traditional trading areas from injurious Japanese competition. Moreover, the GATT rules had specifically prohibited the adoption of new preferences by any member to protect its trading area against a fellow contracting party. The erosion of Commonwealth preferential duties meant that the existing preferences were inadequate safeguards against Japanese competition, thus Britain was compelled to block Japan's GATT entry until a solution could be devised.

Once the British realised that their obstructionist strategy would only succeed in the short-term, they decided to seek effective safeguards within the GATT framework. The period between 1952 and 1954 saw Britain flounder from one safeguard solution to another as it sought a viable mechanism that would both protect its domestic industry and also allow for Anglo-Japanese trade relations to be based on GATT principles. Britain explored various alternatives, from the Article 19 emergency clause to the Article 23 arbitration clause. All attempts at a safeguard solution failed, however, due to the GATT's inability to accept Britain's prerequisite condition for Japan's entry, namely the ability to take unilateral action against what it deemed as disruptive Japanese trade practices. Thus, by 1955, Britain had no other option left but to establish commercial relations on a bilateral basis, outside of the GATT multilateral trading system.

Once Britain had invoked Article 35 of the GATT against Japan, it initiated talks towards a bilateral Anglo-Japanese commercial treaty. Negotiations progressed slowly because there was little economic benefit in expediting the process. Japan's relative importance had always been linked with Britain's interests in Asia. Thus, once the negotiations became limited to an Anglo-Japanese context, Britain had little incentive to see them resolved. And so the wrangling continued for six years as officials exchanged views on differences in their respective treatment of foreign companies and nationals.

The aim of this book has been to illustrate that it was the protectionist component within Britain's trade policy that set precedence over other issues in Anglo-Japanese relations of the 1950s. This resulted in the shadow of protectionism – both perceived and actual – over Britain's sterling and commercial policies, thereby, clouding US and Japanese judgment of

Britain's objectives and intent. Thus those policies that were aimed at helping Japan toward economic recovery and increased inter-regional trade, such as Britain's sterling policy remained obscure. It even had the effect of spilling over to every other policy that might concern trade, such as the debacle over the Yoshida Letter as illustrated in Chapter 2.

The protectionist overtones had a negative effect on Anglo-Japanese diplomacy, which could not flourish because of the strains emanating from Britain's inability to accord favourable trading rights to Japan. An Anglo-Japanese cultural agreement was delayed until the 1960s, in part because formal commercial relations could not be established. The most obvious impact was, however, on those British industries that wished to enter the Japanese market, such as oil, pharmaceuticals, automobiles and chemicals. These industries received little institutional support for their endeavours, because many saw Japan as a manufacturer of cheap products and could not see a potential for British exports. There was little incentive to even visit Japan for exploratory missions to understand its market potential. Thus Britain lost its opportunity in the early postwar period to establish its businesses in the Japanese market. By the time Britain came to realise that there were significant export opportunities in Japan, it was lagging well behind the United States and Germany in many key export areas such as machinery, chemicals and technical assistance. Britain attempted to rectify this situation by expediting commercial relations with Japan in order to ensure equal opportunity for British industries. This aggressive policy had one flaw. It was entirely initiated by the British government and lacked the grassroots support of industry, due to the years of government disinterest, lack of infrastructure and deficient 'institutional' knowledge. Bilateral trade relations after *de jure* MFN rights had been granted therefore remained disappointingly low.

From a wider perspective, the book has considered a period when Western nations were coming to grips with changes in their political and economic influence in the postwar world. The United States found itself the most powerful nation in the Western world. It used this power in an attempt to protect the 'free' world from falling victim to communism, but it also attempted to use its power as leverage to force Western countries to abide by its own blue-print for the world. This included the adoption of the American containment policy and its vision of a multilateral trading system. Furthermore, the US attempted to force the Western bloc to apply a stringent economic embargo on strategic and non-strategic exports to the communist bloc. Western countries agreed to adopt the American-sponsored economic embargo for the duration of the Korean war and while they were in receipt of Marshall Aid. When both war and aid came to an end in 1953, the European powers, in particular, Britain, became restive and applied pressure on the United States to relax the communist embargo, since Japanese and German economic recovery meant increasing competition in the same, limited market. In 1954, COCOM controls were relaxed. CHINCOM controls remained unchanged in that year, but Britain unilaterally abolished the China differential on 27 May 1957. On 16 July of the same year, Japan announced that, as of 30 July, it would follow the British initiative and adopt COCOM levels to all trade with communist China. In June 1958, the Consultative Group declared that there would be a further relaxation on export controls to the communist bloc, and the two lists merged into one. Thus 1958 saw the end of the American-sponsored 'wedge' policy against China, and the US's attempts to enforce export controls on its allies, because all this was causing problems with the Western alliance.

In the postwar period, Japan faced the enormous task of restoring its economy and returning to the international community. Japan had realised from an early stage of the Allied occupation that her immediate future was explicitly linked with the United States. Thus she attempted to play a 'subordinate' role in her relationship with the United States, which meant relying on US economic charity. The United States, however, wished to see Japan become independent of its aid. Once Japan realised this, she began to place greater emphasis on her relations with the non-dollar countries. This included relations with the Sterling Area. Japan also set great store on her relations with Southeast Asia. Despite her ambition to form a peaceful 'greater co-prosperity sphere' under the aegis of the United States, Japan realised that she would have to act in an acceptable and orderly manner if she wished to normalise her relations with Southeast Asia. Thus she embarked on reparation payments to countries in the region, starting with Burma, Indonesia and the Philippines. Furthermore, the Japanese government understood that its investment and aid would be accepted more readily if this were supplied via international organisations; therefore it strove to become a member of various regional organisations. But despite Japan's attempts to return to the comity of nations, the process proved to be gradual. Moreover, by the late 1950s the United States had become less than enthusiastic about increased Japanese influence in Southeast Asia, and dampened repeated Japanese overtures for the consolidation of the region under its economic aegis, opting for the continued fragmentation of the region. Consequently, the 1950s saw the Japanese government concentrate its efforts on increasing domestic demand for its manufactured goods. Moreover, Japan strengthened its economic ties with the United States. Indeed its decision to rely on the American market was due to a combination of disappointment with the Sterling Area's readiness to open its markets to Japan and Southeast Asia's inability to consume Japanese goods in great quantities.

Britain, too, had an enormous economic task ahead, as it sought to find a solution to its balance of payments problems. Politically, it was in search of a role. Unable to attain superpower status, it sought to carve out an economic and political power base which would enable it to continue to influence world affairs. The solution was the Sterling Area and the Commonwealth. Despite Britain's attempts to strengthen its economic foundation in the 1950s, convertibility failed to restore sterling as a major currency, and the Suez debacle served to highlight sterling's weakness. By the late 1950s, with much of its global influence undermined, Britain had decided to withdraw from east of Suez, and now focused on maintaining its position as the leading ally of the United States in Europe, by attempting to join and play a key role in the European Economic Community.

Appendix 1

**Sterling Payments Agreement between the Government of the
United Kingdom of Great Britain and Northern Ireland and the
Government of Japan**

Tokyo, 31st August, 1951

The Government of the United Kingdom of Great Britain and Northern
Ireland (hereafter referred to as 'the Government of the United Kingdom')
and the Government of Japan

Have agreed as follows:

Article 1   All payments between residents of Japan and residents of the
Scheduled Territories, other than such as must necessarily be
made in yen, shall be settled in sterling.

Article 2   The Government of Japan will ensure that their appropriate
authorities shall buy and sell sterling and that the rates of those
authorities for sterling and for the United States dollar shall be
related to one another at the middle rate quoted by the Bank of
England for the United States dollar.

Article 3   All sterling payments to residents of Japan which residents of the
Scheduled Territories or of countries outside the Scheduled
Territories are permitted to make under the Exchange Control
Regulations in force in the United Kingdom shall be made to
Japanese Accounts.

Article 4   (1) The Government of the United Kingdom shall not restrict the
transfer of sterling which is at the disposal of residents of Japan
to other residents of Japan or to residents of the Scheduled
Territories. (2) The Government of the United Kingdom shall not
restrict the availability of sterling under the control of the
Japanese Foreign Exchange Control Board for making payments
in respect of direct current transactions to residents of such countries (other than Japan and the Scheduled Territories) as may be
agreed between the Bank of England and the Japanese Foreign
Exchange Control Board.

Article 5   The Government of Japan shall not restrict the acceptance by
residents of Japan of sterling from residents of the Scheduled

Territories and, as regards payment in respect of direct current transactions from residents of such countries (other than Japan and the Scheduled Territories) as may be agreed between the Bank of England and the Japanese Foreign Exchange Control Board.

Article 6   In so far as the Japanese Exchange Control Regulations from time to time permit, the Government of Japan will facilitate the transfer of yen accruing to residents of the Scheduled Territories from permitted current transactions to other residents of the Scheduled Territories or to residents of Japan, and the transfer of such yen into sterling.

Article 7   For the purposes of the present Agreement –

(a)   the expression 'the Scheduled Territories' shall have the meaning from time to time assigned to it under the United Kingdom Exchange Control Act, 1947;

(b)   the expression 'Japanese Account' shall mean an account of a resident of Japan which is for the time being recognised by the Bank of England as a Japanese Account for the purposes of the present Agreement;

(c)   the expression 'payments in respect of direct current transactions: means payments in respect of transactions of the type defined in Article XIX (i) of the Articles of Agreement of the International Monetary Fund which are made by a principal resident in the country from which payment is made and which relate exclusively (1) to goods (other than gold bullion, gold coin or gold either in semi-manufactured or fully manufactured from) imported into, and for use or consumption in, that country and originating in the country to which payment is made or (2) to services rendered to residents in the former country by residents of the latter country.

Article 8   For the purposes of the present Agreement the Bank of England shall act as agent of the Government of the United Kingdom and the Japanese Foreign Exchange Control Board as agent of the Government of Japan.

Article 9   The present Agreement shall come into force upon the entry into force of a Peace Treaty between the Government of the United Kingdom and the Government of Japan, provided that the Agreement between the Government of the United Kingdom and the Supreme Commander for the Allied Powers acting in respect of Occupied Japan which came into force on 31st August, 1952, shall not previously have terminated. In the event, however, that notice of termination of the latter Agreement shall already have been given but not have expired, the present Agreement shall come into force only for the remainder of the period of such notice and shall then terminate, unless both Contracting Parties agree to the contrary. At any time after the entry into force of the present Agreement either Contracting Party may give notice to the other of its intention to terminate it and the present Agreement shall cease to have effect three months after the date of such notice. It shall terminate, unless both Contracting Parties agree to the contrary, on 31st August, 1952.

In witness whereof the undersigned, being duly authorised by their respective Government, have signed the present Agreement and have affixed thereto their seals.

Done at Tokyo this Thirty-first day of August, 1951, in duplicate.

For the Government of the United Kingdom of Great Britain and Northern Ireland	For the Government of Japan

GEORGE CLUTTON   SHIGERU YOSHIDA

Source: Sterling Payments Agreement between the Government of the United Kingdom of Great Britain and Northern Ireland and the Government of Japan (with Exchange of Notes) 31 August 1951, Parliamentary Papers Volume 31, Cmd 8602 599–604.

Exchange of notes

No. 1   The Acting United Kingdom Political Representative in Japan to the Japanese Minister for Foreign Affairs

United Kingdom Liaison Mission in Japan,
Tokyo, 31st August, 1951

M. le Ministre,

With reference to the Payments Agreement signed today between the Government of the United Kingdom of Great Britain and Northern Ireland and the Government of Japan, I have the honour to set out the understanding which has been reached on the subject of consultation between the parties to the Agreement during its currency in order to assist in its satisfactory operation.

To ensure the smooth working of the Agreement, the Government of the United Kingdom and the Government of Japan mutually recognise the desirability of keeping Japan's sterling balances within reasonable limits. In order that at all times Japan may hold sufficient sterling to meet her requirements, without, however, accumulating an excessive amount, having regard to all the circumstances, both parties will take all reasonable measures to prevent, or correct should it occur, any chronic imbalance of payments in either direction.

With this intention in mind the two parties have agreed, in addition to the informal consultation which will take place between the Government of the United Kingdom and the Government of Japan or their Agents under the Agreement in the normal course of its current operation, to meet at short notice, which maybe given by either party, in order to discuss any aspect of the development of the payments relationship between the two countries which may appear to call for special consideration.

I shall be grateful for your Excellency's confirmation of this understanding.

I avail, &c.

GEORGE CLUTTON

No. 2   The Japanese Minister for Foreign Affairs to the Acting United Kingdom Political Representative

The Gaimusho,
Tokyo, 31st August, 1951

Sir,

I have the honour to acknowledge the receipt of your Note of today's date reading as follows:

(as in No. 1)

I have pleasure in confirming that the understanding of your Government as set out in that Note corresponds to that of the Government of Japan.

I beg, & c.

SHIGERU YOSHIDA

No. 3   The Acting United Kingdom Political Representative in Japan to the Japanese Minister for Foreign Affairs

United Kingdom Liaison Mission in Japan
Tokyo, 31st August, 1951

M. le Ministre,

In connexion with the facilities which will be available to Japan on an administrative basis for transfers of sterling between Japan and countries outside the Scheduled Territories in settlement of direct current transactions during the currency of the Payments Agreement signed today between the Government of the United Kingdom of Great Britain and Northern Ireland

and the Government of Japan, I have the honour to inform your Excellency that, as an extension of these facilities, the United Kingdom

Exchange Control will, so long as that Agreement is in force, be prepared for its part to approve any transfer of sterling in settlement of direct current transactions from Japan to any country in the 'transferable account' system (comprising the countries listed in the Third Schedule to the United Kingdom Exchange Control (Payments) Order, 1950, as amended from time to time) or in the group of 'Other Countries' (comprising territories outside the Scheduled Territories and outside any of the territories specified in the schedules to the United Kingdom Exchange Control (Payments) Order, 1950, as amended from time to time), provided there is no objection on the part of the authorities in the receiving country to settlement in sterling.

I avail & c.

GEORGE CLUTTON

No. 4   The Japanese Minister for Foreign Affairs to the Acting United Kingdom Political Representative

The Gaimusho,
Tokyo, 31st August, 1951

Sir,

I have the honour to acknowledge the receipt of your Note of today's date reading as follows:

(As in No. 3)

I am glad to take note of its contents on behalf of the Government of Japan.

I beg, &c.

SHIGERU YOSHIDA

Source: (Sterling Payments Agreement between the Government of the United Kingdom of Great Britain and Northern Ireland and the Government of Japan [with exchange of notes] 31 August 1951, Parliamentary Papers Volume 31, Cmd 8602 599–604)

Appendix 2

The Yoshida Letter

Dear Ambassador Dulles,

While the Japanese Peace Treaty and the US-Japan Security Treaty were being debated in the House of Representatives and the House of Councillors of the Diet, a number of questions were put and statements made relative to Japan's future policy toward China. Some of the statements, separated from their context and background, gave rise to misapprehensions which I should like to clear up.

The Japanese Government desires ultimately to have a full measure of political peace and commercial intercourse with China which is Japan's close neighbour. At the present time it is, we hope, possible to develop that kind of relationship with the National Government of the Republic of China, which has the seat, voice and vote of China in the United Nations, which exercises actual governmental authority over certain territory, and which maintains diplomatic relations with most of the members of the United Nations. To that end my Government on November 17, 1951, established a Japanese Government Overseas Agency in Formosa, with the consent of the National Government of China. This is the highest form of relationship with other countries which is now permitted to Japan, pending the coming into force of the multilateral Treaty of Peace. The Japanese Government Overseas Agency in Formosa is important in its personnel, reflecting the importance which my government attaches to relations with the National Government of China, if that government so desires, a Treaty which will reestablish normal relations between the two Governments in conformity with the principles set out in the multilateral Treaty of Peace. The terms of such bilateral treaty shall, in respect of the Republic of China, be applicable to all territories which are now, or which may hereafter be, under the control of the National Government of the Republic of China. We will promptly explore this subject with the National Government of China.

As regards the Chinese Communist regime, that regime stands actually condemned by the United Nations of being an aggressor and in consequence, the United Nations has recommended certain measures against that regime, in which Japan is now concurring and expects to continue to concur when the multilateral Treaty of Peace comes into force pursuant to the provisions of Article 5 (a) (iii), whereby Japan has undertaken 'to give the United Nations every assistance in any action it takes in accordance with the Charter and to refrain from giving assistance to any State against which the United Nations may take preventive or enforcement action'. Furthermore, the Sino-Soviet Treaty of Friendship, Alliance and Mutual Assistance concluded in Moscow in 1950 is virtually a military alliance aimed against Japan. In fact there are many reasons to believe that the Communist Party in its program of seeking violently to overthrow the constitutional system and the present Government of Japan. In view of these considerations, I can assure you that the Japanese Government has no intention to conclude a bilateral Treaty with the Communist regime of China.

Yours sincerely,

SHIGERU YOSHIDA
Source: (Letter from the Prime Minister of Japan to Dulles, 24 December 1951, FRUS 1951, vol. 6, part I, 1438)

Appendix 3

The text of GATT Articles 19, 23, 25 and 35

Article 19 Emergency Action on Imports of Particular Products

1(a).   If, as a result of unforeseen developments and of the effect of the obligations incurred by a contracting party under this Agreement, including tariff concessions, any product is being imported into the territory of that contracting party in such increased quantities and under such conditions as to cause or threaten serious injury to domestic producers in that territory of like or directly competitive products, the contracting party shall be free, in respect of such product, and to the extent and for such time as may be necessary to prevent or remedy such injury, to suspend the obligation in whole or in part or to withdraw or modify the concession.

(b).   If any product, which is the subject of a concession with respect to a preference, is being imported into the territory of a contracting party in the circumstances set forth in sub-paragraph (a) of this paragraph, so as to cause or threaten serious injury to domestic producers of like or directly competitive products in the territory of a contracting party which receives or received such preference, the importing contracting party shall be free, if that other contracting party so requests, to suspend the relevant obligation in whole or part or to withdraw or modify the concession in respect of the product, to the extent and for such time as may be necessary to prevent or remedy such injury.

2.   Before any contracting party shall take action pursuant to the provisions of paragraph 1 of this Article, it shall give notice in writing to the CONTRACTING PARTIES as far in advance as may be practicable and shall afford the CONTRACTING PARTIES and those contracting parties having a substantial interest as exporters of the product concerned an opportunity to

consult with it in respect of the proposed action. When such notice is given in relation to a concession with respect to a preference, the notice shall name the contracting party which has requested the action. In critical circumstances, where delay would cause damage which it would be difficult to repair, action under paragraph 1 of this Article may be taken provisionally without prior consultation, on the condition that consultation shall be effected immediately after taking such action.

3(a).   If agreement among the interested contracting parties with respect to the action is not reached, the contracting party which proposes to take or continue the action shall, nevertheless, be free to do so, and if such action is taken or continued, the affected contracting parties shall then be free, not later than ninety days after such action is taken, to suspend, upon the expiration of thirty days from the day on which written notice of such suspension is received by the CONTRACTING PARTIES, the application to the trade of the contracting party taking such action, or, in the case envisaged in paragraph 1(b) of this Article, to the trade of the contracting party requesting such action, of such substantially equivalent concessions or other obligations under this Agreement the suspension of which the CONTRACTING PARTIES do not disapprove.

(b).   Notwithstanding the provisions of sub-paragraph (a) of this paragraph, where action is taken under paragraph 2 of this Article without prior consultation and causes or threatens serious injury in the territory of a contracting party to the domestic producers of products affected by such action, that contracting party shall, were delay would cause damage difficult to repair, be free to suspend, upon the taking of the action and throughout the period of consultation, such concessions or other obligations as may be necessary to prevent or remedy the injury.

Article 23   Nullification or Impairment

1.   If any contracting party should consider that any benefit accruing to it directly or indirectly under this Agreement is being nullified or impaired or that the attainment of any objective of the Agreement is being impeded as the result of
       (a) the failure of another contracting party to carry out its obligations under this Agreement, or
       (b) the application by another contracting party of any measure, whether or not it conflicts with the provisions of this Agreement, or
       (c) the existence of any other situation,

the contracting party, may with a view to the satisfactory adjustment of the matter make written representations or proposals to the other contracting party or parties which it considers to be concerned. Any contracting party thus approached shall give sympathetic consideration to the representations or proposals made to it.

If no satisfactory adjustment is effected between the contracting parties concerned within a reasonable time, or if the difficulty is of the type described in paragraph 1(c) of this Article, the matter may be referred to the CONTRACTING PARTIES. The CONTRACTING PARTIES shall promptly investigate any matter so referred to them and shall make appropriate recommendations to the contracting parties which they consider to be concerned, or give a ruling on the matter, as appropriate. The CONTRACTING PARTIES may consult with contracting parties, with the Economic and Social council of the United Nations and with any appropriate inter-governmental organization in cases where they consider such consultation necessary. If the CONTRACTING PARTIES consider that the circumstances are serious enough to justify such action, they may authorize a contracting party or parties to suspend the application to any other contracting party or parties of such concessions or other obligations under this Agreement as they determine to be appropriate in the circumstances. If the application to any contracting party of any concession or other obligation is in fact suspended, that contracting party shall then be free, not later than sixty days after such action is taken, to give written notice to the Executive Secretary to the CONTRACTING PARTIES of the intention to withdraw from this Agreement and such withdrawal shall take effect upon the sixtieth day following the day on which such notice is received by him.

Article 25   Joint Action by the Contracting Parties

Representatives of the contracting parties shall meet from time to time for the purpose of giving effect to those provisions of this Agreement which involve joint action and, generally, with a view to facilitating the operation and furthering the objectives of this Agreement. Wherever reference is made in this Agreement to the contracting parties acting jointly they are designated as the CONTRACTING PARTIES.

The Secretary-General of the United Nations is requested to convene the first meeting of the CONTRACTING PARTIES, which shall take place not later than March 1, 1948.

Each contracting party shall be entitled to have one vote at all meetings of the CONTRACTING PARTIES.

Except as other wise provided for in this Agreement, decisions of the CONTRACTING PARTIES shall be taken by a majority of the votes cast.

In exceptional circumstances not elsewhere provided for in this Agreement, the CONTRACTING PARTIES may waive an obligation imposed upon a contracting party by this Agreement; provided that any such decision shall be approved by a two-thirds majority of the votes cast and that such majority shall comprise more than half of the contracting parties. The CONTRACTING PARTIES may also by such a vote

    (i)   define certain categories of exceptional circumstances to which other voting requirements shall apply for the waiver of obligations, and

    (ii) prescribe such criteria as may be necessary for the application of this paragraph.

Article 35   Non-Application of the Agreement between particular Contracting Parties

This Agreement, or alternatively Article II of this Agreement, shall not apply as between any contracting party and any other contracting party if the two contracting parties have not entered into tariff negotiations with each other, and either of the contracting parties, at the time either becomes a contracting party, does not consent to such application.

The CONTRACTING PARTIES may review the operation of this Article in particular cases at the request of any contracting party and make appropriate recommendations.

Source: (General Agreement on Tariffs and Trade, Analytical Index: Guide to GATT Law and Practice, Geneva: GATT, 1994)

Appendix 4

**Treaty of Commerce, Establishment and Navigation between
the United Kingdom of Great Britain and Northern Ireland and
Japan (excerpts)**

Article 6

1   The companies of one Contracting Party shall in any territory of the
    other be accorded treatment not less favourable than that accorded to
    the companies of any other foreign country in all matters relative to the
    carring on all kinds of business, including finance, commerce, industry,
    banking, insurance, shipping and transport, as well as in all matters
    relative to the establishment and maintenance for such purpose of
    branches, agencies, offices, factories and other establishments appro-
    priate to the conduct of their business.
2   Neither Contracty Party shall in any territory enforce, as a condition
    for the operation of any company of the other, any requirements as to
    the nationality of the directors, adminstrative personnel, technicians,
    professional consultants, auditors or shareholders of that company
    more retrictive than requirements applied to the companies of any
    other foreign country.

Article 13

The nationals and companies of one Contracting Party shall be
accorded in any territory of the other treatment not less favourable than
that accorded to the nationals and companies of any other foreign
country with respect to the introduction of foreign capital or technology.
Source: (Treaty of Commerce, Establishment and Navigation between
the United Kingdom of Great Britain and Northern Ireland and Japan,
in *Parliamentary Papers*, vol. 38, Cmd 2085, 331–425)

Appendix 5

Annexes to the Board of Trade's government statement on the Anglo-Japanese Commercial Treaty

Annex A:

Japanese note concerning voluntary export control and British reply

November 12, 1962

My Lord,

I have the honour to propose to Your Lordship, on behalf of the government of Japan, that as a result of the consultation held between the representatives of our two Governments on orderly marketing of Japanese products in the United Kingdom, my government will, in accordance with laws and regulations in force in Japan, exercise voluntary export control on the exportation from Japan to the United Kingdom of the specific products enumerated in the list attached hereto.

I should be grateful if Your Lordship would be good enough to inform me that your Government have no objection to the above proposal.

I avail myself of this opportunity to renew to Your Lordship the assurances of my highest consideration.

KATSUMI OHNO

The attached list
1   Cotton yarn
2   Spun yarn of man-made fibres
3   Woven cotton fabrics, except for re-export
4   Woven man-made fibre fabrics, except for re-export
5   Woven and knitted silk fabrics:
     (a) Weighing less than 0.6 oz. per square yard
     (b) Weighing more than 1.9 oz. per square yard
6   Woven wool fabrics
7   Knitted fabrics and apparel (excluding gloves) of knitted, netted or crocheted material of cotton, wool or man-made fibres (including stockings and socks).

8 Outer garments (excluding gloves) and underwear of woven cotton, or man-made fibre fabrics or of silk fabrics weighing less than 0.6 oz. per square yard or more than 19 oz. per square yard: handkerchiefs, shawls, scarves and mufflers except those of silk weighing 0.6 oz to 1.9 oz. per square yard or of linen.

9 Knitted gloves and gloves of textile materials.

10 Miscellaneous textile articles, the following:
  (a) Lace and lace net and embroidery of all types;
  (b) Industrial goods of cotton; and
  (c) Narrow fabrics of all types and articles made therefrom

11 Textile secondary products wholly or mainly of cotton for household use.

12 Nets and netting

13 Radio and television apparatus and parts, the following:
  (a) Semi-conductors;
  (b) Transistorised radio reception apparatus;
  (c) Parts of transistorised radio reception apparatus; and
  (d) Transistorised television reception appartus

14 Domestic pottery (except articles of traditional Japanese design; and ceramic toys and parts thereof (Control to be operated as from 1st January 1968)

November 14, 1962

Your Excellency,

I have the honour to acknowledge the receipt of Your Excellency's Note of today's date on voluntary export control to be applied by the Government of Japan and to inform you that the Government of the United Kingdom have no objection to the proposal set out in your Note.

I have the honour to be, with the highest consideration,
Your Excellency's obedient Servant,

HOME

Annex B: items under voluntary export control: quotas and liberalisation
dates

Table A1

Item	Quotas (annual rate, £thousands)			Liberalisation date
	1963	*1964*	*1965*	
Cigarette lighters (other than thjose of precious metals) and parts	30	40		1.1.65
Knives, forks and spoons and parts thereof, containing iron or steel	50	100	160	1.1.66
Domestic sewing machines and parts (1)	350	600		1.1.65
Fishing tackle (excluding fish-hooks of metal and fishing reels of wood or metal)	50	100		1.1.65
Binoculars and parts (1)	100	200		1.1.65
Microscopes and parts (1) –				
(a) capable of a total magnification ×1,000 and above	60			1.1.64
(b) other		80		1.1.65
Toys and games and parts thereof (excluding ceramic toys and parts thereof and toys made wholly of celluloid, rubber or glass) –				
(a) metallic toys costing less than $3 f.o.b. per piece	500	700	1,000	1.1.68
(b) plastic toys	200	250		1.1.65
(c) others			275	1.1.66
Domestic pottery (except articles of traditional Japanese design); and ceramic toys and parts thereof –				1.1.68
(a) ceramic toys and parts thereof	50	75	100	
(b) other	200	250	300	

Annex C: Exchange of notes between the government of the United
Kingdom and the government of Japan constituting an agreement in accor-
dance with the second protocol concerning trade relations
November 14, 1962

Your Excellency,

I have the honour to refer to the recent discussion between representatives of the Government of the United Kingdom of Great Britain and Northern Ireland and the Goverenment of Japan relative to the Treaty of Commerce, Establishment and Navigation and the Second Protocol concerning Trade Relations signed today. It is the understanding of the Government of the United Kingdom that as a result of these discussions, agreement has been reached in the following terms:

The Government of the United Kingdom may continue to restrict imports of products originating in Japan shown in the first column of the attached schedule, subject to the following conditions:

(a)   During the period commencing on the date of coming into force of the Treaty and ending on 31st December, 1963, the government of the United Kingdom shall issue licences so as to allow importation of Japanese products at the annual rate indicated against each product in the column headed '1963'.

(b)   During succeeding years the amounts to be licensed annually for each product shall be those indicated in the appropriate column of the schedule.

(c)   Where no amounts are shown in the schedule for a year, the amounts to be licensed for that year will be determined, aiming at reasonable increase, under the agreement of the two Governments. If no agreement is reached on a higher level, the amounts to be licensed for that year shall be at least those agreed as the amounts for the preceding year; and

(d)   Restrictions may not be retained on any product after the date shown against that product in the column of the schedule under the heading 'Date of liberalisation'.

If the foregoing equally represents the understanding of the Government of Japan in this matter, I have the honour to propose, that the present Note together with Your Excellency's reply to that effect shall be regarded as constituting an Agreement between the two Governments concluded in accordance with the afore-mentioned Protocol and that it shall come into force on the date of coming into force of the Protocol.

I have the honour to be, with the highest consideration,

Your Excellency's obedient Servant,

HOME

Table A2

Item	Quotas (annual rate)			Liberalisation date
	1963	1964	1965	
Cotton yarn	nil	nil	nil	
Spun yarn of man-made fibres	£25,000	£25,000	£25,000	
Woven cotton fabrics, except for re-export	5.5 million square yards	6 million square yards	7 million square yards	
Woven man-made fibre fabrics, except for re-export	3 million square yards	3.6 million square yards	4.2 million square yards	
Woven and knitted silk fabrics:				
(a) weighing less than 0.6oz per square yard	300,000 square yards	400, 000 square yards	500,000 square yards	1.1.66
(b) weighing more than 1.9oz per square yard	200,000 square yards	300,000 square yards	450,000 square yards	
Woven wool fabrics	400,000 square yards	500,000 square yards	600,000 square yards	
Knited fabrics and apparel (excluding gloves) of knited, netted or crotcheted material of cotton, wool or man-made fibres (including stockings and socks)	£500,000	£600,000	£700,000	

Table A2 contd.

Outer garments (excluding gloves) and underwear of woven cotton, or man-made fibre fabrics or of silk fabrics weighing less than 0.6oz per square yard or more than 1.9oz per square yard: handkerchiefs, shawls, scarves and mufflers except those of silk weighing 0.6oz to 1.9oz per square yard or of linen.	£1,375,000 of which not more than £200,000 for cotton, £250,000 for silk	£1,625,000 of which not more than £250,000 for cotton, £300,000 for silk	£1,875,000 of which not more than £300,000 for cotton, £350,000 for silk
Knited gloves and gloves of textile materials	£125,000	£140,000	£160,000
Miscellaneous textile articles, the following: (a) Lace and lace net and embroidery of all types; (b) Industrial gods of cotton, and (c) Narrow fabrics of all types and articles made therefrom	£150,000 of which maximum to be: £40,000 for (a), £50,000 for (b), £60,000 for (c)	£180,000 of which maximum to be: £48,000 for (a), £60,000 for (b), £72,000 for (c)	£210,000 of which maximum to be: £56,000 for (a), £70,000 for (b), £84,000 for (c)
Textile secondary products wholly or mainly of cotton for household use	£100,000	£120,000	£140,000
Nets and netting	£40,000	£50,000	£100,000
Radio and television apparatus and parts, the following:			1.1.66
(a) semi-conductors	£200,000	£450,000	£700,000
(b) transistorised radio reception and apparatus	£500,000	£750,000	£1,200,000
(c) parts of transistorised radio reception apparatus	£200,000	£450,000	£700,000
(d) transistorised television reception apparatus	£225,000	£450,000	£600,000

November 14, 1962

My Lord,

I have the honour to acknowledge receipt of Your Lordship's Note of today's date, which reads as follows:

[Here follows text of Lord Home's Note]

I have the honour to inform Your Lordship that the foregoing equally represents the understanding of the government of Japan, who therefore regard Your Lordship's Note and the present Note as constituting an Agreement between the two Governments concluded in accordance with the Second Protocol concerning Trade Relations, the Agreement to come into force on the date of coming into force of the Protocol.

I avail myself of this opportunity to renew to Your Lordship the assurances of my highest consideration.

KATSUMI OHNO

Source: (Government statement on the Anglo-Japanese Commercial Treaty, *Parliamentary Papers*, vol. 31, Cmd 1875, 25–36)

Notes

1 Introduction

1 One of the first works on the subject, which has subsequently stood the test of time, is Jerome B. Cohen's *Japan's Postwar Economy*, Bloomington: Indiana University Press, 1958.
2 One example of such work is Chitoshi Yanaga , *Big Business in Japanese Politics*, New Haven and London: Yale University Press, 1968.
3 See for example Kanji Haitani, *The Japanese Economic System: An Institutional Overview*, Lexington: DC Heath and Company, 1976.
4 Ross Mouer and Yoshio Sugimoto, *Images of Japanese Society: A Study in the Structure of Social Reality*, London: KPI, 1986, 2–3.
5 The actual Sterling Area members consisted of Australia, New Zealand, South Africa, India, Pakistan, Ceylon, Burma, Iceland, Iraq, Jordan, Libya, Persian Gulf Territories and the British Colonies. See Catherine R. Shenk, *Britain and the Sterling Area: From Devaluation to convertibility in the 1950s,* London Routledge, 1994, 9.
6 Tôkyô Ginkô Chôsabu, *Tai Sterling Chiikibôeki no kôsatsu*, Tôgin Chôsashiryô dai 17 gô, July 1969 [Study on trade with the Sterling Area, Bank of Tokyo Research Department, Bank of Tokyo Research Study no. 17, July 1969] 4.
7 The figure can be misleading given that Hong Kong was also an entrepôt trading centre, thus the final destination of the exports was not necessarily a Sterling Area member in Southeast Asia.
8 See Thomas W. Zeiler, *American Trade and Power in the 1960s*, New York: Columbia University Press, 1992, 5–22.
9 Aaron Forsberg, *America and the Japanese Miracle: The Cold War Context of Japan's Postwar Economic Revival, 1950–1960*, Chapel Hill: University of North Carolina Press, 2000; Sayuri Shimizu, *Creating People of Plenty: The United States and Japan's Economic Alternatives, 1950–1960*, Kent OH: Kent State University Press, 2001. See also Walter Lafeber, *The Clash: US-Japanese Relations throughout History*, New York and London: Norton, 1997; and Burton I. Kaufman, *Trade and Aid Eisenhower's Foreign Economic Policy, 1953–1961*, Baltimore: Johns Hopkins University Press, 1982.
10 See Roger Buckley, *Occupation Diplomacy: Britain, the United States and Japan 1945-52,* Cambridge: Cambridge University Press, 1982.
11 See Peter Lowe, *Containing the Cold War in East Asia: British Policies towards Japan, China and Korea, 1948–53*, Manchester and New York: Manchester University Press, 1997.
12 R. P. T. Davenport-Hines and Geoffrey Jones (eds) *British Business in Asia since 1860*, Cambridge: Cambridge University Press, 1989; Christopher Madeley, 'A Case Study of Anglo-Japanese Cooperation in the Motor Vehicle Industry:

Ishikawajima, Wolseley, Isuzu and Rootes', in Janet E. Hunter and S. Sugiyama (eds) *The History of Anglo-Japanese Relations, 1600–2000: Volume 4, Economic and Business Relations*, London: Palgrave, 2002; John Weste, 'Facing the Unavoidable – Great Britain, the Sterling Area and Japan: Economic and Trading Relations, 1950–1960', in *ibid.*; and Marie Conte-Helm, 'Anglo-Japanese Investment in the Postwar Period', in *ibid.*

13 See for example P. J. Cain and A. G. Hopkins, *British Imperialism: Innovation and Expansion, 1688–1914* and *British Imperialism: Crisis and Deconstruction, 1914–1990*, London and New York: Longman, 1993.

14 Schenk, *Britain and the Sterling Area*; and John Singleton and Paul L. Robertson, *Economic Relations between Britain and Australasia, 1945–1970*, Hampshire: Palgrave, 2002.

15 Hosoya Chihiro, *San Francisco Kôwa e no Michi* [The Road to the San Francisco Peace Treaty], Tokyo: Chûô Kôrônsha, 1984; Kibata Yôichi, *Teikoku no Tasogare: Reisenka no Igirisu to Ajia* [The Twilight of the Empire: British Policy towards Japan and Malaya, 1947–1955], Tokyo: University of Tokyo Press, 1996.

16 See Akaneya Tatsuo, *Nihon no GATT Kanyû Mondai: Regîmu Riron no Bunseki Shikaku ni yoru Jirei Kenkyû* [The Problem of Japanese Accession to the GATT: A Case Study in Regime Theory], Tokyo: University of Tokyo Press, 1992.

17 See for example, Fukushima Teruhiko, 'Sengo Nihon no Bôeki Senryaku ni okeru Australia 1947–54' [Japan's Postwar Trade Strategy towards Australia, 1947–1954], in *Gendai Nihon Gaikô no Bunseki* [An Analysis of Japan's Foreign Diplomacy], eds Kusano Atsushi and Umemoto Testuya, Tokyo: University of Tokyo Press, 1995.

18 Junko Tomaru , *The Postwar Rapprochement of Malaya and Japan, 1945–61: The Roles of Britain and Japan in South-East Asia*, Hampshire: Macmillan, 2000, 159.

19 See ch. 3 of Nakamura Takafusa, *The Postwar Japanese Economy: Its Development and Structure, 1937–1994*, Tokyo: University of Tokyo Press, 1995, 53–108.

20 See Chalmers Johnson, *MITI and the Japanese Miracle: The Growth of Industrial Policy, 1925–1975*, Stanford: Stanford University Press, 1982; Daniel I. Okimoto, *Between MITI and the Market: Japanese Industrial Policy for High Technology*, Stanford: Stanford University Press, 1989; Laura E. Hein, *Fueling Growth: The Energy Revolution and Economic Policy in Postwar Japan*, Cambridge MA: Harvard University Press, 1990.

2   The Open Payments Agreement with Japan

1 See Robert Gilpin, *The Political Economy of International Relations*, Princeton: Princeton University Press, 1987, 127–31; James Foreman-Peck, *A History of the World Economy: International Economic Relations since 1850*, Hemel Hempstead: Harvester Wheatsheaf, 1995, 203–4.

2 Gilpin, *The Political Economy of International Relations*, 131.

3 Foreman-Peck, *A History of the World Economy*, 131.

4 For further detail on Anglo-American negotiations, see Richard Gardner, *Sterling-Dollar Diplomacy in Current Perspective: the Origins and the Prospects of our International Economic Order*, New York: Columbia University Press, 1980.

5 Foreman-Peck, *A History of the World Economy*, 240.

6 *Ibid.*, 242.

7 Disagreements between Britain and the United States on the rules of the charter led to the widening of 'loopholes' in the proposed rules until the charter no longer satisfied anyone. As a consequence, the Truman Administration decided not to submit the charter to Congress, which led to the demise of the ITO. See Gardner, *Sterling-Dollar Diplomacy*, 378.

184   *Notes*

8 Foreman-Peck, *A History of the World Economy*, 240.
9 The Lend-Lease Programme (1941–5) authorised the President to 'sell, transfer title to, exchange, lease, lend or otherwise dispose of any defence articles to any country whose protection seemed vital to the US security'. The terms of the settlement were to have some benefit to the United States. See Gardner, *Sterling-Dollar Diplomacy*, 55–6.
10 *Ibid.*, 199–208.
11 It should be noted that Lend-Lease payments were also settled during these negotiations. Over $20 billion was written off, and Britain was instead asked to pay $650 million at the same interest rate as the financial agreement. *Ibid.*, 205.
12 *Ibid.*, 313.
13 See Schenk, *Britain and the Sterling Area*, 9–10.
14 Gardner, *Sterling-Dollar Diplomacy*, 360.
15 See Marc Gallicchio, *The Cold War Begins in Asia: American East Asian Policy and the Fall of Japanese Empire*, New York: Columbia University Press, 1988, for the beginning of the Cold War in East Asia.
16 For this period of China's history, see Odd Arne Westad, *Cold War and Revolution: Soviet-American Rivalry and the Origins of the Chinese Civil War, 1944–1946*, New York: Columbia University Press, 1993; and Lanxin Xiang, *Recasting the Imperial Far East: Britain and America in China, 1945–1950*, London and New York: M. E. Sharpe, 1995.
17 Michael Schaller, *The American Occupation of Japan: the Origins of the Cold War in East Asia*, Oxford: Oxford University Press, 1985, 24.
18 See Stephen S. Large, *Emperor Hirohito and Shôwa Japan: A Political Biography*, London and New York: Routledge, 1992; and Herbert P. Bix, *Hirohito and the Making of Modern Japan*, New York: HarperCollins, 2000, concerning this topic.
19 Schaller, *The American Occupation of Japan*, 79.
20 *Ibid.*, 35.
21 Toru Nakakita, 'Trade and Capital Liberalization Policies in Postwar Japan' in *The Japanese Experience of Economic Reforms*, eds Jurô Teranishi and Yutaka Kosai, London: Macmillan, 1993, 333.
22 Schaller, *The American Occupation of Japan*, 179.
23 On Kennan's containment strategy, see John Lewis Gaddis, *Strategies of Containment: A Critical Appraisal of Postwar America National Security Policy*, Oxford: Oxford University Press, 1982, 25–53.
24 Foreman-Peck, *A History of the World Economy*, 242–3.
25 William S. Borden, *The Pacific Alliance: United States Foreign Economic Policy and Japanese Trade Recovery, 1947–1955*, Wisconsin: The University of Wisconsin Press, 1984. 70.
26 *Ibid.*, 71.
27 Howard Schonberger, *Aftermath of War: Americans and the Remaking of Japan, 1945–1952*, Kent OH: Kent State University Press, 1989, 209–10.
28 See Nakamura, *The Postwar Japanese Economy*, 40–1.
29 See Andrew J. Rotter, *The Path to Vietnam: Origins of the American Commitment to Southeast Asia*, Ithaca NY: Cornell University Press, 1987, 49–69.
30 Other factors also have to be taken into account when analysing Japan's competitive advantage over Britain's textiles industry. For example, the overvaluation of the pound in the 1920s and the devaluation of the yen in the 1930s which made Japanese textiles far more attractive to buyers. Japan had the advantage of a surplus unskilled labour force due to the rural depression in the late 1920s, whereas by this time Britain had developed other industries and so labour was more scarce and expensive. See Lars G. Sandberg, *Lancashire in Decline: A Study in Entrepreneurship, Technology and International Trade*, Columbus OH: Ohio State University Press, 1974, 213–16; see also Shimizu, Hiroshi *Anglo-Japanese*

Trade Rivalry in the Middle East in the Inter-war period, London: Ithaca Press, 1986, 31.

31 *Ibid.*, 38.

32 *Ibid.*, 54. See also John Sharkey's thesis, 'The Influence of British Business Interests on Anglo-Japanese Relations, 1933–1937', Ph.D. thesis, London School of Economics and Political Science, 1994, in which he argues that the imperial preferences were ineffective, 91.

33 In regard to the British perception in the 1930s, see Antony Best, *Britain, Japan and Pearl Harbor: Avoiding War in East Asia, 1936–41*, London and New York: Routledge, 1995, 39.

34 T. Nakamua, *The Postwar Japanese Economy*, 38.

35 Buckley, *Occupation Diplomacy*, 166.

36 Memorandum of the ONC, 21 June 1949, ON(49)220, CAB134/565, Public Record Office, Kew (hereafter PRO).

37 Memorandum of the ONC, 6 February 1948, ON(48)72, CAB134/558, PRO.

38 Memorandum of the ONC, 10 February 1948, ON(48)88, CAB134/558, PRO.

39 Minutes of the 74th meeting of the ONC, 29 July 1948, CAB 134/556, PRO.

40 Telegram from FO to Tokyo, 27 January 1948, FO371/69803 FI484/4/23, PRO. Final draft of the trade arrangement between certain countries in the Sterling Area and occupied Japan, 11 August 1948, pp. 65–68, subseries 1, *Nichiei Boeki Shiharai Ikken* [Japan-UK Trade Payments Agreement], reel B-0020, Public Release Series 8, Diplomatic Records on Microfilm (hereafter DRM), Japan Ministry of Foreign Affairs Archives, Tokyo (hereafter JMFAA).

41 Memorandum of the ONC, 27 May 1949, ON(49)186, CAB134/565, PRO.

42 Memorandum of the ONC, 10 February 1948, ON(48)88, CAB134/558, PRO.

43 See Alan S. Milward and George Brennan, *Britain's Place in the World: A Historical Enquiry into Import Controls, 1945–60*, London and New York: Routledge, 1996, 37–8. For background on Japanese import controls, see Tokyo Embassy to Department of State (hereafter DOS), 13 August 1959, Decinal File (DF) 394.41/ 8–1359 RG59, National Archives II, College Park, Maryland (hereafter NA).

44 *Ibid.*

45 See minutes of the 55th meeting of the ONC, 7 July 1949, CAB134/563 and the note by the working party, 10 October 1949, ON(49)331, CAB 134/567, PRO.

46 The inter-ministerial group was made up of representatives of the Board of Trade, the Foreign Office, the Treasury, the Ministry of Food, the Colonial Office, the Commonwealth Relations Office, the Bank of England and the Ministry of Supply.

47 Memorandum of the ONC, 16 July 1949, ON(49)242, CAB134/566, PRO.

48 See Schenk, *Britain and the Sterling Area*, 63.

49 Nakamura, *The Postwar Japanese Economy*, 40–1.

50 Johnson, *MITI and the Japanese Miracle*, 190.

51 They were the Foreign Advisory Trade Commission, the Logan and the IMF missions. See Borden, *The Pacific Alliance*, 96.

52 *Ibid.*

53 Memorandum attached to the minutes of the 10th Cabinet Far Eastern Committee, 10 October 1950, CAB134/289, PRO.

54 Minutes of the 40th meeting of the ONC, 5 May 1950, CAB134/568, PRO.

55 Note from Boehringer to DOS, 30 November 1950, DF 441.9431/11–3050, RG59, NA.

56 Minutes of meeting of the Japanese panel of the overseas policy committee of the Federation of British Industries, 12 April 1950, MSS.200/F/3/D2/1/12, Papers of the Federation of British Industries (hereafter FBI), Modern Records Centre, Warwick University (hereafter MRC).

57 Memorandum by the Board of Trade, 15 May 1950, ON(50)129, CAB 134/571, PRO.
58 *Ibid.*
59 *Ibid.*
60 *Ibid.*
61 Minutes of the 20th meeting of the EPC, 28 July 1950, CAB134/224, PRO.
62 Minutes of the fifth meeting of the EPC, 17 January 1950, CAB134/568, PRO.
63 Correspondence from Petch to Croome, 17 October 1949, T236/2854 OF63/119/07M, PRO.
64 *Ibid.*
65 *Ibid.*
66 *Ibid.*
67 Minutes of the 57th meeting of the ONC, 4 July 1950, CAB134/568, PRO.
68 A report on the IWA compiled by MOFA and the Ministry of Agriculture, Forestry and Fisheries, September 1951, 63–81, subseries 6, *Dai Hakkai Kokusai Komugi Kyôtei Kankei Ikken* [the eighth session of the IWA], reel B-0029, Public Release Series 8, DRM JMFAA.
69 Memorandum on Japan's accession to the International Wheat Agreement, 27 February 1950, SCAP Files Box 5979, RG331, NA.
70 After Japan's application was turned down in November, SCAP advised the Japanese government to seek IWA membership for 900,000 metric tons of wheat rather than the 12,000,000 metric tons it originally sought. This led to a debate within the Japanese government, especially between MITI and the Food Agency. The Food Agency sought the original supply of wheat from the IWA whereas MITI thought Japan should accept the new amount recommended by SCAP. Eventually it was agreed that Japan should settle for 900,000 metric tons. Kaiire Hoshôshûryô *Sakugen ni kansuru ken* [Report on the Reduction of Guaranteed Amount of Purchase], 3 December 949, pp. 201–208, subseries 3, *Dai Hakkai Kokusai Komugi Kyôtei Kankei Ikken* [the eighth session of the IWA], reel B-0029, Public Release Series 8, DRM, JMFAA.
71 Minutes of the first meeting of the EPC, 5 January 1950, CAB134/224, PRO.
72 Minute by Jackling, 10 January 1950, FO371/82973 UES1303/13, PRO.
73 *Kokusai Komugi Kyôtei e no Kanyû ni Kansuru Kaigi* [A meeting on Japan's Entry to the IWA], 25 May 1950, 284–287, subseries 5, *Dai Hakkai Kokusai Komugi Kyôtei Kankei* Ikken [the eighth session of the IWA], reel B-0029, Public Release Series 8, DRM, JMFAA.
74 Telegram from Washington DC to SCAP, 24 June 950, SCAP Files, Box 6805, RG331, NA.
75 Akaneya *Nihon no GATT Kanyû Mondai*, 92.
76 *Ibid.*, 88.
77 Conference between British Commonwealth and US Representatives on MFN Treatment for Japan, 10 November 1948, SCAP Files, Box 6725, RG331, NA.
78 A single exchange rate between the dollar and the yen was established from 25 April 1949, when the yen was set at 360 yen to the dollar. The yen was set at 1,450.8 yen to the pound from 24 June of the same year. See MOF (ed.) *Shôwa Zaiseishi: Shûsen kara kowa made vol. 15 (Shôwa Financial History: From the end of the war to the San Francisco Peace Treaty)* Tôkyô: Tôkyô Keizai Shinpôsha, 1976, 366.
79 Report on MFN treatment for Japan to the Under Secretary of the Army, 22 March 1950, attached to 394.31/3–3050, RG59, NA.
80 Memorandum by the President of the Board of Trade, 5 September 1950, EPC(50)87, CAB134/226, PRO.
81 *Ibid.*

82 In 1950, one of the leaders of the Japanese Communist Party, Nosaka Sanzô was criticised by the Cominform for his belief in the establishment of communism in Japan through peaceful and constitutional means. Thus there was a high probability that the Japanese Communist Party would resort to more revolutionary means. The outbreak of the Korean War meant that many of the occupation forces were dispatched to Korea. It provided an opportunity for the communists to increase their activity. A series of anti-occupation demonstrations in Japan led General MacArthur to shut down several communist newspapers for thirty days and to dismiss communists and communist sympathisers from various industries. See correspondence from A. Gascoigne to the Principal Secretary of State for Foreign Affairs, 18 March 1950, FO371/83807 FJ1017/27, PRO; correspondence from Chancery to the Far Eastern Department, 9 August 1950, FO371/8308 FJ1017/68, PRO.

83 Note by the FO, 14 September 1950, FO371/92065 UEE177/4, PRO.

84 Office memorandum from Allison to McClurkin, 21 July 1952, in FO371/99393 FJ1016/32, PRO.

85 Minutes of the 21st meeting of the EPC, 15 September 1950, CAB134/224, PRO.

86 Note by Milward, 20 September 1950, FO371/82965 UEE177/5, PRO.

87 Telegram from Torquay to DOS, 4 December 1950, DF 394.31/12–450, NA.

88 Robin Gray, 'The Anglo-Japanese Commercial Treaty: A British Perspective', in Ian Nish (ed.) *Britain and Japan: Biographical Portraits. Volume II*, Sussex: Japan Library, 1995, 311.

3   Embarking on the Sterling Payments Agreement

1 Michael Mastanduno, *Economic Containment: CoCom and the Politics of East-West Trade*, London and Ithaca NY: Cornell University Press, 1992, 83–4.

2 Telegram from Tokyo to FO, 6 July 1951, FO371/92642 FJ1121/1, PRO and Report from Singapore to DOS, 1 August 1951, DF 494.9731/8–151, NA.

3 The working party was made up of a central group of officials which consisted of the representatives of the Central Economic Planning Staff within the Economic Intelligence Department of the Foreign Office, the Overseas Finance Division of the Treasury and the Economic Section of the Cabinet Office. See Minutes of the Cabinet working party on long-term economic relations with Japan, 26 June 1950, GEN326/1 in Japan, OV16/63, Bank of England Archives (hereafter BoE).

4 Memorandum of the ESC on the long-term economic relations with Japan, 6 February 1951, ES(51)7, CAB134/264, PRO.

5 *Ibid.*

6 *Ibid.*

7 See note by the Chairman for the Cabinet working party on long term economic relations with Japan, 22 February 1951, GEN 326/13, CAB130/61, PRO and Minutes of the ONC, 23 February 1951, ON(51)9, CAB134/573, PRO.

8 Telegram from Washington to FO, 8 March 1951, FO371/92629 FJ1121/48, PRO.

9 See correspondence from Thomas to Serpell, 19 March 1951 and 21 March 1951 in T236/4130 OF63/208/05B, PRO.

10 Note from Boehringer to DOS, 6 April 1951, DF 441.9431/4–651, NA.

11 *Ibid.*

12 Report by the Bank of Japan enclosed in a note from Boehringer to DOS, 6 April 1951, DF 441.9431/4–651, NA.

13 *Ibid.*

14 *Ibid.*

15 *Ibid.*

16 The Bank of England believed that Thomas needed a Bank of England official with knowledge about the mechanics of sterling to be on the British team to negotiate the first Sterling Payments Agreement in East Asia. Note by G.M. Watson, 8 March 1951, OV16/70, BoE.
17 Note by the Treasury, ONC, 6 April 1951, ON(51)52, CAB134/574, PRO.
18 Correspondence from Thomas to Serpell, 23 July 1951, T236/4134 OF63/208/05F, PRO.
19 Telegram from Clutton to the FO, 9 August 1951, FO371/92634 FJ1121/180, PRO.
20 Correspondence from Thomas to Serpell, 30 April 1951, T236/4131 OF63/208/05C, PRO.
21 Peter Lowe, 'Herbert Morrison, the Labour Government, and the Japanese Peace Treaty, 1951', in 'Britain, the United States and Japan's Return to Normal, 1951–1972', *International Studies*, vol. 93, no. 258 (1993): 9.
22 Correspondence from Thomas to Serpell, 23 July 1951, T236/4134 OF63/208/05F, PRO.
23 See also Sterling Payments Agreement between the Government of the United Kingdom of Great Britain and Northern Ireland and the Government of Japan (with Exchanges of Notes), 31 August 1951, *Parliamentary Papers*, 1951–1952, vol. 31, 599–604.
24 A copy of the correspondence from UKLM to FO, 1 October 1951 in T236/4137 OF63/208/05I, PRO.
25 *Ibid.*
26 Correspondence from Loynes to Grafftey Smith, 31 July 1951, OV16/74, BoE.
27 Note from Boehringer to DOS, 26 April 1951, DF 441.94/4–2651, NA.
28 The drafting committee consisted of Kiuchi, Ishida and Yukawa on the Japanese side, Thomas and Loynes on the British side and a SCAP observer. Telegram from Tokyo to FO, 26 July 1951, FO371/92633 FJ1121/151, PRO.
29 Telegram from Grantham to the Secretary of State for the Colonies, 15 August 1951, in T236/4135 OF63/208/05G, PRO.
30 Telegram from Tokyo to FO, 9 August 1951, FO371/92634 FJ1121/180, PRO.
31 Telegram from SCAP to Washington, 1 August 1951, SCAP Files, Box 6727, RG331, NA.
32 Telegram from SCAP to Washington, 30 July 1951, SCAP Files, Box 6727, RG331, NA.
33 Telegram from SCAP to Army Department, 27 August 1951, SCAP Files, Box 6718, RG331, NA.
34 A copy of the correspondence from the UKLM to FO, 1 October 1951, in T236/4137 OF63/208/05I, PRO.
35 Kiuchi Nobutane, *Kuni no Kosei* [The Character of a Nation], Tokyo: President-sha, 1986, 22–3.
36 Telegram from Tokyo to BT, 30 November 1951, in T236/4137 OF63/208/05K, PRO.
37 Extract from *Nippon Times*, 24 November 1951, in T236/3185 OF63/119/011C, PRO.
38 On the EPU, see Jacob J. Kaplan and Günther Schleiminger, *The European Payments Union: Financial Diplomacy in the 1950s*, Oxford: Clarendon Press, 1989.
39 Note from Loynes to Grafftey Smith, 7 November 1951, OV16/78, BoE.
40 Telegram from Tokyo to FO, 5 December 1951, FO371/92638 FJ1121/292, PRO.
41 Draft statement of the UK and UK governments, 19 June 1951, FRUS 1951, vol. 6, part I, p. 1389.
42 John Dower, *Empire and Aftermath: Yoshida Shigeru and the Japanese Experience, 1878–1954*, Cambridge MA: Harvard University Press, 1988, 406;

Dower, see Hosoya, 'Japan, China, the United States and the United Kingdom'; Howard Schonberger, 'Peacemaking in Asia', 59–73; Michael Schaller, *Altered States: The United States and Japan since the Occupation*, Oxford: Oxford University Press, 1997, 42; Lowe, *Containing the Cold War in East Asia.*

43 On the Anglo-American differences over the recognition of China, see David McLean, 'American Nationalism, the China Myth, and the Truman Doctrine: The Question of Accommodation with Peking, 1949–50', *Diplomatic History*, vol. 10, no. 1 (1986): 25–42; Richard Ovendale, 'Britain, the United States, and the Recognition of Communist China', *Historical Journal*, vol. 26, no. 1 (1983): 139–58; on the fate of British firms in communist China, see Aaron Shai, 'Imperialism Imprisoned: The Closure of British Firms in the People's Republic of China', *English Historical Review*, vol. 105 (1989): 88–109.

44 Memorandum by Perkins to Rusk, 30 October 1951, FRUS 1951, vol. 6, part I, p. 1389.

45 Oral history interview, Livingston T. Merchant, 13 March–17 April 1965, p. 11, the JFD Oral History Project, Seeley G. Mudd Library, Princeton, New Jersey (hereafter Princeton); and telegram from Dulles to Acheson, 7 November 1951, FRUS 1951, vol. 6, part I, p. 1393.

46 *Ibid.*

47 *Ibid.*

48 *Ibid.*

49 Telegram from Ringwalt to Merchant, 17 November 1951, FRUS 1951, vol. 6, part I, pp. 1406–7.

50 Telegram from FO to Tokyo, 14 November 1951, FO371/92604 FJ10310/29, PRO.

51 Dean Acheson, *Present at the Creation: My Years in the State Department*, London: W. W. Norton & Company, 1969, 576.

52 Correspondence from Acheson to Eden, 22 November 1951, FO371/92605 FJ10310/29, PRO.

53 Memorandum by Dulles, 26 December 1951, FRUS 1951, vol. 6, part I, p. 1467.

54 Memorandum by Merchant to Dulles, 26 November 1951, FRUS 1951, vol. 6, part 1, p. 1415.

55 *Ibid.*

56 Correspondence from Eden to MacDonald, 16 November 1951, FO371/92642 FJ1127/17, PRO.

57 Telegram from Tokyo to FO, 13 December 1951, FO371/92605 FJ10310/29, PRO.

58 *Ibid.*

59 *Ibid.*

60 Telegram from FO to Washington, 16 December 1951, FO371/92605 FJ10310/38, PRO.

61 Telegram from FO to Tokyo, 14 December 1951, FO371/92605 FJ10310/38, PRO.

62 Telegram from Washington to FO, 18 December 1951, FO371/92605 FJ10310/43 PRO and Telegram from Acheson to Sebald, 18 December 1951, FRUS 1951, vol. 6, part 1, p. 1450.

63 Telegram from Tokyo to FO, 18 December 1951, FO371/92605 FJ10310/42, PRO.

64 *Ibid.*

65 Memorandum of conversation by Sebald, 18 December 1951, FRUS 1951, vol. 6, part 1, p. 1444. Yoshida wrote in his memoirs that he wanted more time to consider the China issue, but the atmosphere prevailing in the US senate meant that without a signed letter, the peace treaty might not have been ratified. See

Shigeru Yoshida, *Kaisô Jûnen* [Memoirs of the former Prime Minister of Japan], vol. 3, Tokyo: Shinchô-sha, 1957, 71–3.

66 Telegram from Tokyo to FO, 21 December 1951 FO371/92605 FJ10310/45, PRO.
67 Memorandum by Dulles, 9 January 1952, FRUS 1952–54, vol. 14, p. 1071.
68 Editorial note, FRUS 1952–1954, vol. 14, p. 1069.
69 Memorandum of conversation by Allison, 9 January 1952, FRUS 1952–1954, vol. 14, p. 1076. There is nothing concerning the Anglo-American debacle over China in Alex Danchev's *Oliver Franks: Founding Father*, Oxford: Clarendon Press, 1993.
70 Memorandum of conversation by Allison, 10 January 1952, FRUS 1952–1954, vol. 14, p. 1077.
71 Telegram from Washington to FO, 10 January 1952, FO371/99403 FJ10310/4, PRO.
72 Telegram from Acheson to Sebald, 11 January 1952, FRUS 1952–1954, vol. 14, p. 1083.
73 Correspondence from Dening to Scott, 18 February 1952, FO371/99404 FJ10310/54, PRO.
74 See Anthony Eden, *Full Circle: The Memoirs of Sir Anthony Eden*, London: Cassell, 1960, 19–20; and Acheson, *Present at the Creation*, 603–5.
75 Note from Dulles to Acheson, 28 February 1952, February 1952(1) Box 3, JFD-JMA Chronological Series, John Foster Dulles Papers, Eisenhower Library.
76 Memorandum by Dulles, 6 March 1952, March 1952(3) Box 3, JFD-JMA Chronological Series, John Foster Dulles Papers, Eisenhower Library.

4 Learning the rules of engagement

1 Ishii Osamu, *Reisen to Nichibei Kankei: Patonashippu no Keisei* [The Cold War and US/Japan Relations: Formation of a Partnership], Tokyo: Japan Times, 1989, 82–3; Sayuri Shimizu, 'Perennial Anxiety: Japan-US Controversy over Recognition of the PRC, 1952–1958', *The Journal of American-East Asian Relations*, vol. 4, no. 3 (Fall 1995): 223–48.
2 Report by ONC, 17 April 1952, ON(52)72, CAB134/108, PRO.
3 Note from Heasman to Loynes, 25 January 1952, OV16/79, BoE.
4 Second conclusions of the Cabinet, 10 January 1952, CAB128/24, PRO.
5 *Ibid.*
6 Memorandum of the UK Delegation, Meeting of Commonwealth Finance Ministers, 8 January 1952, FM (2) 4, T236/4137 OF63/208/05K, PRO.
7 Minutes of meeting, 18 March 1952, p. 105, subseries 2, *Nichiei Bôeki Shiharai Kankei Ikken* [Japan-UK Trade Agreements], reel B-0021, Public Release Series 8, DRM, JMFAA.
8 Note from Brook to the Prime Minister, 26 January 1952, PREM 11/21, PRO.
9 See postwar trade chronology in MITI (ed.) *Nihon Boeki no Tenkai: Sengo Ionen no ayumikara* [Development of Japan's Trade: A Review of the Postwar Decade], Tokyo: Shôkô Shuppan, 1956, 672.
10 Briefing for the Supreme Commander, 25 February 1952, SCAP Files, Box 7692, RG 331, NA.
11 *Ibid.*
12 *Ibid.*
13 *Ibid.*
14 Telegram from Tokyo to FO, 25 March 1952, FO371/99431 FJ1121/15, PRO.
15 See summary of the Sterling Payments Review of 18–25 March 1952, T236/4138 OF63/208/05L, PRO.
16 *Ibid.*
17 *Ibid.*

18 *Ibid.*

19 Report by the ONC, 17 April 1952, ON(52)72, CAB 134/108, PRO.

20 See telegram from Tokyo to FO, 25 March 1952, FO371/99431 FJ1121/15, PRO.

21 Correspondence from Hampson to Serpell, 9 June 1952, T236/4139 OF63/208/05M, PRO.

22 Correspondence from Dening to FO, 10 June 1952 in T236/4139 OF63/208/05M, PRO.

23 Note by Kerr to DOS, 30 July 1952, Box 7 RG 84, NA. See also the memorandum from Tokyo to DOS on preparation for GATT Article 12, 13 August 1959, DF 394.41/8–1359, NA.

24 See revision of the current Anglo-Japanese payments agreement, 17 July 1952, pp. 168–172, subseries 5, *Nichei Boeki Shiharai Kankei Ikken* [Japan-UK Trade Agreements], reel B-0021, Public Release Series 8, DRM, JMFAA.

25 Correspondence from Hampson to Serpell, 10 July 1952, T236/4139 OF63/208/05M, PRO.

26 Tetsuya Kataoka, *The Price of a Constitution: The Origins of Japan's Postwar Politics*, New York: Taylor and Francis, 1991, 104.

27 Correspondence from Hampson to Serpell, 10 July 1952, T236/4139 OF63/208/05M, PRO.

28 Japanese Observations on the Anglo-Japanese Sterling Payments Agreement attached to the *note verbale* from the MOFA, 1 August 1952, T236/4139 OF63/208/05M, PRO.

29 Note from Flett to Serpell, 14 October 1952, T236/4140 OF63/208/05M, PRO.

30 Oda replaced Yukawa Morio, who was appointed Councillor at the Japanese Embassy in Paris. A copy of the correspondence from Hampson to Ogilvy-Webb, 9 September 1952 in OV16/83, BoE.

31 Note from Bolton to Rowan 26 November 1952, OV16/84, BoE.

32 Telegram from Tokyo to FO, 27 November 1952, FO371/99433 FJ1121/87, PRO.

33 A copy of the *note verbale* from MOFA, 26 November 1952, in OV16/84, BoE.

34 Telegram from FO to Tokyo, 29 November 1952, FO371/99433 FJ1121/89, PRO.

35 A copy of the telegram from Tokyo to FO, 2 December 1952, in OV16/84, BoE.

36 Nichiei Shiharai, *Kyotei no Koshin ni kansuru Ken* [On the Renewal of the UK-Japan Payments Agreement], 15 December 1952, pp. 62–63, subseries 8, *Nichiei Bôeki Shiharai Kankei Ikken* [Japan-UK Trade Agreements], reel B-0021, Public Release Series 8, DRM, JMFAA.

37 Note from Ogilvy-Webb to Serpell, 19 November 1952, T236/4140 OF63/208/05N, PRO.

38 See postwar trade chronology in MITI (ed.) *Nihon Boeki no Tenkai*, 675.

39 Telegram from FO to Tokyo, 5 December 1952, FO371/99433 FJ1121/114, PRO.

40 *Note verbale* from MOFA to UKLM, Japan, 26 April 1952, FO371/99441 FJ1152/2, PRO.

41 Article 12 stipulated that Japan would grant MFN treatment on a reciprocal basis to allied powers for four years after the ratification of the treaty, pending the conclusion of the relevant treaty or agreement. See *note verbale* from MOFA to UKLM Japan, 26 April 1952, FO371/99441 FJ1152/2, PRO.

42 *Ibid.*

43 Correspondence from Dening to FO, 6 May 1952, FO371/99441 FJ1152/2, PRO.

44 *Ibid.*

45 Circular letter from the CO, 22 September 1952, in FO371/99441 FJ1152/19, PRO.

46 FO Minute by Snellgrove, 24 July 1952, FO 371/998985 UEE67/12, PRO.

47 Schenk, *Britain and the Sterling Area*, 61.

48 Donald McDougall and Rosemary Hutt, 'Imperial Preference: A Quantitative Analysis', *The Economic Journal*, vol. LXIV, no. 254 (June 1954): 256.

49 Note on Japan and the GATT, 7 October 1952, BT11/4979 CRE33435/1952, PRO.
50 Correspondence from Dening to Scott, 21 January 1952, FO371/99441 FJ1152/1, PRO.
51 *Ibid.*
52 *Ibid.*
53 Note from Percival to Scott, 19 June 1952, FO371/99441 FJ1152/6, PRO.
54 Japan and the GATT, 12 January 1953, in Japanese Competition: General Policy, BT11/4918 CRE10959/1951, PRO.
55 *Ibid.*
56 GATT (ed.) *Analytical Index: Guide to GATT Law and Practice*, Geneva: GATT, 1994, 945.
57 *Ibid.*
58 Note from Kerr, 13 July 1952, p. 105, subseries 2, *Kanzei oyobi Boeki ni kansuru Ippan Kyotei Kankei Ikken* [The Problem of Japanese entry into the GATT], reel E-0010, Public Release Series 10, DRM, JMFAA.
59 *Ibid.*
60 The twenty-eight countries were Australia, Belgium, the Netherlands, Luxembourg, Brazil, Burma, Canada, Ceylon, Chile, Cuba, Finland, France, West Germany, India, Indonesia, Italy, Liberia, Norway, New Zealand, Pakistan, Peru, South Africa, Southern Rhodesia, Sweden, the UK, the United States, South Korea and the Philippines. See letter from Hagiwara to Wyndham White, 18 July 1952, pp. 67–69, subseries 2, *Kanzei oyobi Boeki ni Kansuru Ippan Kyotei Kankei Ikken* [The Problem of Japanese Entry into the GATT], reel E-0010, Public Release Series 10, DRM, JMFAA.
61 Minutes of the 23rd meeting of the EPC, 30 July 1952, CAB134/842, PRO.
62 *Ibid.*
63 Memorandum for the President, 20 August 1952, WHCF: CF, State Department, trade agreements negotiations, 1952; Truman Papers, Truman Library.
64 Telegram from Washington to FO, 2 September 1952, FO371/98987, UEE67/153, PRO.
65 *Ibid.*
66 Minutes of the seventh meeting of the CPCE Conference, 11 September 1952, CAB 133/131, PRO.
67 *Ibid.*
68 Minutes of the seventh meeting of the CPCE, 11 September 1952, CAB133/131, PRO.
69 Memorandum by the Minister of State, 17 September 1952, C(52)302, CAB129/55, PRO.
70 *Ibid.*
71 80th Conclusions of the Cabinet, 18 September 1952, CAB128/25, PRO.
72 Telegram from Washington to FO, 22 September 1952, FO 371/98987 UEE67/60, PRO.
73 *Ibid.*
74 Minutes of TN (G)(52) 34th meeting, 10 November 1952, BT11/4979 CRE33435/1952, PRO.
75 Telegram from the Secretary of State to the American Embassy in Tokyo, 3 October 1952, RG84 Box 6, NA.

5   Britain at the helm?

1 Aaron Forsberg, 'Eisenhower and Japanese Economic Recovery: The Politics of Integration with the Western Bloc, 1952–1955', *The Journal of American-East Asian Relations*, vol. 5, no. 1 (1996): 62.

2 For Churchill's ill-health and declining political enthusiasm, see John Colville, *The Fringes of Power: Downing Street Diaries vol. II, 1941–April 1955*, Kent: Sceptre, 1987, 323–43.

3 Schaller, *Altered States*, 63.

4 Watanabe Akio (ed.) *Sengo Nihon no Saishô tachi* [The Postwar Japanese Prime Ministers], Tokyo: Chûô Kôronsha, 1995, 57–8.

5 The collective approach was based on the principle of sterling convertibility at a flexible exchange rate between the dollar and sterling. Under the plan, convertibility would be limited to resident holders of sterling, and it would only apply to newly acquired sterling in current and capital transactions. Furthermore, the IMF was required to provide an extra support fund to enable a smooth system of operation. The idea was objectionable to the United States because it would have to pursue good creditor policies to maintain reasonable equilibrium in the balance of payments between the United States and the rest of the world. Conversely, European governments were expected to become convertible according to the UK timetable, which did not go down well with them either. Thus American and European opposition to the idea led to the failure of the collective approach. See 'A Collective Approach to Freer Trade and Currencies: Summary of the United Kingdom proposals, 31 October 1953', US President's Commission on Foreign Economic Policy: Records 1953–1954 (Randall Commission) Box 61, Eisenhower Library; Schenk, *Britain and the Sterling Area*, 121–2.

6 Telegram from Tokyo to FO, 2 February 1953, in OV16/85, BOE.

7 Two thirds in this case meant of the 1951 level.

8 Memorandum by the President of the Board of Trade to the EPC, 24 February 1953, EA(53) 33, CAB134/847, PRO.

9 Minutes of the 7th meeting of the EPC, 4 March 1953, CAB134/846, PRO.

10 *Ibid.*

11 *Ibid.*

12 *Ibid.*

13 Telegram from FO to Washington, 6 March 1953, and a note from Rowan to the Chancellor of the Exchequer, 8 March 1953 in T236/4142/OF63/208/05, PRO.

14 Memorandum by the Secretary of State for Commonwealth Relations, 8 March 1953, C(53)88, CAB129/59, PRO.

15 Memorandum by the Economic Secretary of the Treasury, 6 March 1953, C(53)91, CAB129/59, PRO.

16 *Ibid.*

17 Telegram from Tokyo to FO, 25 March 1953 in T236/4143 OF63/208/05Q, PRO.

18 Note from Ogilvy-Webb to Flett, 17 March 1953 in T236/4143 OF63/208/05Q, PRO.

19 Note from Hogg to Watson and Parson, 30 March 1953, and note from Crawshaw to Cunnell, 9 April 1953, OV16/86, BoE.

20 Annex C in the confidential Treasury record: minutes of fifth meeting with Tôjô, 7 April 1953, T236/3442 OF63/208/09A, PRO.

21 *Ibid.*

22 Confidential Treasury record: minutes of seventh meeting with Tôjô, 16 April 1953, T236/3442 OF63/208/09A, PRO.

23 Note from Hogg to Watson, Cunnell, Crawshaw and Miller, 29 April 1953, T236/3442 OF63/208/09A, PRO.

24 Correspondence from Phelps to Serpell, 27 May 1953, T236/4144 OF63/208/05R, PRO.

25 From Waring to DOS, 26 February 1953, DF 4441.9431/2–2653, NA.

26 *Ibid.*

27 *Ibid.*

28 *Ibid.*
29 Memorandum by the Secretary of State for Foreign Affairs and the President of the Board of Trade with regard to Japan and the GATT, 16 January 1953, C(53) 20, CAB 129/58, PRO.
30 *Ibid.*
31 Correspondence from Wright to Sanders, 15 January 1953, FO371/105031 UEE38/5, PRO.
32 Telegram from London to Secretary of State, 13 January 1953, 394.31/1–1353, RG59, NA.
33 *Ibid.*
34 *Ibid.*
35 Minutes of the fourth Cabinet Conclusions, 22 January 1953, CAB 128/26, Part I, PRO.
36 Minute by Snellgrove, 31 January 1953, FO371/105032 UEE38/53, PRO.
37 See for example, telegram from Oslo to FO, 26 January 1953, FO371/105031 UEE38/15, PRO.
38 See telegram from Santiago to FO, 28 January 1953, FO371/105031 UEE38/27, PRO.
39 See telegram from Havana to FO, 27 January 1953, FO371/105031 UEE38/27, PRO.
40 Note from Eden to Thorneycroft, 3 February 1953, FO371/105032 UEE38/49, PRO.
41 Memorandum of Conversation, 28 January 1953, 394.31/1–2853, RG59, NA. The Reciprocal Trade Program placed the tariff ratemaking power in the hands of the President, but his authority only extended for three years. The extension of this programme depended on the approval of Congress. See 'the Question of Renewing the Administration's Reciprocal Trade Program', *Congressional Digest*, vol. 30, no. 4 (April 1951): 99–128.
42 Raymond A. Bauer, Ithiel De Sola Pool and Lewis Anthony Dexter, *American Business and Public Policy: The Politics of Foreign Trade*, Chicago: Aldine Atherton, 1972, 26.
43 Kaufman, *Trade and Aid*, 17.
44 Forsberg, 'Eisenhower and Japanese Economic Recovery', 61.
45 Kaufman, *Trade and Aid*, 17.
46 The meeting was chaired by Johan Melander, the Director of Commercial Policy in the Norwegian ministry of Foreign Affairs. See GATT press release, GATT/108, 27 January 1953, in FO371/105032 UEE 38/43, PRO.
47 Correspondence from Snellgrove to Turpin, 4 February 1953, FO371/105033, UEE38/58, PRO.
48 Telegram from Geneva to FO, 4 February 1953, FO371/105032 UEE38/42, PRO.
49 Correspondence from Snellgrove to Wright, 12 February 1953, FO371/105033 UEE38/63, PRO.
50 Telegram from Geneva to FO, 12 February 1953, FO371/195933 UEE38/58, PRO.
51 Correspondence from Snellgrove to Turpin, 9 February 1953, FO371/105033 UEE38/59, PRO.
52 The members consisted of officials from MOFA, MOF and MITI. See *GATT dai nana, hakkai teiyakukokudankaigikan kikaniinkai kaigi hôkokusho* [Report of the Intersessional Committee Meeting of the seventh and eighth GATT sessions of the Contracting Parties], compiled by Hagiwara, 29 February 1953, 138–72, subseries 1, *Kanzei oyobi Bôeki ni kansuru Ippan Kyôtei Kankei Ikken* [The Problem of Japanese Entry into the GATT], reel E-0011, Public Release Series 10, DRM, JMFAA.

53 Report of the accession of Japan, L/76, 13 February 1953, FO371/105033 UEE38/69, PRO.

54 Minutes of the first meeting of the Cabinet Tariff Policy on Japan, 5 June 1953, CAB 130/87, PRO.

55 Minutes of the 41st meeting of the ONC, 14 July 1953, CAB134/1091, PRO.

56 Memorandum by the ONC, 16 July 1953, ON(53)136, CAB134/1095, PRO.

57 Note by the Chancellor of the Exchequer, 28 July 1953, C(53)215, CAB129/62, PRO.

58 See Akaneya, *Nion no GATT Kanyû Mondai*, 181.

59 *Ibid.*, 181–2.

60 Memorandum from Robertson to Linder, 30 April 1953, DF 394.31/4–3053, NA.

61 Record of a meeting between Hagiwara and Wyndham White, 13 July 1953, 178–88, subseries 2, *Kanzei oyobi Bôeki ni kansuru Ippan Kyôtei Kankei Ikken* [The Problem of Japanese Entry into the GATT], reel E-0011, Public Release Series 10, DRM, JMFAA. Records of meetings between Hagiwara and Wyndham White are microfilmed in reel E-0011 and E-0012.

62 See note from Lee to Coulson, 5 August 1953, FO371/105035, UEE 38/140; telegram from FO to Washington, 7 August 1953, FO 371/105035, UEE 38/140; note from Brittain to Lee, 7 August 1953, FO371/105035 UEE38/140; and airgram from Geneva to BT, 5 August 1953, FO371/105035 UEE38/141, PRO.

63 Telegram from FO to Washington, 7 August 1953, FO371/105035 UEE38/140, PRO.

64 See telegram from Washington to FO, 11 August 1953, FO371/105035 UEE38/142 and correspondence from Parker to Sanders, 11 August 1953, BT11/5056, PRO.

65 Letter from Thorneycroft to Salisbury, 17 August 1953, FO371/105035 UEE38/150, PRO.

66 Minutes of the 50th conclusions of the Cabinet, 25 August 1953, CAB 128/26 Part II, PRO.

67 The session was convened between 17 and 20 August. See Akaneya, *Nihon no GATT Kanyû Mondai*, 191–2.

68 Telegram from Geneva to FO, 23 September 1953, FO371/105036 UEE38/174, PRO.

69 See minutes of the second meeting of the UK delegation to the GATT, 24 September 1953, FO371/105088 UEE80/145, PRO.

70 Minute by Wright, 30 September 1953, FO371/105037, UEE38/180, PRO.

71 Note from Jardine to Wakefield, 16 October 1953, FO371/105038 UEE38/226, PRO.

72 Minute by Wright, 17 October 1953, FO371/105038 UEE38/226(A), PRO.

73 Minutes of the 59th conclusions of the Cabinet, 22 October 1953, CAB128/26 Part II, PRO.

74 See Akaneya, *Nihon no GATT Kanyû Mondai*, 206–7.

75 Minutes of the 60th conclusions of the Cabinet, 22 October 1953, CAB 128/26 Part II, PRO.

76 *GATT Kari Kanyû no Seiritsu ni tsuite*, 24 October 1953, p. 149 subseries 3, *Kanzei oyobi Bôeki ni kansuru Kyôtei Kankei Ikken* [The Problem of Japanese Entry into the GATT], reel E-0012, Public Release Series 10, DRM, JMFAA.

77 Correspondence from Serpell to Levine, 19 June 1953, T236/4144 OF63/208/05R, PRO.

78 Note by Serpell, 30 July 1953, T236/4144 OF63/208/05R, PRO.

79 Note from Wies to Watson, 26 August 1953, OV16/89, BoE.

80 See note by Hogg, 16 October 1953, OV16/90, BoE.

81 *Ibid.*

82 Telegram from FO to Tokyo, 29 October 1953 in T236/4146 OF63/208/05T, PRO.

83 Minute of 71st meeting of the ONC, 6 November 1953, CAB134/1091, PRO.
84 Note by the Treasury for the ONC, 4 November 1953, ON(53)196, CAB134/1096, PRO.
85 Minute of 71st meeting of the ONC, 6 November 1953, CAB134/1091, PRO.
86 Minutes of the third meeting of the Cabinet Tariff Policy on Japan, 1 December 1953, CAB 130/87, PRO.

6 Limits to Britain's policy towards Japan

1 Japan's release from its secret bilateral agreement remained nominal, however, as CHINCOM controls were far more stringent than those of COCOM. The disparity between the two trade controls became wider as a result of a British proposal in March 1954 to cut items under COCOM's International List I by 50 per cent and the virtual abolition of International Lists II and III. The British proposal culminated in talks in Paris, and as a result of the 475 items reviewed, only seventy remained embargoed. Scholars are divided over whether the trade relaxation was initiated by the British and the Europeans, or whether the Eisenhower administration initiated a fundamental revision of the American policy to enable a relaxation to take place. Those who argue that it was a British initiative include Forland, ' "Selling firearms to the Indians" '; and another scholar who supports this argument is Takamotsu Motoyuki, '*China Differential Kanwa Mondai wo megutte no Eisenhower Seiken no Taiô*' [The Eisenhower Administration's Response to the China Differential, 1955–57], *Kokusai Seiji*, vol. 105 (1994): 60–79; those who argue that it was an American initiative include Spaulding, 'A Gradual and Moderate Relaxation', and Shimizu, *Creating People of Plenty*. On the British position towards COCOM, see John W. Young, 'Winston Churchill's Peacetime Administration and the Relaxation of East-West Trade Controls, 1953–54', *Diplomacy and Statecraft*, vol. 7, no. 1 (1996): 125–40. See also minutes of the Ministry of Defence, Joint War Production Committee, Security Export Controls Working Party, 15 October 1954, SX/M(54) 13, DEFE10/316, PRO.
2 Shimizu, *Creating People of Plenty*, 86.
3 *Ibid.*
4 See Shimizu, *Creating People of Plenty*, 94.
5 Minutes of the 20th Conclusions of the Cabinet, 17 March 1954, CAB128/27 Part I, PRO.
6 Singleton, *Lancashire on the Scrapheap*, 118.
7 Memorandum by the Chancellor of the Exchequer, 7 December 1953, C(53)314, CAB129/64, PRO.
8 *Ibid.*
9 Minutes of the 77th conclusions of the Cabinet, 8 December 1953, CAB128/26 Part II, PRO.
10 A telegram was sent from the Colonial Office to Nigeria on 11 December. See outward telegram from the Secretary of State for Colonies to Nigeria, 11 December 1953, in T236/4148 OF63/208/05V, PRO.
11 *Ibid.*
12 See annex C attached to the minutes of the plenary meeting held in the Treasury, 10 December 1953, T236/4148 OF63/208/05V, PRO.
13 The revised minutes of the fourth plenary meeting held in the Treasury, 17 December 1953, T236/4148 OF63/208/05V, PRO.
14 See annex A and B attached to the revised minutes of the fourth plenary meeting held at the Treasury, 17 December 1953, T236/4148 OF63/208/05V, PRO.
15 Revised minutes of the fourth plenary meeting held at the Treasury, 17 December 1953, T236/4148 OF63/208/05V, PRO.

16 Inward telegram from Nigeria to the Secretary of State for the Colonies, 23 December 1953, in T236/4148 OF63/208/05V, PRO.
17 Minutes of the 81st conclusions of the Cabinet, 29 December 1953, CAB128/26 Part II, PRO.
18 *Ibid.*
19 Ushiba, *Gaikô no Shunkan: Watakushi no Rirekisho* [A Moment in Diplomacy: My Memoir], Tokyo: Nihon Keizai Shimbun-sha, 1984, 82.
20 Note from Serpell to Percival, 25 January 1954, T236/4149 OF63/208/05W, PRO.
21 *Ibid.*
22 Note from Serpell to Playfair, 6 January 1954, T236/4149 OF63/208/05W, PRO.
23 See memorandum by the Board of Trade, 24 January 1954, C(54)30, CAB129/64 and minutes of the 6th conclusion of the Cabinet, 28 January 1954, CAB128/27, PRO.
24 See annex C attached to minutes of the 6th plenary meeting held at the Treasury, 29 January 1954, T236/4150 OF63/208/05X, PRO.
25 Record of a meeting held at the Treasury, 28 January 1954, T236/4150 OF63/208/05X, PRO.
26 For the actual details of the agreement, see Appendix 5 for the agreed minute.
27 These speakers had the support of the Cotton Spinners and Manufacturers' Association, the Rochdale Weavers and Winders' Association, the British Pottery Manufacturers' Federation and the North Staffordshire Chamber of Commerce, to name but a few. See 'Views on Japanese Trade Agreement' in *The Times*, 1 February 1954, 2.
28 See *Hansard Parliamentary Debates*, 5th series, vol. 523 (1953–4), cols 31–8.
29 The misunderstanding that Streat knew all about the negotiations but had not informed the interested parties led to a crisis of confidence in Streat and the Cotton Board. This culminated in the Federation of Master Cotton Spinners, the Yarn Spinners' Association and the Cotton Spinners' and Manufacturers' Association bypassing the Cotton Board in their attempt to see the President of the Board of Trade, which was most unusual. See Marguerite Dupree (ed.) *Lancashire and Whitehall: The Diary of Sir Raymond Streat, Volume Two, 1939–57*, Manchester: Manchester University Press, 1987, 708–12.
30 It was rejected because the issue in contention (i.e. the Sterling Payments Agreement) had already been signed.
31 Wilson, Statement to the House of Commons, 1 February 1954, *Hansard Parliamentary Debates*, 5th series, vol. 523 (1953–4), col. 36.
32 See *Hansard Parliamentary Debates*, 5th series, vol. 523 (1953–4), cols 1315–24.
33 Memorandum by the Secretary of State for Foreign Affairs, 8 March 1954, C(54)92, CAB129/65, PRO.
34 Correspondence from Dening to Allen, 27 January 1954, FO371/110496 FJ1631/2, PRO.
35 Telegram from FO to Tokyo, 5 February 1954, FO371/110496 FJ1631/2, PRO.
36 Letter from Stark to Colville, 23 April 1954, FO371/110496 FJ1631/11, PRO.
37 Letter from Percival to Crowe, 23 May 1954, FO371/110434 FJ1152/4, PRO.
38 Minutes of meeting of the Board of Directors, 12 April 1954, M8/5/70, Manchester Chamber of Commerce (hereafter MCC).
39 Letter from Percival to Crowe, 24 May 1954, FO371/110434 FJ1152/15, PRO.
40 Note by Colegate, 27 May 1954, BT11/5286 CRE5985/1954, PRO.
41 Memorandum by the President of the Board of Trade to the EPC, 21 June 1954, EA(54)72, CAB134/852, PRO.
42 Minutes of the 15th meeting of the EPC, 24 June 1954, CAB134/850, PRO.
43 *Currency retention*: Retention was permitted for 10 per cent of the foreign exchange earned on exports of manufactured goods. The 10 per cent could be used to import various industrial materials.

Tax relief:

    (a) An income tax exemption allowed on 50 per cent of export profits or 3 per cent of export turnover, whichever was less.

    (b) Firms recognised as exporters or as manufacturers for export were allowed to set aside reserves as a charge on income before taxation.

    (c) Depreciation at especially favourable rates was allowed on assets abroad.

Link System: The system whereby the right to import a commodity was linked with the export of a Japanese product. For example sugar imports were linked with export of ships, locomotives and raw silk. As import right commanded a premium of 25–35 per cent, exporters of linked goods were able to sell their goods at a discount. See annex B attached to memorandum by the President of the Board of Trade, 21 June 1954, EA(54)72, CAB134/852, PRO.

44 Letter from Levine to Crowe, 30 June 1954, FO371/110435 FJ1152/29, PRO.

45 Note of meeting by Le Goy, 7 July 1954, FO371/110435 FJ1152/30, PRO.

46 Forsberg, *America and the Japanese Miracle* 138–40.

47 Note from Sinclair to Wilson, 6 July 1954, FO371/110160 UEE1021/9, PRO.

48 Record of a meeting at the State Department, 29 June 1954, in a letter from Lloyd to Butler of 20 July 1954, FO371/110435 FJ1152/35, PRO.

49 Memorandum by the Treasury, 12 July 1954 ON(54)95, CAB134/1100, PRO.

50 Minutes of the second meeting of the Committee on EEP, 19 July 1954, CAB134/869, PRO.

51 *Ibid.*

52 Minute by Wilson, 26 July 1954, FO371/110435 FJ1152/44, PRO.

53 Minute of the 3rd meeting of the Committee on EEP, 27 July 1954, CAB134/869, PRO.

54 Minutes of an informal meeting of the ONC, 28 July 1954, ON(54)105, CAB134/1100, PRO.

55 Minute by Wilson, 28 July 1954, FO371/110435 FJ1152/45(B), PRO.

56 See memorandum by the Chancellor of the Exchequer, 10 August 1954, C(54)268, CAB129/70, PRO.

57 Letter from Crowe to Brain, 10 September 1954, FO371/110436 FJ1152/61, PRO.

58 Memorandum of conversation, 27 September 1954, 510.1 GATT, RG84, NA.

59 Telegram from Washington to FO, 30 September 1954, FO371/110161 UEE1021/50 and notes of meeting at the Board of Trade, 4 October 1954, BT11/5298 CRE10409/1954, PRO.

60 Correspondence from White to Kerr, 21 October 1954, 510-.1GATT, RG84, NA.

61 *Ibid.*

62 See minutes by Lord Reading, 23 October 1954, FO371/110436 FJ1152/82 and telegram from Tokyo to FO, 23 October 1954, FO371/110161 UEE 1021/60, PRO.

63 In spite of the minor differences over the objectives of the trip, it can be said that Yoshida's goodwill tour to Britain, Canada, France, Germany, Italy and the United States was successful in that it enhanced Japan's image with the host countries. The trip, however, had no impact on Yoshida's embattled image in Japan, and not long after his return he was forced out of office, and Hatoyama Ichirô became the new Prime Minister of Japan. For an account of Yoshida's visit, see 503–68, subseries 2, *Yoshida Sôri Ôbei Hômon Kankei Ikken* [Prime Minister Yoshida's European and American trip], reel A-0136, Public Release Series 11, DRM, JMFAA; see also his account of the trip in Yoshida, *Kaisô Jûnen*, vol. 1, 218–27.

64 Record of a meeting held at the Foreign Office, 28 October 1954, FO371/110161 UEE1021/63, PRO.

65 *Ibid.*

66 Telegram from Geneva to FO, 29 October 1954, FO371/110161 UEE1021/64, PRO.

67 Lalita Prasad Singh, *The Politics of Economic Cooperation in Asia: A Study of Asian International Organisations*, Missouri: University of Missouri Press, 1966, 53.

68 Associate membership was granted to British Borneo, Burma, Ceylon and Hong Kong.

69 On the origins of the Colombo Plan see Remme, *Britain and Regional Cooperation in South-East Asia*; David Lowe, 'Percy Spender and the Colombo Plan 1950', *Australian Journal of Politics and History*, vol. 40, no. 2 (1994): 162–76; and Nicholas Tarling, 'The United Kingdom and the Origins of the Colombo Plan', *Journal of Commonwealth and Comparative Politics*, vol. 24, no. 1 (1986): 3–34.

70 Kajima, *Nihon Gaikôshi* [The Diplomatic History of Japan] *Vol. 30, Kôwago no Gaikô II Keizai iyô* [Diplomacy after the Peace Treaty (II) Economics Part I], Tokyo: Kajima Kenkyûjyo Shuppankai, 1972, 258.

71 Singh, *The Politics of Economic Cooperation in Asia*, 172.

72 FO minutes, 20 December 1951, FO371/92642 FJ1127/19, PRO.

73 Kajima, *Nihon Gaikôshi*, 260.

74 See Hatano Sumio, 'Tônan Ajia Kaihatsu wo meguru Nichieibei Kankei: Nihon no Korombo Plan Kannyû (1954) wo chûshinni' [Japan-US-UK Relations Centering on the Development of Southeast Asia in the 1950s], *Kindai Nihon Kenkyû*, vol. 16 (1994): 218.

75 *Ibid.*, 220–1.

76 *Ibid.*

77 See minutes of 5th and 7th meetings of the working party on Economic Development in South and Southeast Asia, 25 August and 8 September 1954, CAB134/868, PRO.

78 Ronald C. Keith, *The Diplomacy of Zhou Enlai*, Basingstoke and London: Macmillan Press, 1989, 58–87. For further readings, see Chen Jian, 'China and the First Indo-China War, 1950–1954', *The China Quarterly*, no. 113 (1993): 85–110; George C. Herring, ' "A Good Stout Effort": John Foster Dulles and the Indochina Crisis, 1954–1955', in Richard H. Immerman (ed.) *John Foster Dulles and the Diplomacy of the Cold War*, Princeton: Princeton University Press, 1990, 213–33; Melanie Billings-Yun, *Decision Against War. Eisenhower and Dien Bien Phu, 1954*, New York: Columbia University Press, 1988; Laurence Kaplan, Denise Artaud and Mark Rubin (eds) *Dien Bien Phu and the Crisis of Franco-American Relations, 1954–1955*, Wilmington: Scholarly Sources, 1990; and Kevin Ruane, ' "Containing America": Aspects of British Foreign Policy and the Cold War in South-East Asia, 1951–54', *Diplomacy and Statecraft*, vol. 7, no. 1 (1996): 141–74.

79 See Report on Asian Economic Working Group, August 1954, Box 67, White House Central Files, Eisenhower Library; see also Hatano, 'Tônan Ajia Kaihatsu wo meguru Nichieibei Kankei', 223.

7 Britain and Japan's GATT entry

1 On the normalisation of relations with the Soviet Union, see Tanaka Takahiko, *Nisso Kokkô Kaifuku no Shiteki Kenkyû: Sengo Nisso Kankei no Kiten, 1945–1956* [A Historical Study of the Normalisation of Relations between the Soviet Union and Japan: The Origins of the Postwar Soviet-Japanese Relations, 1945–1956], Tokyo: Yûhikaku, 1993; Akio Watanabe (ed.) *Sengo Nihon no Saishô Tachi*, Tokyo: Chûô Kôronsha, 1995, 92–108.

2 See Shimizu, *Creating People of Plenty*, 39–42; and Forsberg, *America and the Japanese Miracle*, 153–5.
3 The overall ceiling on Japan's cotton cloth exports to the United States was agreed at 150 million square yards for 1956. Shimizu, *Creating People of Plenty*, 120.
4 See report by the Official Committee on the Review of the GATT, 7 January 1955, E (55)4, CAB134/855, PRO.
5 Britain had liberalised 84 per cent of its import restrictions against OEEC countries by 30 June 1955. See Alan S. Milward and George Brennan, *Britain's Place in the World*, 127.
6 Serious injury was defined as widespread unemployment in an industry or a part of an industry, and would also include the shutting down of production in an important section of an industry. *Ibid.*
7 Britain's attempts to overturn the no-new-preference rule to protect Commonwealth trade against Japanese competition had little support from the Commonwealth countries, particularly those in Asia. Waiver was granted in exceptional cases concerning colonial commodities. See Singleton and Robertson, *Economic Relations between Britain and Australia, 1945–1960*, 106–7.
8 Report by the Official Committee on the Review of the GATT, 7 January 1955, EA(55)4, CAB134/855, PRO.
9 Comments on the Report by the Official Committee on the Review of the GATT, 10 January 1955, EA(55)5, CAB134/855, PRO.
10 See report by the Official Committee on the Review of the GATT, 7 January 1955, EA(55)4, CAB134/855, PRO.
11 Minutes of the 3rd meeting of the Cabinet Economic Policy Committee, 18 January 1955, CAB134/854, PRO.
12 Minutes of the sixth conclusions of the Cabinet, 24 January 1955, CAB128/28; Memorandum by the President of the Board of Trade, 19 January 1955, C(55)14, CAB129/73; and memorandum by the Secretary of State for Foreign Affairs, 21 January 1955, C(55)17, CAB129/73, PRO.
13 Minutes of the first meeting of the Cabinet committee on Japan and the General Agreement on Tariffs and Trade, CAB130/109, PRO.
14 Minutes of the eighth conclusions of the Cabinet, 31 January 1955, CAB128/28, PRO.
15 *Ibid.*
16 Telegram from Tokyo to FO, 16 February 1955, FO371/114927 UEE1022/38, PRO.
17 Telegram from Tokyo to FO, 10 February 1055, FO371/114927 UEE1022/33, PRO.
18 Telegram from Washington to FO, 21 February 1955, FO371/114927 UEE1022/46, PRO.
19 Note by Lord Reading to the Foreign Secretary, 17 March 1955, FO371/114928 UEE1022/69, PRO.
20 Telegram from FO to Tokyo, 18 April 1955, FO371/114929 UEE1022/98, PRO.
21 Copy of the announcement in *Nichiei Tsûshô Kyôtei Kankei* [Japan-UK Commercial Treaty], reel B-0095, Public Release Series 14, DRM, JMFAA.
22 *Ibid.*
23 *Ibid.*
24 Shimizu, *Creating People of Plenty*, 45.
25 Telegram from Tokyo to FO, April 22, 1955, FO371/114929 UEE1022/108, PRO; correspondence from Sir Esler Dening to Harold Macmillan, 4 May 1955, FO371/114930 UEE1022/119, PRO.
26 See Forsberg, *America and the Japanese Miracle*, 154.

27 Burma, Canada, Chile, Denmark, the Dominican Republic, Finland, FRG, Greece, Indonesia, Italy, Nicaragua, Norway, Pakistan Peru, Sweden, the United States and Uruguay took part in the tariff negotiations. See Press Release GATT/234, 7 June 1955 in FO371/114930 UEE1022/135, PRO.

28 Forsberg, *America and the Japanese Miracle*, 155. See also p. 162 for further elaboration of the triangular negotiations. The triangular negotiations were conducted with Canada, Denmark, Finland, Italy, Norway and Sweden. See Willoughby to DOS, 26 May 1955, DF 394.41/5–2655.

29 Note from C. W. Sanders to Mr Galsworthy, 28 June 1955, FO371/114930 UEE1022/151, PRO.

30 Memorandum by the Secretary of State for Foreign Affairs, 11 June 1955, CP(55)34, CAB129/75, PRO.

31 Memorandum by the President of the Board of Trade, 13 June 1955, CP(55)37, CAB129/75, PRO.

32 The German textiles industry could not understand why Britain, the Benelux countries and France were willing to invoke Article 35 of the GATT against Japan to protect its domestic textiles industries, but its government was unwilling to provide the same level of protection to its own industry and protested vigorously. See Memorandum of conversation on Japanese-German Tariff Negotiations, 13 May 1955, DF 394.41/5–1355, NA.

33 Germany requested the inclusion of special safeguards under Article 23 in its bilateral agreement with Japan. Memorandum of conversation on Japanese-German negotiations, 26 May 1955, DF 394.41/5–2655, NA. See also Akaneya, *Nihon no GATT Kanyû Mondai*, 265.

34 Minutes of the 26th conclusions of the Cabinet, 26 July 1955, CAB128/29, PRO.

35 The countries were the United Kingdom, Australia, New Zealand, South Africa, the Federation of Rhodesia and Nyasaland, Belgium, the Netherlands, Luxembourg, France, Brazil, Cuba, Haiti, Austria and India. See Office Memorandum from Robertson to McClurkin, 4 October 1955, DF 394.41/10–455, NA.

36 See minutes of meeting of the Contracting Parties, 19 November 1955, in BT11/5384, CRE/13874/1955 PRO.

37 Memorandum by the Chancellor of the Exchequer, 26 July 1955, EP(55)33, CAB134/1227, PRO.

38 Minutes of the seventh meeting of the EPC, 27 July 1955, CAB 134/1226, PRO.

39 Memorandum by the Economic Secretary, 8 September 1955, EP(55)39, CAB134/1227, PRO.

40 Minutes of the eighth meeting of the EPC, 28 September 1955, CAB134/1226, PRO.

41 Note by the Treasury, 25 January 1955, ON(55)2, CAB 134/1103, PRO.

42 *Ibid.*

43 *Ibid.*

44 Note by the Joint Secretaries, 22 March 1955, ON(55)34, CAB134/1103, PRO.

45 Paper by the Board of Trade and the Treasury, 17 March 1955, ON(55)33, CAB134/1103, PRO.

46 *Ibid.*

47 *Ibid.*

48 Note by the Treasury, 17 June 1955, ON(55)69, CAB134/1104, PRO.

49 *Ibid.*

50 Note by the Secretaries, 12 August 1955, ON(55)84, CAB134/1105, PRO.

51 Note by the Treasury, 17 June 1955, ON(55)69, CAB134/1104, PRO.

52 Minutes of the second meeting of the EPC, 15 June 1955, CAB 134/1226, PRO.

53 Note by the Board of Trade, 16 July 1955, ON(55)82, CAB134/1105, PRO.

54 Note by the Joint Secretaries, 28 July 1955, ON(55)83, CAB134/1105, PRO.

55 Minutes of the 35th meeting of the ONC, 27 July 1955, CAB134/1102, PRO.

56 Note by the Chancellor of the Exchequer, 12 August 1955, CP(55)103, CAB129/77, PRO.
57 *Ibid.*
58 Memorandum by the Chancellor of the Exchequer, 12 August 1955, CP(55)103, CAB129/77, PRO.
59 Memorandum by the Chancellor of the Exchequer, 2 September 1955, CP(55)114, CAB129/77, PRO.
60 Minutes of the 28th conclusions of the Cabinet, 15 August 1955, CAB128/29, PRO.
61 Minutes of the 41st meeting of the ONC, 19 August 1955, CAB134/1102, PRO.
62 Memorandum by the Foreign Office, 24 August 1955, ON(55)86, CAB134/1105, PRO.
63 Minutes of the 29th conclusions of the Cabinet, 26 August 1955, CAB128/29, PRO.
64 Memorandum by the Chancellor of the Exchequer, 1 October 1955, CP(55)142, CAB129/77, PRO.
65 *Ibid.*
66 The breakdown of the main items were as follows: wool, 22 million; foodstuffs, 20 million; cotton, 14 million; sugar, 2.5 million; Open General Licence, 32 million; invisibles, 25 million. See memorandum by the Chancellor of the Exchequer, 1 October 1955, CP(55)142, CAB129/77, PRO.
67 *Ibid.*
68 See 'Exchange of Notes between the Government of the United Kingdom of Great Britain and Northern Ireland and the Government of Japan prolonging until 30th September 1956 the Sterling Payments Agreement of the 29th of January 1954', *Parliamentary Papers*, 1955–6, vol. 44, Cmd. 9658, London: HMSO, 1956.
69 Note by the Joint Secretaries, 24 November 1955, ON(55)113, CAB134/1105, PRO.
70 *Ibid.*

8 A period of lull

1 On Kishi Nobusuke, see John Welfield, *An Empire in Eclipse: Japan in the Postwar American Alliance System. A Study in the Interaction of Domestic Politics and Foreign Policy*, London and Atlantic Highlands: Athlone Press, 1988, 116–25; Akio Watanabe, *Sengo Nihon no Saishô tachi*, 122–47.
2 Welfield, *An Empire in Eclipse*, 120.
3 For background on the Australia-Japan Commercial Trade Agreement, see Alan Rix, *Coming to Terms: The Politics of Australia's Trade with Japan 1945–57*, Sydney: Allen & Unwin, 1986, 204–10; for the New Zealand-Japan Commercial Trade Agreement, see Singleton and Robertson, *Economic Relations between Britain and Australasia, 1945–1970*, 129–85.
4 See FRUS 1955–1957, vol. 10, Washington DC: US Government Printing Office, 1989, 205–508; Qing Simei, 'The Eisenhower Administration and Changes in Western Embargo Policy Against China, 1954–1958', in Warren I. Cohen and Akira Iriye (eds) *The Great Powers in East Asia, 1953–1960*, New York: Columbia University Press, 1990, 121–42: Shimizu, *Creating People of Plenty*, 145–7; Forsberg, *America and the Japanese Miracle*, 213–18.
5 Shimizu, *Creating People of Plenty*, 158; Forsberg, *America and the Japanese Miracle*, 213.
6 The Kishi plan, or the Southeast Asian Development Fund, was a yen-based regional credit union. It was the brainchild of MITI and MOF. Membership was restricted to the Colombo Plan members and Taiwan. The fund had three

components. The first component consisted of a $500 million finance corporation fund, which was a low-interest long-term development loan for implementation in private and public projects in Southeast Asia. The second component consisted of an institution capitalised at $100 million to rediscount long- and medium-term export credit bills at low interest rates for Asian traders. Third, the Asian trade fund, which consisted of $100 million, was to assist countries which were dependent on one or two seasonal exports with six-month foreign exchange loans. All the components of the fund provided for the needs of the region, which were either not met or were provided for too slowly by the IMF, World Bank and the US Export-Import Bank. The United States' rejection of the Kishi Plan eventually led Japan to seek a unilateral approach to Southeast Asian economic development. See Shimizu, *Creating People of Plenty*, 194; Tomaru, *The Postwar Rapprochement of Malaya and Japan, 1945–1961*, 166–9.

7 On the Suez crisis, see Diane B. Kunz, *The Economic Diplomacy of the Suez Crisis*, Chapel Hill and London: University of North Carolina Press, 1991; and W. M. Roger Louis and Roger Owen (eds) *Suez 1956: The Crisis and Its Consequences*, Oxford: Clarendon Press, 1989; Lewis Johnman, 'Defending the Pound: The Economics of the Suez Crisis, 1956', in Anthony Gorst, Leis Johnman and W. Scott Lucas (eds) *Post-war Britain, 1945–64: Themes and Perspectives*, London and New York: Pinter Publishers, 1989, 166–81.

8 On Britain's policy towards European integration, see Richard Lamb, 'Macmillan and Europe', in Richard Aldous and Sabine Lee (eds) *Harold Macmillan: Aspects of a Political Life*, Basingstoke: Macmillan Press, 1999, 75–94; Sabine Lee, 'Staying in the Game? Coming into the Game? Macmillan and European Integration', in Richard Aldous and Sabine Lee (eds) *Harold Macmillan and Britain's World Role*, Basingstoke: Macmillan Press, 1996, 123–47; David Reynolds, *Britannia Overruled: British Policy and World Power in the 20th Century*, New York and London: Longman, 1991, 216–21.

9 See John Fforde, *The Bank of England and Public Policy, 1941–1958*, Cambridge: Cambridge University Press, 1992, 566–605; Derek W. Unwin, *The Community of Europe: A History of European Integration since 1945*, London and New York: Longman, 1991.

10 Memorandum of the Review of Anglo-Japanese Trade and Payments Arrangements for the ONC, 23 February 1956, ON(56)6, CAB134/1309, PRO.

11 *Ibid.*

12 *Ibid.*

13 Memorandum by the Board of Trade and the Treasury to the ONC, 24 August 1956, ON(56)38, CAB134/1309, PRO.

14 *Ibid.*

15 *Ibid.*

16 Dispatch from American Embassy London to DOS, 11 January 1957, DF 44 1.944,1/1–1157, NA.

17 *Ibid.*

18 Memorandum by the Board of Trade on United Kingdom-Japan Trade Negotiations, 24 January 1957, ON(57) 6, CAB134/2351, PRO.

19 *Ibid.* On Anglo-Japanese cooperation in the motor vehicle industry, see Madeley, 'A Case Study of Anglo-Japanese Cooperation in the Motor vehicle Industry' 219–48.

20 Correspondence from Esler Dening to Selwyn Lloyd, 4 April 1957, FO37/127562 FJ1152/64, PRO.

21 *Ibid.*

22 Minutes of the second meeting of the Cabinet Overseas Negotiations Committee, 28 January 1957, CAB134/2351, PRO.

23 Correspondence from O.C. Morland to Esler Dening, 9 February 1957, FO371/127562 FJ1152/30, PRO.

24 Letter from Dening to Nobusuke Kishi, 29 March 1957, FO371/127562 FJ1152/64, PRO.

25 Draft of a brief on Japanese Ambassador's visit to Chancellor of the Exchequer, 9 June 1958, FO371/133598 FJ1051/239, PRO.

26 See minutes of the Anglo-Japanese Trade Negotiations, 21 February to 25 April, in FO371/133616 FJ1151/12, PRO.

27 The sale was made possible as a result of the conclusion of the United Kingdom-Japanese Atomic Energy Agreement in June 1958. See Note by P. G. F. Dalton, 23 June 1958, FO371/133598 FJ1057/27, PRO.

28 John Weste, 'Facing the Unavoidable', 304.

29 Hein, *Fueling Growth*, 281–4.

30 Weste, 'Facing the Unavoidable', 304.

31 Note by J. E. Chadwick, 24 February 1956, BT11/5389 CRE500/3/56, PRO.

32 Note from A. L. Mayall to S. Levine, 1 February 1956, BT11/5359 CRE 500/3/56 PRO.

33 Correspondence from J. E. Chadwick to S. H. Levine, 2 March 1956, BT11/5389 CRE500/3/56, PRO.

34 This question was too laborious a task for Britain at this stage of the negotiations, given that the Japanese officials had not elaborated on the exact information needs from Britain. Moreover, the Board of Trade did not wish to 'drift into piecemeal' questions and answers in advance of the conclusion of the treaty. See correspondence from S. H. Levine to J. E. Chadwick, n.d., BT11/5389 CRE500/3/56; telegram from Tokyo to FO, 25 February 1956, FO371/121056 FJ1151/29, PRO.

35 Note by J. E. Chadwick, 24 February 1956, BT11/5389 CRE500/3/56, PRO.

36 Correspondence from S. H. Levine to C. T. Crowe, 8 March 1956, FO371/121056 FJ1151/29, PRO.

37 Note by W. Harpham, 20 July 1956, BT11/ 5392 CRE500/6/56, PRO.

38 See Minutes of agreed record of meeting on Treaty of Commerce and Navigation between the United Kingdom and Japan, 12 June 1956, BT11/5391 CRE500/5/56; and note of meeting on the draft Treaty of Commerce and Navigation between the United Kingdom and Japan, 21 December 1956, BT11/ 5393 CRE501/1956, PRO.

39 Correspondence from S. H. Levine to W. Harpham, 18 September 1956, FO371/121058 FJ1151/94, PRO.

40 See Memorandum of Conversation of State Department and Japanese delegation, 12 September 1960, *FRUS, 1958–1960*, vol. 4, Washington DC: US Government Printing Office, 1992, 401–3.

41 Note by P. H. Gore-Booth on Relations with Japan, 29 January 1959, FO371/141470 FJ1152/11, PRO.

42 Memorandum by the President of the Board of Trade to the EPC, 29 February 1960, EA(60)25,CAB134/1686, PRO.

43 John Singleton and Paul L. Robertson, *Economic Relations Between Britain and Australasia 1945–1970*, 111.

44 For a thorough treatment of this issue, see *ibid.*, ch. 5, 'Stresses in the Ottawa System', 99–122.

45 Memorandum by the Board of Trade on Imports of Cotton Textiles from Asian Commonwealth Countries to the Cabinet Economic Policy Committee, 13 April 1962, EA (62) 57, CAB134/1676, PRO.

46 India and Pakistan agreed to the voluntary export restriction on the condition that duty-free exports from mainland China were abolished. See minutes of 28th meeting of the EPC, 5 December 1957, CAB134/1674, PRO; Memorandum by

the President of the Board of Trade on Imports of Cotton Textiles from India, Pakistan and Hong Kong for the EPC, 27 June 1957, EA(57)69, CAB134/1676, PRO.

47 Minutes of the 18th meeting of the EPC, 10 July 1957, CAB134/1674, PRO.
48 *Ibid.*
49 Minutes of the 56th Conclusions of the Cabinet, 23 July 1957, CAB128/31, PRO.
50 India's annual ceiling was 140 million yards and Pakistan's was 30 million yards. See minutes of the third meeting of the Cabinet Cotton Imports Committee, 7 July 1958, CAB130/145, PRO.
51 See 84th conclusions of the Cabinet, 10 December 1958; and 86th conclusions of the Cabinet, 18 December 1958, CAB128/32, PRO.
52 DOS to the American Embassy Tokyo, 6 July 1959, DF 394.41/7–659, NA.
53 *Ibid.*
54 See Report to the Secretary of State by the Chairman of the US Delegation to the 14th Session of the GATT, DF 394.41/10–959, NA.
55 Minutes of 25th conclusions of the Cabinet, 23 April 1959, CAB128/33, PRO.
56 See memorandum by the Chancellor of the Exchequer on Liberalisation of dollar imports, 17 April 1959, C(59)70, CAB129/97, PRO.
57 Minutes of 25th conclusions of the Cabinet, 23 April 1959, CAB128/33, PRO.
58 See minutes of the 31st conclusions of the Cabinet, 12 May 1959, CAB128/33, PRO.
59 Balance of Payments Studies: Trade Discrimination, CFEP 595/1, 20 May 1960, FRUS 1958–1960 vol. 4, Washington DC: US Government Printing Office, 1992, 249–54.
60 American Embassy Tokyo to DOS, 21 August 1959, DF 394.41/8–1359, NA.
61 They were lard, beef tallow, hides and skins, soybeans, iron and steel scrap, pig iron, copper alloy scrap, lauan logs, abaca and gypsum. *Ibid.*
62 Other commodities mentioned by the United States were automobiles, motorcycles, sewing machines, writing instruments, television receivers, crude oil, cotton, equipment for Singer sewing machines, company investment in Japan, motion pictures, Bourbon whiskey, raisins, lemons, cheese and wood pulp. See *ibid.*
63 Balance of Payments Studies: Trade Discrimination, CFEP 595/1, 20 May 1960, FRUS 1958–1960, vol. 4, 249–254.
64 Telegram from Tokyo to FO, 13 January 1959, FO371/ 141470 FJ1152/35, PRO.
65 *Ibid.*
66 Telegram from Tokyo to FO, 30 January 1959, FO371/141470 FJ1152/10, PRO.
67 MITI was pressurised by domestic industries such as the wool and glass industries. In addition, it was under increasing pressure from the United States. See correspondence from A. N. MacCleary to Macphail, 13 February 1959, FO371/141471 FJ11512/15, PRO.
68 Record of conversation by A. N. McCleary, 28 January 1958, FO371/133618 FJ1154/28, PRO.
69 Correspondence from W. Hughes to Mr T. Nakagawa, 25 March 1959, FO371/141471 FJ1152/24, PRO.
70 Note by J. E. Chadwick on his conversation Mr Nakamura, 19 March 1959, FO371/141471 FJ1152/19, PRO.
71 Telegram from FO to Tokyo, 28 May 1959, FO371/141472 UEE 10414/97, PRO.
72 Article 5 of the Australian-Japanese Commercial Agreement read as follows:

> If, nevertheless, as a result of unforeseen developments, the government of either country finds that any product is being imported from the other country under such conditions as to cause or threaten serious injury to producers in the country of importation of like or directly competitive products, that Government may, in respect of such product, suspend obligations

under this Agreement to the extent and for such time as may be necessary to prevent or remedy the injury.

See note by M. E. Heath, 22 April 1959, FO371/141472 FJ1152/33, PRO.

73 Note of a Board of Trade meeting, 23 July 1959, BT11/5727 CRE6034/1959, PRO.
74 Record of conversation between the Prime Minister and the Prime Minister of Japan, 27 July 1959, PREM11/2738, PRO.
75 *Ibid.*
76 Note of a Board of Trade meeting, 23 July 1959, BT11/5727 CRE6034/1959, PRO.
77 Note by the Board of Trade on MFN treatment for Japan, 15 October 1959, BT11/5727, CRE6034/1959,PRO.
78 Copy of a memorandum by the Board of Trade on MFN treatment for Japan, 15 October 1959, FO371/141473 FJ1152/98, PRO.
79 *Ibid.*
80 Correspondence from Hughes to C. B. Reynolds, 5 November 1959, BT11/5727 CRE6034/1959, PRO.
81 *Ibid.*
82 Minutes of the 6th meeting of the UK Delegation to the 15th Session of the Contracting Parties to the GATT, 5 November 1959, BT11/5727 CRE6034/1959, PRO.
83 *Aide-mémoire* from Ohno Katsumi to Reginald Maudling, 9 November 1959, FO371/141473 FJ1152/61, PRO.
84 Telegram from FO to Tokyo, 12 November 1959, FO371/141473 FJ1152/61, PRO.
85 See extract from the Mainich, 11 November 1959, FO371/141474 FJ1152/60, PRO.
86 Correspondence from Reginald Maudling to Selwyn Lloyd, 24 November 1959, FO371/141474 FJ1152/78, PRO.
87 Telegram from FO to Tokyo, 17 December 1959, FO371/141474 FJ1152/83, PRO.

9   The Anglo-Japanese Commercial Treaty

1 See N. Piers Ludlow, 'A Mismanaged Application: Britain and the EEC, 1961–1963', in Anne Deighton and Alan S. Milward (eds) *Widening, Deepening and Acceleration: The European Economic Community, 1957–1963*, Baden-Baden: Nomos, 1999, 271–86.
2 Memorandum by the President of the Board of Trade to the EPC, 8 February 1960, EA (60) 9, CAB134/1686, PRO.
3 Calculated from memorandum by the President of the Board of Trade to the EPC, 7 March 1960, EA(60)31, CAB134/1687, PRO.
4 The purpose of the 1959 Cotton Industry Act was to boost Conservative prospects in Lancashire ahead of the general election, but the industry would rather have seen a cap on foreign textiles imports rather than receive a re-equipment subsidy which 'was equivalent to an effect rate of protection of a mere 5 per cent for two years'. See John Singleton, 'Showing the White Flag: The Lancashire Cotton Industry, 1945–65', *Business History*, vol. 32, no. 4 (1990): 141–2.
5 Memorandum by the President of the Board of Trade to the EPC, 7 March 1960, EA(60)31, CAB134/1687, PRO.

6 Memorandum by the President of the Board of Trade to the EPC, 27 June 1960, EA(60)57, CAB134/1687, PRO.

7 *Ibid.*

8 Memorandum by the President of the Board of Trade to the Cabinet, 2 August 1961, C(61)127, CAB129/106, PRO.

9 Memorandum by the Board of Trade to the EPC, 23 October 1961, EA(61)87, CAB134/1692, PRO.

10 *Ibid.*

11 Correspondence from Hughes to Phillips, 27 July 1962, BT11/5944 CRE1444/2/1962, PRO.

12 Note by E. L. Phillips on the visit of Mr Ohno, 19 October 1962, BT11/5945 CRE1444/3/1962, PRO.

13 Memorandum by the President of the Board of Trade to the EPC, 15 February 1960, EA(60)13, CAB134/1686, PRO.

14 Memorandum by the President of the Board of Trade to the EPC, 29 February 1960, EA(60)23, CAB134/1686, PRO.

15 Minutes of the 16th conclusions of the Cabinet, 10 March 1960, CAB128/34, PRO.

16 Note by the President of the Board of Trade to the EPC, 28 November 1960, EA(60)97, CAB134/1688, PRO.

17 *Ibid.*

18 *Ibid.*

19 *Ibid.*

20 Note by the President of the Board of Trade to the EPC, 28 November 1960, EA(60)96, 28 November, 1960, CAB134/1688, PRO.

21 Memorandum by the President of the Board of Trade to the EPC, 25 November 1960, EA(60)94, CAB134/1688, PRO.

22 *Ibid.*

23 *Ibid.*

24 Memorandum by the Chancellor of the Exchequer to the Cabinet, 2 December 1960, C(60)181, CAB129/103, PRO.

25 Minutes of the 62nd conclusions of the Cabinet, 8 December 1960, CAB128/34, PRO.

26 Note by A. J. De La Mare on visit of the Foreign Minister, Mr Kosaka, 5 July 1961, BT11/5838 CRE/4572/61, PRO.

27 Christopher Braddick, 'Distant Friends: Britain and Japan since 1958–the Age of Globalization', in Ian Nish and Kibata Yoichi (eds) *The History of Anglo-Japanese Relations, 1600–2000, Volume II: The Political-Diplomatic Dimension, 1931–2000*, Basingstoke: Macmillan Press, 2000, 270.

28 *Ibid.*

29 Memorandum by the President of the Board of Trade to the EPC, 27 July 1961, CAB134/1891, PRO.

30 *Ibid.*

31 *Ibid.*

32 Memorandum from the Chancellor of the Exchequer to the Cabinet, 2 August 1961, C(62)37, CAB129/106, PRO.

33 Note of a meeting of FBI, 16 June 1961, F/3/D3, FBI, MRC.

34 Letter from Kipping to Directors of Certain Trade Associations, 21 May 1961, F/3/D3, FBI, MRC.

35 Gray, 'The Anglo-Japanese Commercial Treaty of 1962', 309; Sosuke Hanaoka, 'Memories of the Anglo-Japanese Commercial Treaty: A Japanese Perspective', in Ian Nish (ed.) *Britain and Japan: Biographical Portraits Volume II*, Richmond: Japan Library, 1997, 308.

36 See Gray, 'The Anglo-Japanese Commercial Treaty of 1962', 314.

37 Correspondence from W. Hughes to Sir Edgar Cohen, 22 December 1961, BT11/5945 CRE1444/3/1962, PRO.
38 *Ibid.*
39 Correspondence from W. Hughes to Sir Edgar Cohen, 9 February 1962, BT11/5947 CRE1563/1962, PRO.
40 Correspondence from W. Hughes to C. G. Harris, 27 June 1962, BT11/5943 CRE1444/1/1962, PRO.
41 Correspondence from E. L. Phillips to R. D. Poland, 12 April 1962, BT11/5746 CRE8731/1959, PRO.
42 Correspondence from S. M. A. Banister to E. L. Phillips, 3 July 1962, BT11/5746 CRE8731/1959, PRO.
43 Note of Informal Meeting with Japanese held on 29 May 1962, BT11/5746 CRE8731/1959, PRO.
44 Robin Gray, 'The Anglo-Japanese Commercial Treaty of 1962: A British Perspective', in Ian Nish (ed.) *Britain and Japan: Biographical Portraits Volume II*, Surrey: Japan Library, 1997, 305.
45 *Ibid.*
46 Department of State, 'Treaty of Friendship, Commerce and Navigation between the United States and Japan', *United States Treaties and Other International Agreements*, vol. 4, part 2 (1953): 2066–82.
47 *Ibid.*, p. 156; see also Marie Conte-Helm, 'Anglo-Japanese Investment in the Postwar Period', in Janet E. Hunter and S. Sugiyama (eds) *The History of Anglo-Japanese Relations, 1600–2000*, 319.
48 Robin Gray, 'The Anglo-Japanese Commercial Treaty of 1962: A British Perspective', 307.
49 *Ibid.*
50 See Hughes' notes on an informal meeting with Mr Seki and Mr Suzuki, 3 August 1962, BT11/5944 CRE1444/2/1962 PRO.
51 *Ibid.*
52 Note of meetings between the President and Mr Zentaro Kosaka, 26 April and 4 May1962, 7 May 1962, BT11/5910 CRE583/2/1962, PRO.
53 See note by W. Hughes on the main outstanding points of the treaty, 5 April 1962, BT11/5947 CRE1563/1962, PRO.
54 Hughes' notes on informal meeting with Mr Seki and Mr Suzuki, 3 August 1962, BT11/5944 CRE1444/2/1962, PRO.
55 Note by the President of the Board of Trade to the Cabinet's Economic Policy Committee, 17 May 1962, EA(62)70, CAB134/1695, PRO.
56 *Ibid.*
57 Note of a meeting with representatives of the wool textile industry, 11 July 1962, PREM11/5156, PRO.
58 See minutes of the 48th conclusions of the Cabinet, 19 July 1962, CAB128/36, PRO.
59 Correspondence from Ohno to Erroll, 6 November 1962, BT11/5943 CRE1444/1/1962, PRO.
60 Government Statement on the Anglo-Japanese Commercial Treaty, *Parliamentary Papers*, vol. 31, Cmd 1875, 25–36.
61 See Joint Communiqué on the visit of the Japanese Prime Minister, 14 November 1962, PREM11/4329, PRO.
62 See Janet Hunter and S. Sugiyama, 'Anglo-Japanese Economic Relations in Historical Perspective, 1600–2000', in Hunter and Sugiyama, *The History of Anglo-Japanese Relations*, 71.
63 Marie Conte-Helm, 'Anglo-Japanese Investment in the Postwar Period', in Hunter and Sugiyama, *The History of Anglo-Japanese Relations*, 320.
64 *Ibid.*, 340.

65 See R. P. T. Davenport-Hines, 'British Business in Japan since 1868', in *British Business in Asia since 1860*, 240–2; Madeley, 'A Case Study of Anglo-Japanese Cooperation in the Motor Vehicle Industry: Ishikawajima, Wolseley, Isuzu and Rootes', in Hunter and Sugiyama, *The History of Anglo-Japanese Relations*, 237–43; Helm, 'Anglo-Japanese Investment in the Postwar Period', in *ibid.*, 318–21.

66 Laura E. Hein, *Fueling Growth*, 214.

67 See Hunter and Sugiyama, 'Anglo-Japanese Economic Relations in Historical Perspective 1600–2000: Trade and Industry, Finance, Technology and the Industrial Challenge', in Hunter and Sugiyama, *The History of Anglo-Japanese Relations*, 84.

68 See correspondence from O. C. Morland to Sir Frank Lee, 29 September 1959, and J. E. Chadwick to W. Hughes, 7 October 1959, BT11/5768 CRE12429/59, PRO.

69 See Hunter and Sugiyama, 'Anglo-Japanese Economic Relations in Historical Perspective 1600–2000: Trade and Industry, Finance, Technology and the Industrial Challenge', in Hunter and Sugiyama, *The History of Anglo-Japanese Relations*, 95.

70 Copy of correspondence from J. A. Turpin, n.a., BT11/5744 CRE8311/1959, PRO.

Bibliography

Primary sources

Bank of England, London
OV16: Japan: Financial (including trade) Relations with the UK.
Eisenhower Library, Abilene, Kansas
Central files.
US President's Commission on Foreign Economic Policy.
Whitman files.
Manchester Central Library, Manchester
Manchester Chamber of Commerce
Ministry of Foreign Affairs Archives, Tokyo
A-0136: *Yoshida Sôri Ôbei Hômon Kankei Ikken* [Prime Minister Yoshida's European and American trip].
A-0357: *Ôhira Gaimu Ôbei Hômon Kankei* [Foreign Minister Ohira's European and American trip].
A-0362: *Kosaka Gaimu Yôroppa Hômon Kankei* [Foreign Minister Kosaka's European trip].
A-0363: *Ikeda Sôri Yôroppa Hômon Kankei Ikken* [Prime Minister Ikeda's European trip].
B-0020: *Nichiei Bôeki Shiharai Kankei Ikken* [Japan-UK Trade Agreements].
B-0021: *Nichiei Bôeki Shiharai Kankei Ikken* [Japan-UK Trade Agreements].
B-0029: *Dai Hakkai Kokusai Komugi Kyôtei Kankei Ikken* [the Eighth Session of the International Wheat Agreement].
B-0093: *Nichigô Tsûshô Kyôtei Kankei* [Japan-Australia Commercial Treaty].
B-0095: *Nichiei Tsûshô Kyôtei Kankei* [Anglo-Japanese Commercial Treaty].
E-0010: *Kanzei oyobi Bôeki ni kansuru Ippan Kyôtei Kankei Ikken* [The Problem of Japanese Entry into the GATT].
E-0011: *Kanzei oyobi Bôeki ni kansuru Ippan Kyôtei Kankei Ikken* [The Problem of Japanese Entry into the GATT].
E-0012: *Kanzei oyobi Bôeki ni kansuru Ippan Kyôtei Kankei Ikken* [The Problem of Japanese Entry into the GATT].
E-0013: *Kanzei oyobi Bôeki ni kansuru Ippan Kyôtei Kankei Ikken* [The Problem of Japanese Entry into the GATT].
E-0015: *Tai-Kyôsanken Yushutsu Tôsei Iinkai Kankei Ikken* [Coordinating Committee Related].
Modern Records Centre, Warwick University

MSS.200F: Federation of British Industries.
National Archives II, College Park, Maryland
Record Group 59: State Department Decimal Files.
Record Group 84: Record of the Foreign Service Post of the Department of State.
Record Group 331: Records of Allied Operational and Occupation Headquarters, World War II.
Public Record Office, Kew
BT 11: Board of Trade Commercial Department.
BT 175: Cotton Board and Textile Council.
CAB 128: Cabinet Minutes.
CAB 129: Cabinet Memoranda.
CAB 130: Cabinet Miscellaneous Committees.
CAB 133: Cabinet Office: Commonwealth and International Conferences and Ministerial visits to and from the United Kingdom.
CAB 134: Cabinet Miscellaneous Committees.
CO 537: Colonial Office: Confidential General and Original Correspondence.
CO 852: Colonial Office: Economic: Original Correspondence.
CO 1022: Colonial Office: South East Asia Department: Original Correspondence.
CO 1023: Colonial Office: Hong Kong and Pacific Department: Original Correspondence.
CO 1030: Colonial Office: Far East Department: Original Correspondence.
DEFE 10: Ministry of Defence: Major Committees, Minutes, Papers: 1942-1976.
DO 35: Dominions Office and Commonwealth Relations Office: Original Correspondence.
FO262: Foreign Office: Embassy and Consulates, Japan: General Correspondence.
FO371: Foreign Office: Political Department.
PREM 8: Prime Minister's Office: Correspondence and Papers, 1945–1951.
PREM 11: Prime Minister's Office: Correspondence and Papers, 1951–1964.
T236: Treasury: Overseas Finance Division.
T238: Treasury: Overseas Negotiations Committee Division: Registered Files.
Truman Library, Independence, Missouri
President's Secretary's Files.
Official File.

Private papers

Dean Acheson Papers, Truman Library, Independence, Missouri.
Clement Attlee Papers, Bodleian Library, Oxford.
Ernest Bevin Papers, Public Record Office, Kew.
Richard Austen Butler Papers, Trinity College, Cambridge.
Winston Churchill Papers, Churchill College, Cambridge.
John Foster Dulles Papers, Eisenhower Library, Abilene, Kansas and at Mudd Library, Princeton.
Anthony Eden Papers, Birmingham University Library and the Public Record Office, Kew.
Alan Lennox-Boyd Papers, Bodleian Library, Oxford.
Oliver Lyttelton Papers, Public Record Office, Kew.
Malcolm MacDonald Papers, Durham University, Durham.
Herbert Morrison Papers, Public Record Office, Kew.

H. Alexander Smith Papers, Mudd Library, Princeton.
Harry S. Truman Papers, Truman Library, Independence, Missouri.

Oral Histories

Rhodes House Library, Oxford
Sir Alexander Grantham.
Seeley G. Mudd Library, Princeton
The JFD Oral History Project.
Oliver Franks.
U. Alexis Johnson.
George F. Kennan.
Livingstone T. Merchant.
Okazaki Katsuo.
William J. Sebald.
Truman Library, Independence, Missouri
Lucius Battle.
Niles W. Bond.
John F. Melby.
John W. Snyder.
R. Allen Thorp.
Willard L. Thorp.

Published documents

Bank of Tokyo, *Tai Stâringu Chiiki Bôeki no kôsatsu* [A Study on Trade Relations with the Sterling Area], vol. 3, no. 17. Tokyo: Tôkyô Ginkô Chôsa bu [Bank of Tokyo Research Department], 1968.

Bank of Tokyo, *Tai Sterling Chîkibôeki no kôsatsu, Tokyo Ginkô Chôsabu, Tôgin Chôsashiryô dai 17 gô, July 1969* [Study on trade with the Sterling Area, Bank of Tokyo Research Department, Bank of Tokyo Research Study no. 17, July 1969], 2–35.

General Agreement on Tariffs and Trade, *Analytical Index: Guide to GATT Law and Practice*, Geneva: GATT, 1994.

State Department, *Foreign Relations of the United States*, 1951, vol. 6, part 1, Washington DC: US Government Printing Office, 1977.

——*Foreign Relations of the United States*, 1952–1954, vol. 1, part 1, Washington DC: US Government Printing Office, 1983.

——*Foreign Relations of the United States*, 1952–1954, vol. 12, part 1, Washington DC: US Government Printing Office, 1984.

——*Foreign Relations of the United States*, 1952–1954, vol. 14, part 2, Washington DC: US Government Printing Office, 1985.

——*Foreign Relations of the United States*, 1955–1957, vol. 9, Washington DC: US Government Printing Office, 1987.

——*Foreign Relations of the United States*, 1955–1957, vol. 11, Washington DC: US Government Printing Office, 1988.

——*Foreign Relations of the United States*, 1955–1957, vol. 23, part 1, Washington DC: US Government Printing Office, 1991.

——*Foreign Relations of the United States*, 1958–1960, vol. 4, Washington DC: US Government Printing Office, 1992.

——*Foreign Relations of the United States*, 1958–1960, vol. 18, Washington DC: US Government Printing Office, 1994.

——*Foreign Relations of the United States*, 1961–1963, vol. 9, Washington DC: US Government Printing Office, 1995.

——*Foreign Relations of the United States*, 1961–1963, vol. 22, Washington DC: US Government Printing Office, 1996.

Kajima Morinosuke (ed.) *Nihon Gaikôshi* [The Diplomatic History of Japan], vol. 30, *Kôwago no Gaikô (II) Keizai (jyo)* [Diplomacy after the Peace Treaty (II) Economics, Part I], Tokyo: Kamima Kenkyûjo Shuppankai, 1972.

Ministry of Finance (ed.) *Shôwa Zaiseishi* [Showa Financial History] vol. 15, *Shûsen kara Kôwa made* [From the end of the war to the Peace Treaty], Tokyo: Tôyô Keizai Shinpôsha, 1976.

——*Shôwa Zaiseishi* [Showa Financial History] vol. 19, *Shûsen kara Kôwa made* [From the end of the war to the Peace Treaty], Tokyo: Tôyô Keizai Shinpôsha, 1978.

Ministry of International Trade and Industry (ed.) *Nihon Bôeki no Tenkai: Sengo 10 nen no Ayumikara* [Development of Japan's Trade: A Review of the Postwar Decade], Tokyo: Shôkô Shuppan, 1956.

——*Tsûshô Sangyô Seisakushi* [The History of Trade and Industrial Policy], vol. 6, *Dai Niki Kiritsu Kiban Kakuritsuki (2)* [The Second Stage – Establishing the Foundation for self-efficiency (2)], Tokyo: Tsûshô Sangyô Chôsakai, 1990.

Sterling Payments Agreement between the Government of the United Kingdom of Great Britain and Northern Ireland and the Government of Japan (with Exchange of Notes) *Parliamentary Papers* vol. 31, Cmd 8602, London: HMSO, 1951.

United Kingdom, *Hansard Parliamentary Debates* (Commons) 5th series, vol. 473 (1950).

——*Hansard Parliamentary Debates* (Commons) 5th series, vol. 523 (1953–4).

Treaty of Peace with Japan, Treaty Series no. 33, *Parliamentary Papers*, vol. 31, Cmd. 8601, London: HMSO, 1952.

United Kingdom Balance of Payments 1949 to 1952, *Parliamentary Papers*, vol. 18, Cmd. 8808, London: HMSO, 1953.

United Kingdom Balance of Payments 1946 to 1955, *Parliamentary Papers*, vol. 29, Cmd. 9731, London: HMSO, 1956.

Treaty of Commerce, Establishment and Navigation between the United Kingdom of Great Britain and Northern Ireland and Japan, *Parliamentary Papers*, vol. 38, Cmd. 2085, London: HMSO, 1962.

United Nations, *Yearbook of International Trade Statistics, 1951*, New York: United Nations, 1952.

——*Yearbook of International Trade Statistics, 1951–1956*, New York: United Nations, 1952–1957.

——*Yearbook of International Trade Statistics, 1954*, New York: United Nations, 1955.

——*Yearbook of International Trade Statistics, 1957, vol. 1*, New York: United Nations, 1958.

——*Yearbook of International Trade Statistics, 1961*, New York: United Nations, 1963.

——*Yearbook of International Trade Statistics, 1965*, New York: United Nations, 1965.

Newspapers

Asahi Shimbun.
Economist.
Manchester Guardian.
The Times.

Journals

Cotton Board Quarterly Statistical Review.
Congressional Digest.
Bulletin.

Published memoirs and diaries

Acheson, Dean, *Present at the Creation: My Years in the State Department*, New York: Norton, 1967.

Butler, Richard Austin, *The Art of the Possible: The Memoirs of Lord Butler*, London: Hamish Hamilton, 1971.

Cairncross, Alec (ed.) *The Robert Hall Diaries, 1954–1961*, London: Unwin Hyman, 1991.

Colville, John, *The Fringes of Power: Downing Street Diaries. Vol. II 1941–April 1955*, Kent: Sceptre, 1987.

Dupree, Marguerite (ed.) *Lancashire and Whitehall: The Diary of Sir Raymond Streat Volume Two 1939–57*, Manchester: Manchester University Press, 1987.

Eden, Anthony, *Full Circle*, London: Cassell and Company, 1960.

Eisenhower, Dwight D., *The White House Years: Mandate for Change 1953–1956*, London: William Heinemann, 1963.

Grantham, Alexander, *Via Ports: From Hong Kong to Hong Kong*, Hong Kong: Hong Kong University Press, 1965.

Ihara, Takashi, *Ihara Takashi Ikôshu* [The Unpublished Writings of Ihara Takashi], Tokyo: Yokohama Ginkô, 1977.

Kiuchi Nobutane, *Kuni no Kosei* [The Character of a Nation], Tokyo: President-sha, 1986.

Macmillan, Harold, *Pointing the Way 1959–1961.* New York: Harper & Row, 1972.

Maudling, Reginald, *Memoirs*, London: Sidgwick & Jackson, 1978.

Morrison, Herbert, *An Autobiography*, London: Odhams Press, 1960.

Plowden, Edwin, *An Industrialist in the Treasury: The Post-War Years*, London: Andre Deutsch: 1989.

Sebald, William J., with Russell Brines, *With MacArthur in Japan: A Personal History of the Occupation*, London: Cresset Press, 1967.

Truman, Harry S., *The Memoirs of Harry S. Truman Volume Two: Years of Trial and Hope 1946–1953*, Suffolk: Hodder and Stoughton, 1956.

Ushiba, Nobuhiko, *Gaikô no Shunkan: Watakushi no Reirekisho* [A moment in Diplomacy: My Memoirs], Tokyo: Nihon Keizai Shimbun-sha, 1984.

——*Keizaigaikô e no Shôgen* [A Testimony to Economic Diplomacy], Tokyo: Diamond-sha, 1985.

Williams, Philip M. (ed.) *The Diary of Hugh Gaitskell 1945–1956*, London: Jonathan Cape, 1983.

Yoshida Shigeru, *Kaisô Jûnen* [Memoirs of the former Prime Minister of Japan], vols 1 and 3, Tokyo: Shinchô-sha, 1957.

Secondary Sources

Aaronson, Jonathan David and Peter F. Cowhy, *Trade in Services: A Case for Open Markets*, Washington DC: American Enterprise Institute for Public Policy Research, 1984.

Adler-Karlsson, Gunnar, *Western Economic Warfare 1947–1967: A Case Study in Foreign Economic Policy*, Stockholm: Almqvist & Wiksells, 1968.

Akaneya Tatsuo, *Nihon no GATT Kanyû Mondai: Rejimu Riron no Bunseki shikaku ni yoru Jirei Kenkyû* [The Problem of Japanese Accession to the GATT: A Case Study in Regime Theory], Tokyo: University of Tokyo Press, 1992.

Aldous, Richard and Sabine Lee (eds) *Harold Macmillan and Britain's World Role* London: Macmillan, 1996.

——*Harold Macmillan: Aspects of a Political Life*, London: Macmillan, 1999.

Allen, G. C., *Japan's Economic Expansion*, London: Oxford University Press, 1965.

——*A Short Economic History of Modern Japan*, London: Macmillan, 1981.

——*The Japanese Economy*, New York: St Martin's Press, 1981.

Bartlett, C. J., *'The Special Relationship': A Political History of Anglo-American Relations since 1945*, London and New York: Longman, 1992.

Bauer, Raymond A., Ithiel De Sola Pool and Lewis Anthony Dexter, *American Business and Public Policy: The Politics of Foreign Trade*, Chicago: Aldine Atherton Inc., 1972.

Bell, Philip W., *The Sterling Area in the Postwar World: Internal Mechanism and Cohesion 1946–1952*, Oxford: Clarendon Press, 1956.

Best, Antony, *Britain, Japan and Pearl Harbor: Avoiding War in East Asia, 1936–41*, London and New York: Routledge, 1995.

Billings-Yun, Melanie, *Decision Against War. Eisenhower and Dien Bien Phu, 1954*, New York: Columbia University Press, 1988.

Blaker, Michael (ed.) *The Politics of Trade: US and Japanese Policymaking for the GATT Negotiations*, New York: Columbia University Press, 1978.

Blank, Stephen, *Industry and Government in Britain: The Federation of British Industries in Politics, 1945–1965*, Massachusetts: Lexington Books, 1973.

Borden, William S., *The Pacific Alliance: United States Foreign Economic Policy and Japanese Trade Recovery, 1947–1955*, Madison: University of Wisconsin Press, 1984.

Brown, Kenneth D., *Britain and Japan: A Comparative Economic and Social History since 1900*, Manchester: Manchester University Press, 1998.

Buckley, Roger, *Occupation Diplomacy: Britain, the United States and Japan 1945–1952*, Cambridge: Cambridge University Press, 1982.

Bullock, Allan, *Ernest Bevin: Foreign Secretary 1945–1951*, London: William Heinemann, 1983.

Cain, P. J. and A. G. Hopkins, *British Imperialism: Innovation and Expansion, 1699–1914*, London and New York: Longman, 1993.

——*British Imperialism: Crisis and Deconstruction 1914–1990*, London and New York: Longman, 1993.

Cairncross, Alec, *Years of Recovery: British Economic Policy 1945–1951*, London and New York: Methuen, 1985.

Calder, Kent E., *Crisis and Compensation: Public Policy and Political Stability in Japan, 1948–1986*, Princeton: Princeton University Press, 1986.

Chen, Jian, *China's Road to the Korean War: The Making of the Sino-American Confrontation*, New York: Columbia University Press, 1994.

Childs, David, *Britain since 1945: A Political History*, London: Methuen, 1986.

Clayton, David, *Imperialism Revisited: Political and Economic Relations between Britain and China, 1950–54*, London and New York: Macmillan Press, 1997.

Cohen, Jerome B., *Japan's Postwar Economy*, Bloomington: Indiana University Press, 1960.

Cohen, Theodore, *Remaking Japan: The American Occupation as New Deal*, New York: Free Press, 1987.

Craig, F. W. S. (ed.) *British Parliamentary Election Results 1950–1970*, Chichester: Political Reference Publications, 1971.

Cumings, Bruce, *The Origins of the Korean War: Liberation and the Emergence of Separate Regimes 1945–1947*, Princeton: Princeton University Press, 1981.

——*The Origins of the Korean War: The Roaring of the Cataract 1947–1950*, Princeton: Princeton University Press, 1990.

Danchev, Alex, *Oliver Franks: Founding Father*, Oxford: Clarendon Press, 1993.

Darwin, John, *The End of the British Empire: The Historical Debate*, Oxford: Blackwell, 1991.

Davenport-Hines, R. P. T. and Geoffrey Jones (eds) *Business in Asia since 1860*, Cambridge: Cambridge University Press, 1989.

Deighton, Anne and Alan S. Milward (eds) *Widening, Deepening and Acceleration: The European Economic Community 1957–1963*, Baden-Baden: Nomos, 1999.

Dobson, Alan P., *The Politics of the Anglo-American Economic Special Relationship, 1940–1987*, Sussex: Wheatsheaf Books, 1988.

Dower, J. W., *Empire and Aftermath: Yoshida Shigeru and the Japanese Experience, 1878–1954*, Cambridge MA and London: Harvard University Press, 1988.

——*Embracing Defeat: Japan in the Wake of World War II*, New York: Norton, 1999.

Drifte, Reinhard, *Japan's Foreign Policy*, London: Routledge, 1990.

Finn, Richard B., *Winners in Peace: MacArthur, Yoshida and Postwar Japan*, Berkley: University of California Press, 1991.

Fforde, John, *The Bank of England and Public Policy, 1941–1958*, Cambridge: Cambridge University Press, 1992.

Foot, Rosemary, *The Wrong War: American Policy and the Dimensions of the Korean Conflict, 1950–1953*, Ithaca NY: Cornell University Press, 1985.

Foreman-Peck, James, *A History of the World Economy: International Economic Relations since 1850*, Hemel Hempstead: Harvest Wheatsheaf, 1995.

Forsberg, Aaron, *America and the Japanese Miracle: The Cold War Context of Japan's Postwar Economic Revival, 1950–1960*, London and Chapel Hill: University of North Carolina Press, 2000.

Frankel, Joseph, *British Foreign Policy 1945–1975*, Oxford: Oxford University Press, 1975.

Gaddis, John Lewis, *The United States and the Origins of the Cold War, 1941–1947*, New York: Columbia University Press, 1972.

——*Strategies of Containment: A Critical Appraisal of Postwar American National Security Policy*, Oxford: Oxford University Press, 1982.

Gallicchio, Marc, *The Cold War begins in Asia: American East Asian Policy and the Fall of Japanese Empire*, New York: Columbia University Press, 1988.

Gardner, Richard, *Sterling-Dollar Diplomacy in Current Perspective: The Origins and the Prospects of Our International Economic Order*, New York: Columbia University Press, 1980.

Gilpin, Robert, *The Political Economy of International Relations*, Princeton: Princeton University Press, 1987.

Goncharov, Sergei N., John W. Lewis and Xue Litai, *Uncertain Partners: Stalin, Mao and the Korean War*, Stanford: Stanford University Press, 1993.

Gorst, Anthony, Lewis Johnman and W. Scott Lucas (eds) *Post-war Britain, 1945–64: Themes and Perspectives*, London and New York: Pinter Publishers, 1989.

Haitani, Kanji, *The Japanese Economic System: An Institutional Overview*, Massachusetts: Lexington Books, 1976.

Hayes, Samuel P. (ed.) *The Beginning of American Aid to Southeast Asia: The Griffin Mission of 1950*, Lexington: DC Heath, 1971.

Harris, Kenneth, *Attlee*, London: Weidenfeld & Nicolson, 1995.

Hashimoto, Jurô, *Sengo no Nihon Keizai* [Japan's Postwar Economy], Tokyo: Iwanami Shinshô, 1995.

Hein, Laura E., *Fueling Growth: The Energy Revolution and Economic Policy in Postwar Japan*, Cambridge MA: Harvard University Press, 1990.

Hennessy, Peter, *Whitehall*, London: Fontana Press, 1990.

Hiwatari, Yumi, *Sengo Seiji to Nichibei Kankei* [Postwar Politics and Japan-US Relations], Tokyo: Tôkyô Daigaku Shuppankai, 1990.

Horne, Alistaire, *Macmillan, 1957–1986: Vol. II of the Official Biography*, London: Macmillan London Ltd., 1989.

Hosoya, Chihiro and Ariga Tadashi (eds) *Kokusai Kankyô no Henyô to Nichibei Kankei* [Changes in the International Environment and US/Japan Relations], Tokyo: Tôkyô Daigaku Shuppankai, 1987.

Hosoya Chihiro and Tomohito Shinoda (eds) *Redefining the Partnership: The United States and Japan in East Asia*, Maryland: University Press of America, 1998.

Hosoya, Chihiro, *San Francisco Kôwa e no Michi*, [The Road to the San Francisco Peace Treaty], Tokyo: Chûô Kôronsha, 1984.

Hunter, Janet E., *The Emergence of Modern Japan: An Introductory History since 1853*, London and New York: Longman, 1989.

Hunter, Janet E. and S. Sugiyama (eds) *The History of Anglo-Japanese Relations 1600–2000. Volume 4: Economic and Business Relations*, London: Palgrave, 2002.

Immerman, Richard H. (ed.) *John Foster Dulles and the Diplomacy of the Cold War*, Princeton: Princeton University Press, 1990.

Inoguchi, Takashi and Daniel I. Okimoto (eds) *The Political Economy of Japan. Volume 2. The Changing International Context*, Stanford: Stanford University Press, 1988.

Iriye, Akira and Yônosuke Nagai (eds) *The Origins of the Cold War in Asia*, New York: Columbia University Press, 1977.

Ishii, Osamu, *Reisen to Nichibei Kankei Pâtonâshippu no Keisei* [The Cold war and US/ Japan Relations: Formation of a Partnership], Tokyo: Japan Times, 1989.

Itô, Masaya, *Ikeda Hayato*, Tokyo: Jiji Tsûshinsha, 1985.

Jackson, John H., *The World Trading System: Law and Policy of International Economic Relations*, Cambridge MA: MIT Press, 1998.

Kaplan, Jacob J., and Günther Schleiminger, *The European Payments Union: Financial Diplomacy in the 1950s*, Oxford: Clarendon Press, 1989.

Kaplan, Lawrence, Denise Artaud and Mark Rubin (eds) *Dien Bien Phu and the Crisis of Franco-American Relations, 1954–1955*, Wilmington: Scholarly Sources, 1990.

Kataoka, Tetsuya, *The Price of a Constitution: The Origins of Japan's Postwar Politics*, New York: Taylor & Francis, 1991.

Kaufman, Burton I., *Trade and Aid Eisenhower's Foreign Economic Policy, 1953–1961*, Baltimore and London: Johns Hopkins University Press, 1982.

Kelly, Saul and Anthony Gorst (eds) *Whitehall and the Suez Crisis*, London: Frank Cass, 2000.

Kent, John, *British Imperial Strategy and the Origins of the Cold War, 1944–49*, Leicester: Leicester University Press, 1993.

Kibata Yôichi: *Teikoku no Tasogare: Reisenka no Igirisu to Ajia* [The Twilight of the Empire: British Policy towards Japan and Malaya, 1947–1955], Tokyo: University of Tokyo Press, 1996.

Kunz, Diane B., *The Economic Diplomacy of the Suez Crisis*, Chapel Hill and London: University of North Carolina Press, 1991.

Kusano, Atsushi and Umemoto Testuya (eds) *Gendai Nihon Gaikô no Bunseki* [An Analysis of Modern Japanese Diplomacy], Tokyo: Tôkyô Daigaku Shuppankai, 1995.

Large, Stephen S., *Emperor Hirohito and Shôwa Japan: A Political Biography*, London and New York: Routledge, 1992.

Livingstone, J. M., *Britain and the World Economy*, Harmondsworth: Penguin Books, 1966.

Louis, Roger W. M. and Roger Owen (eds) *Suez 1956*, Oxford: Clarendon Press, 1989.

Lowe, Peter, *Containing Cold War in East Asia: British Policies towards Japan, China and Korea, 1948–53*, Manchester: Manchester University Press, 1997.

——*Origins of the Korean War*, New York and London: Longman, 1986.

Maga, Timothy P., *Hands Across the Sea? US/Japan Relations, 1961–1981*, Athens OH: Ohio University Press, 1997.

Mason, Mark, *American Multinationals and Japan: The Political Economy of Japanese Capital Controls, 1899–1980*, Cambridge MA: Harvard University Press, 1992.

Mastanduno, Michael, *Economic Containment: CoCom and the Politics of East-West Trade*, Ithaca NY and London: Cornell University Press, 1992.

McDermott, Geoffrey, *The Eden Legacy*, London: Leslie Frewin, 1989.

McGlothlen, Ronald L., *Controlling the Waves: Dean Acheson and US Foreign Policy in Asia*, New York: Norton, 1993.

McIntyre, W. David, *Background to the ANZUS Pact*, London: Macmillan Press, 1995.

Mendl, Wolf, *Issues in Japan's China Policy*, London: Macmillan, 1978.

——*Japan's Asia Policy: Regional Security and Global Interests*, London and New York: Routledge, 1995.

Milward, Alan S. and George Brennan, *Britain's Place in the World: A Historical Enquiry into Import Controls 1945–60*, London: Routledge, 1996.

Mouer, Ross and Sugimoto Yoshio, *Images of Japanese Society: A Study in the Structure of Social Reality*, London: KPI Ltd., 1986.

Munn, Glenn G. *et al.* (eds) *The St James Encyclopedia of Banking and Finance*, Chicago: St James Press, 1991.

Nagaoka, Shinkichi and Nishikawa Hiroshi (eds) *Nihon Keizai to Higashi Ajia: Senji to Sengo no Keizaishi* [The Japanese Economy and East Asia: The Economic History of the Interwar and Postwar Period], Tokyo: Minerva Shobô, 1995.

Nakamura Takafusa, *Shôwashi II 1945–1989* [Showa History II 1945–1989], Tokyo: Tôyô Keizai Shinpôsha, 1993.

——*The Postwar Japanese Economy: Its Development and Structure, 1937–1994*, Tokyo: University of Tokyo Press, 1995.

Nish, Ian, *Alliance in Decline: A Study in Anglo-Japanese Relations, 1908–23*, London: Athlone Press, 1972.

Nish, Ian (ed.) *Anglo-Japanese Alienation 1919–1952*, Cambridge: Cambridge University Press, 1982.

——*Britain and Japan: Biographical Portraits. Volume Two*, Richmond: Japan Library, 1997.

Nish, Ian and Yoichi Kibata (eds) *The History of Anglo-Japanese Relations, 1600–2000. Volume II: The Political-Diplomatic Dimension, 1931–2000*, Basingstoke: Macmillan Press, 2000.

Okimoto, Daniel I., *Between MITI and the Market: Japanese Industrial Policy for High Technology*, Stanford: Stanford University Press, 1989.

Ostry, Sylvia, *The Post-Cold War Trading System: Who's On First?*, London and Chicago: Chicago University Press, 1997.

Pimlott, Ben, *Harold Wilson*, London: HarperCollins, 1992.

Polk, Judd, *Sterling: Its Meaning in World Finance*, New York: Harper & Brothers, 1956.

Remme, Tilman, *Britain and Regional Cooperation in South-East Asia, 1945–1949*, London and New York: Routledge, 1995.

Reynolds, David, *Britannia Overruled: British Policy and World Power in the 20th Century*, London and New York: Longman, 1991.

Rix, Alan, *Coming to Terms: The Politics of Australia's Trade with Japan 1945–57*, Sydney: Allen & Unwin, 1986.

Rotter, Andrew J., *The Path to Vietnam. Origins of the American Commitment to Southeast Asia*, Ithaca NY: Cornell University Press, 1987.

Saitô Shirô, *Japan at the Summit: Japan's Role in the Western Alliance and Asian Pacific Co-operation*, London and New York: Routledge, 1990.

Sandberg, Lars G., *Lancashire in Decline: A study in Entrepeneurship, Technology and International Trade*, Columbus OH: Ohio State University Press, 1974.

Sanger, Clyde, *Malcolm MacDonald: Bringing an End to Empire*, Montreal: McGill-Queen's University, 1995.

Schaller, Michael, *The American Occupation of Japan: the Origins of the Cold War in East Asia*, Oxford: Oxford University Press, 1985.

——*Altered States: The United States and Japan since the Occupation*, New York and Oxford: Oxford University Press, 1997.

Schenk, Catherine R., *Britain and the Sterling Area: From Devaluation to Convertibility in the 1950s*, London: Routledge, 1994.

——*Hong Kong as an International Financial Centre: Emergence and Development 1945–65*, London: Routledge, 2001.

Schonberger, Howard B., *Aftermath of War: Americans and the Remaking of Japan. 1945–1952*, Kent OH: Kent State University Press, 1989.

Shimizu, Hiroshi, *Anglo-Japanese Rivalry in the Middle East in the Inter-war Period*, London: Ithaca Press, 1986.

Shimizu, Sayuri, *Creating People of Plenty: The United States and Japan's Economic Alternatives, 1950–1960*, Kent OH and London: Kent State University Press, 2001.

Shiraishi, Takashi, *Japan's Trade Policies, 1945 to the Present Day*, London: Athlone Press, 1989.

Shonfield, Andrew, *British Economic Policy since the War*, London: Penguin, 1958.

Singh, Lalita Prasad, *The Politics of Economic Cooperation in Asia: A Study of Asian International Organizations*, Missouri: University of Missouri Press, 1966.

Singleton, John, *Lancashire on the Scrapheap: The Cotton Industry 1945–1970*, Oxford: Oxford University Press, 1991.

Singleton, John and Paul L. Robertson, *Economic Relations between Britain and Australia 1945–1970*, London: Palgrave, 2002.

Smith, Michael, Steve Smith and Brian White, *British Foreign Policy Tradition. Change and Transformation*, London: Unwin Hyman, 1988.

Stueck, William, *The Korean War: An International History*, Princeton: Princeton University Press, 1995.

Tanaka, Takahiko, *Nisso Kokkô Kaifuku no Shitekikenkyu: Sengo Nisso Kankei no Kiten 1945–1956* [A Historical Study of the Normalization of Relations between the Soviet Union and Japan: the Origins of the Postwar Soviet-Japanese relations, 1945–1956], Tokyo: Yûhikaku, 1993.

Tarling, Nicholas, *The Fall of Imperial Britain in South-East Asia*, Oxford: Oxford University Press, 1993.

——*Britain, Southeast Asia and the Onset of the Cold War, 1945–1950*, Cambridge: Cambridge University Press, 1998.

Teranishi, Juno and Yutaka Kosa (eds) *The Japanese Experience of Economic Reforms*, London and Basingstoke: Macmillan Press, 1993.

Thorpe, D. R., *Selwyn Lloyd*, London: Jonathan Cape, 1989.

Tomaru, Junko, *The Postwar Rapprochement of Malaya and Japan, 1945–61: The Roles of Britain and Japan in South-East Asia*, Basingstoke: Macmillan, 2000.

Tsutsui, William M., *Banking Policy in Japan: American Efforts at Reform during the Occupation*, London and New York: Routledge, 1988.

Urwin, Derek, *The Community of Europe: A History of European Integration since 1945*, London and New York: Longman, 1991.

Ward, Robert E. and Sakamoto Yoshikazu, *Democratizing Japan: The Allied Occupation*, Honolulu: University of Hawaii Press, 1987.

Warner, Fred, *Anglo-Japanese Financial Relations: A Golden Tide*, Oxford: Blackwell, 1991.

Watanabe, Akio and Seigen Miyasato (eds) *San Francisco Kôwa* [The San Francisco Peace Treaty], Tokyo: Tokyo Daigaku Shuppankai, 1986.

——*Ajia/Taiheiyô no Kokusai Kankei to Nihon* [Japan's Diplomacy and International Relations in the Asia-Pacific Region], Tokyo: Tokyo University Press, 1992.

——*Sengo Nihon no Saishô tachi* [The Postwar Japanese Prime Ministers], Tokyo: Chuo Korônsha, 1995.

Welfield, John, *An Empire in Eclipse: Japan in the Postwar American Alliance System: A Study in the Interaction of Domestic Politics and Foreign Policy*, London: Athlone Press, 1988.

Westad, Odd Arne, *Cold War and Revolution: Soviet-American Rivalry and the Origins of the Chinese Civil War, 1944–1946*, New York: Columbia University Press, 1993.

White, Nicholas J., *Decolonisation: The British Experience Since 1945*, London: Longman, 1999.

Wheeler-Bennett, John, *Action This Day: Working with Churchill*, London: Macmillan, 1968.

Xiang, Lanxin, *Recasting the Imperial Far East: Britain and America in China, 1945–1950*, London and New York: M. E. Sharpe, 1995.

Yanaga, Chitoshi, *Big Business in Japanese Politics*, New Haven and London: Yale University Press, 1968.

Yoshitomi, Masaru and Edward M. Graham (eds) *Foreign Direct Investment in Japan*, Cheltenham: Edward Elgar, 1996.

Young, Stephen, Neil Hood and James Hamill, *Foreign Multinationals and the British Economy*, New York: Croom Helm, 1988.

Zeiler, Thomas W., *American Trade and Power in the 1960s*, New York: Columbia University Press, 1992.

Zhai, Qiang, *The Dragon, the Lion and the Eagle: Chinese-British-American Relations, 1949–1958*, Kent OH and London: Kent State University Press, 1994.

Zubok, V. M., *Inside the Kremlin's Cold War: From Stalin to Khrushchev*, Cambridge MA: Harvard University Press, 1996.

Articles

Buckley, Roger, 'Joining the Club: The Japanese Question and Anglo-American Peace Diplomacy, 1950–1951', *Modern Asian Studies*, vol. 19, no. 2 (1985): 299–319.

——'From San Francisco to Suez and Beyond: Anglo-Japanese Relations, 1952–1960', in *The Great Powers in East Asia, 1953–1960*, eds Warren I. Cohen and Akira Iriye, New York: Columbia University Press, 1990.

——'In Proper Perspective: Sir Esler Dening (1897–1977) and Anglo-Japanese Relations 1951–1957', in *Britain and Japan 1859–1991: Themes and Personalities*, eds Hugh Cortazzi and Gordon Daniels, London and New York: Routledge, 1991.

Bulpitt, Jim and Peter Burnham, 'Operation Robot and the British Political Economy in the Early 1950s: The Politics of Market Strategies', *Contemporary British History*, vol. 13, no. 1 (1999): 1–31.

Cain, Frank, 'Exporting the Cold War: British Responses to the USA's Establishment of COCOM, 1947–51', *Journal of Contemporary History*, vol. 29 (1994): 501–22.

——'The US-Led Trade Embargo on China: The Origins of CHINCOM, 1947–52', *Journal of Strategic Studies*, vol. 18, no. 4 (1995): 33–54.

Chen, Jian, 'China and the First Indo-China War, 1950–54', *The China Quarterly*, no. 133 (1993): 85–110.

Cortazzi, Hugh, 'Britain and Japan: A Personal View of Postwar Economic Relations', in *Conflict and Amity in East Asia: Essays in Honour of Ian Nish*, eds T. G. Fraser and Peter Lowe, London: Macmillan, 1992.

Dingman, Roger, 'Truman, Attlee, and the Korean War Crisis', in 'The East Asian Crisis, 1945–1951: The Problem of China Korea and Japan', *International Studies*, vol. 82, no. 49 (1982): 1–42.

Dower, John, 'Occupied Japan and the Cold War in Asia', in *The Truman Presidency*, ed. Michael J. Lacey, New York: Cambridge University Press, 1989.

Forland, Tor Egil, ' "Selling Firearms to the Indians": Eisenhower's Export Control Policy, 1953–54', *Diplomatic History*, vol. 15, no. 2 (1991): 221–44.

Forsberg, Aaron, 'Eisenhower and Japanese Economic Recovery: The Politics of Integration with the Western Trading Bloc, 1952–1955', *The Journal of American-East Asian Relations*, vol. 5, no. 1 (1996): 57–75.

Fukao, Mitsuhiro, Oumi Masao and Etoh Kimihiro, 'Japan's Experience in the Immediate Postwar Period: Movint toward a Single Exchange Rate and Dena-tionalization of Trade', in *The Japanese Experience of Economic Reforms*, eds Ternishi Juro and Kosai Yutaka, Basingstoke: Macmillan Press, 1993.

Fukushima, Teruhiko, 'Sengo Nihon no Bdeki Senryaku ni okeru Australia 1947–54' [Japan's post-war trade strategy towards Australia, 1947–1954], in *Gendai Nihon Gaikô no Bunseki* [An Analysis of Japan's Foreign Diplomacy], eds Kusano Atsushi and Umemoto Tetsuya, Tokyo: Tokyo Daigaku Shuppankai, 1995.

Gray, Robin, 'The Anglo-Japanese Commercial Treaty of 1962: A British Perspec-tive', in *Britain and Japan: Biographical Portraits, Volume II*, ed. Ian Nish, Sussex: Japan Library, 1997.

Hanaoka, Sosuke, 'Memories of the Anglo-Japanese Commercial Treaty: A Japanese Perspective', in *Britain and Japan: Biographical Portraits, Volume II*, ed. Ian Nish, Sussex: Japan Library, 1997.

Hatano, Sumio, 'Tônan Ajia Kaihatsu wo meguru Nichibeiei Kankei' [Japan-US-UK Relations Centering on the Development of southeast Asia in the 1950s], *Kindai Nihon Kenkvû*, vol. 16 (1994): 215–42.

Hein, Laura E., 'Free Floating Anxieties on the Pacific: Japan and the West Revis-ited', *Diplomatic History*, vol. 20, no. 3 (1996): 411–37.

Hinds, Allister E., 'Sterling and Imperial Policy, 1945–1951', *The Journal of Imperial and Commonwealth History*, vol. 15, no. 2 (1987): 148–69.

——'Imperial Policy and Colonial Sterling Balances 1943–56', *The Journal of Impe-rial and Commonwealth History*, vol. 19, no. 1 (1991): 24–44.

Hosoya, Chihiro, 'Japan, China, the United States and the United Kingdom, 1951–2: the Case of the "Yoshida Letter" ', *International Affairs*, vol. 60, no. 2 (1984): 247–59.

Kaufman, Burton I., 'Eisenhower's Foreign Economic Policy with Respect to East Asia', in *The Great Powers in East Asia 1953–1960*, eds Warren I. Cohen and Akira Iriye, New York: Columbia University Press, 1990, 104–20.

Kitaoka, Shinichi, 'Yoshida Shigeru ni okeru Senzen to Sengo' [Pre-War and PostWar Period in the Diplomacy of Yoshida Shigeru], *Kindai Nihon Kenkvû*, vol. 16 (1994): 105–31.

Komine, Takao, 'The Role of Economic Planning in Japan', in *The Japanese Experi-ence of Economic Reforms*, eds Teranishi Juno and Kosai Yutaka, Basingstoke: Macmillan Press, 1993.

Lafeber, Walter, *The Clash: US-Japanese Relations throughout History*, New York and London: Norton, 1997.

Lowe, David, 'Percy Spender and the Colombo Plan 1950', *Australian Journal of Politics and History* vol. 40, no. 2 (1994): 162–76.

Lowe, Peter, 'Herbert Morrison, the Labour Government, and the Japanese Peace Treaty, 1951', in 'Britain, the United States and Japan's Return to Normal 1951–1972', *International Studies*, vol. 93, no. 58 (1993): 1–27.

——'The Settlement of the Korean War', in *The Foreign Policy of Churchill's Peace-time Administration 1951–1955*, ed. John W. Young, Leicester: Leicester University Press, 1988.

——'Great Britain and the Japanese Peace Treaty, 1951', in *Western Interactions with Japan: Expansion, the Armed Forces and Readjustment 1859–1956*, eds Peter Lowe and Herman Moeshart, Folkstone: Japan Library, 1990.

——'Challenge and Readjustment: Anglo-American Exchanges over East Asia, 1949–53', in *Conflict and Amity in East Asia. Essays in Honour of Ian Nish*, eds T. G. Fraser and Peter Lowe, Basingstoke: Macmillan, 1992.

——'The British Liaison Mission and SCAP, 1948–1952: Exchanges during the Latter Part of the Occupation', *Japan Forum*, vol. 5, no. 2 (1993): 245–56.

——'Sir Alvary Gascoigne in Japan, 1946–1951', in *Britain and Japan: Biographical Portraits*, ed. Ian Nish, Folkstone: Japan Library, 1994.

McDougall, Donald and Rosemary Hutt, 'Imperial Preference: A Quantitative Analysis', *Economic Journal*, vol. LXIV, no. 254 (1954): 233–57.

McLean, David, 'American Nationalism, the China Myth, and the Truman Doctrine: The Question of Accommodation with Peking, 1949–50', *Diplomatic History*, vol. 10, no. 1 (1986): 25–42.

Miwa, Ryoichi, 'Government and the Japanese Shipping Industry, 1945–64', *Journal of Transport History*, vol. 9, no. 1 (1988): 37–49.

Nakakita, Toru, 'Trade and Capital Liberalization Policies in Postwar Japan', in *The Japanese Experience of Economic Reforms*, eds Juro Teranishi and Yutaka Kosai, London: Macmillan, 1993.

Nakanishi, Hiroshi, 'Sengo Ajia/Taiheiyô no Anzen Hoshô Wakugumi no Mosaku to Nihon' [Searches for an Asia-Pacific Security Framework and Japan: 1949–1951], *Kindai Nihon Kenkvu*, vol. 16 (1994): 69–104.

Ovendale, Richard, 'Britain, the United States, and the Cold War in South-East Asia, 1949–1950', *International Affairs*, vol. 58, no. 3 (1982): 447–64.

——'Britain, the United States, and the Recognition of Communist China', *The Historical Journal*, vol. 26, no. 1 (1983): 139–58.

Qing, Simei, 'The Eisenhower Administration and Changes in Western Embargo Policy Against China, 1954–1958', in *The Great Powers in East Asia, 1953–1960*, eds Warren I. Cohen and Akira Iriye, New York: Columbia University Press, 1990.

Rix, Alan, 'Ushiba Nobuhiko: A Japanese "Economic Diplomat"', *Pacific Economic Papers*, no. 170 (1989): 1–32.

——'Australia and Most-favoured Nation Treatment for Japan 1947–1955', *Pacific Economic Papers*, no. 115 (1984): 1–60.

Robertson, Paul L., 'The Decline of Economic Complementarity? Australia and Britain 1945–1952', *Australian Economic History Review*, vol. 37, no. 2 (1997): 91–116.

Ruane, Kevin, '"Containing America": Aspects of British Foreign Policy and the Cold War in South-East Asia, 1951–54', *Diplomacy and Statecraft*, vol. 7, no. 1 (1996): 141–74.

Schaller, Michael, 'Securing the Great Crescent: Occupied Japan and the Origins of Containment in Southeast Asia', *Journal of American History*, vol. 69 (1982): 392–414.

Schenk, Catherine, 'The Sterling Area and British Policy Alternatives in the 1950s', *Contemporary Record*, vol. 6, no. 2 (1992): 266–86.

——'Closing the Hong Kong Gap: The Hong Kong Free Dollar Market in the 1950s', *Economic History Review*, vol. 47, no. 2 (1994): 335–53.

——'Decolonization and European Economic Integration: The Free Trade Area Negotiations, 1956–58', *Journal of Imperial and Commonwealth History*, vol. 24, no. 3 (1996): 444–63.

Schonberger, Howard, 'Peacemaking in Asia: The United States, Great Britain, and the Japanese Decision to Recognize Nationalist China, 1951–52', *Diplomatic History*, vol. 10, no. 1 (1986): 59–73.

Shai, Aaron, 'Imperialism Imprisoned: The Closure of British Firms in the People's Republic of China', *English Historical Review*, vol. 109 (1989): 88–109.

Shimizu, Sayuri, 'Posto-Senryôki no Nichibei Kankei: Tônan Ajia Keizai Kaihatsu Kôsôwo chushin ni' [Post-Occupation US-Japan Relations: The Asian Marshall Plan], *Amerika to Nihon*, Tokyo: Sairyusha, 1993.

——'Perennial Anxiety: Japan/US Controversy over Recognition of the PRC, 1952–1958', *The Journal of American/East Asian Relations*, vol. 4, no. 3 (1995): 223–48.

Singh, D. S. Ranjit, 'British Proposals for a Dominion of Southeast Asia, 1943–1957', *Journal of the Malaysian Branch of the Royal Asiatic Society*, vol. 71, no. 1 (1998): 27–40.

Singleton, John, 'Lancashire's Last Stand: Declining Employment in the British Cotton Industry, 1950–70', *Economic History Review*, vol. 39, no. 1 (1986): 92–107.

——'Planning for Cotton, 1945–1951', *Economic History Review*, vol. 43, no. 1 (1990): 62–78.

——'Showing the White Flag: The Lancashire Cotton Industry, 1945–65', *Business History*, vol. 32, no. 4 (1990): 129–49.

——'New Zealand's Economic Relations with Japan in the 1950s', *Australian Economic History Review*, vol. 37, no. 1 (1997): 1–18.

——'New Zealand, Britain and the Survival of the Ottawa Agreement, 1945–77', *Australian Journal of Politics and History*, vol. 43, no. 2 (1997): 168–82.

Spaulding, Robert Mark Jr, ' "A Gradual and Moderate Relaxation": Eisenhower and the Revision of American Export Control Policy, 1953–1955', *Diplomatic History*, vol. 17, no. 2 (1993): 223–49.

Stockwell, A. J., 'British Imperial Policy and Decolonization in Malaya, 1942–52', *Journal of Imperial and Commonwealth History*, vol. 13, no. 1 (1984): 68–87.

——'Insurgency and Decolonisation during the Malayan Emergency', *Journal of Commonwealth and Comparative Politics*, vol. 25, no. 1 (1987): 71–81.

——' "A Widespread and Long-concocted plot to overthrow government in Malaya"? The Origins of the Malayan Emergency', *Journal of Imperial and Commonwealth History*, vol. 21, no. 3 (1993): 66–88.

Sugihara, Kaoru, 'Sengo Nihon Mengyô wo Meguru Kokusai Kankyô: Ajia kan Kyôsô Fukkatsu no Kôzô', *Kindai Nihon Kenkvû*, vol. 19 (1997): 84–110.

Takamatsu, Motoyuki, 'China Differential Kanwa Mondai wo Megutte no Eisenhower Seiken no Taiô' [The Eisenhower Administration's Response to the China Differential, 1955–57], *Kokusai Seiji*, vol. 105 (1994): 60–79.

Tarling, Nicholas, 'The United Kingdom and the Origins of the Colombo Plan', *Journal of Commonwealth and Comparative Politics*, vol. 24, no. 1 (1986): 3–34.

Tiratsoo, Nick, 'The United States Technical Assistance Programme in Japan, 1955–62', *Business History*, vol. 42, no. 4 (2000): 117–36.

Tucker, Nancy Bernkopf, 'American Policy Toward Sino-Japanese Trade in the Postwar Years: Politics and Prosperity', *Diplomatic History*, vol. 8, no. 3 (1984): 183–208.

Warner, Geoffrey, 'The Settlement of the Indochina War', in *The Foreign Policy of Churchill's Peacetime Administration 1951–1955*, ed. John W. Young, Leicester: Leicester University Press, 1988.

White, Nicholas J., 'Britain and the Return of Japanese Economic Interests to Southeast Asia after the Second World War', *South East Asia Research*, vol. 6, no. 3 (1998): 281–307.

Yasuhara, Yôko, 'Japan, Communist China, and Export Controls in Asia, 1948–52', *Diplomatic History*, vol. 10, no. 1 (1986): 75–89.

Yoshida, Shigeru, 'Japan and the Crisis in Asia', *Foreign Affairs*, vol. 29, no. 2 (January 1951): 171–81.

Young, John W., 'Winston Churchill's Peacetime Administration and the Relaxation of East-West Trade Controls, 1953–54', *Diplomacy and Statecraft*, vol. 7, no. 1 (1996): 125–40.

Zeiler, Thomas W., 'Managing Protectionism: American Trade Policy in the Early Cold War', *Diplomatic History*, vol. 22, no. 3 (1998): 337–60.

Unpublished thesis

Sharkey, John, 'The Influence of British Business Interests in Anglo-Japanese Relations, 1933–1937', Ph.D. thesis, London School of Economics and Political Science, 1994.

Index of Key Persons

Japan

Asakai, Kôichirô	Ministry of Foreign Affairs Representative in the UK (1951); Ambassador to the UK (1951)
Hagiwara, Tôru	Japanese Ambassador to France (1950–1952); Leader of the Japanese Delegation to the GATT prior to Japanese membership; Japanese Ambassador to Canada (1957–1961)
Hatoyama, Ichirô	Prime Minister from December 1954 to December 1956
Ichimada, Hisato	18th Governor of the Bank of Japan (1946–1954)
Iguchi, Sadao	Vice Minister of the Ministry of Foreign Affairs (1951–1952); Ambassador to Canada (1952–1954); Ambassador to the United States (1954–1959)
Ikeda, Hayato	Finance Minister (1952–1954); Various cabinet ministerial posts between 1956–1959 including Minister of Finance, Minister of State and Minister of International Trade and Industry; Prime Minister (1960–1964)
Ishibashi, Tanzan	Prime Minister (1956–1957)
Kishi, Nobusuke	Prime Minister (1957–1960)
Kiuchi, Nobutane	Chairman of the FECB (1949–1952)
Matsumoto, Shunichi	Japanese Ambassador to the UK (1952–1955)
Oda, Takei	Director of the Economic Affairs Bureau, Ministry of Foreign Affairs
Ohno, Katsumi	Japanese Ambassador to the UK (1958–1964)
Okazaki, Katsuo	Chief Cabinet Secretary; Minister of State and Ministry of Foreign Affairs during Yoshida's Premiership (1948–1954)
Takeuchi, Ryuji	International Trade Administrator, Ministry of International Trade and Industry (1951); Ministry of Foreign Affairs Representative in the United States (1951); Ambassador to the United States (1952 and 1953)
Tôjô, Takei	Head of the Foreign Exchange Bureau, Ministry of Finance
Ushiba, Nobuhiko	Director-General for the International Trade Bureau of the MITI (1949–1951); Councilor at the Ministry of

Foreign Affairs (1951–1957), Economic Division Chief at the Ministry of Foreign Affairs (1957–1967)

Yoshida, Shigeru   Prime Minister 1946–1954 (break in premiership1947–1948)

United Kingdom

Allen, W.D. — Foreign Office

Attlee, Clement — Labour Prime Minister 1945–1951

Churchill, Winston — Conservative Prime Minister 1951–1955

Cohen, E.A. — Board of Trade

Dening, Sir Esler — British Ambassador to Japan (1952–1957)

Eden Anthony — Conservative Prime Minister 1955–1957

Gascoigne, Alvary — Head of UK Liaison Mission to Japan (1946–51)

Loynes, J.B. — Assistant Chief Cashier (1949–1955), Adviser (1955–1965), Adviser to the Governor of the Bank of England (1965)

Bank of England

Macmillan, Harold — Conservative Prime Minister 1957–1963

Makins, Roger — Assistant Under Secretary of State for Foreign Affairs (1947–48); Deputy Under Secretary (1948-52) Ambassador to the United States (1952–56)

Maudling, Reginald — Minister of Supply (1955–57); Paymaster-General (1957–59); President of the Board of Trade (1959–61); Colonial Secretary (1961–62)

Morrison, Herbert — Foreign Secretary 1951

Percival A.E. — Board of Trade

Scott R.H. — Chief of the Japan and Pacific Department, Foreign Office

Serpell, David — Treasury

Streat, Raymond — SirChairman of the Cotton Board

Thomas, Hugh — Financial Counselor at the Japanese Embassy

Thorneycroft, Peter — President of the Board of Trade (1951–1957); Chancellor of the Exchequer (1957–1958)

Wilson, Harold — President of the Board of Trade (1947–1951)

United States

Acheson, Dean — Secretary of State (1949–1952)

Allison, John — Chief of the Division of Far Eastern Affairs at the State Department (1947–198); Director of Northeast Asian

Index